Coaching Baseball For Dummies®

Cheat Sheet

What to Bring to Practice

- Properly stocked first-aid kit (see Chapter 16 for a complete rundown of the items that should be in the kit)
- Extra water
- Practice plan for the day, broken down by time segments, detailing drills you'll be running
- Bats, balls, and other equipment you need

What to Bring to Games

- A fully stocked first-aid kit
- Cell phone in case of an injury emergency
- Extra water for players
- Your roster of players, the positions they'll be playing, and your batting order
- Scorebook and pencil
- Sheet with your substitution rotation to ensure equal playing time for all the kids
- Knee cushion for coach-pitch leagues where you may pitch from one knee

Tips for Making Practice Fun

- Ensure lots of repetitions for each child.
- Keep kids active; don't force them to stand in lines.
- Involve parents in drills once in awhile to rev up the excitement.
- Introduce some new drills at each practice to keep the kids' interest.
- When drills turn out to be boring or ineffective, discard them and switch to something else.
- Stop practice briefly to point out when players do something well — not when they made a mistake.
- Solicit feedback and ideas from the kids on drills to use.
- Applaud the slightest improvements to maintain the kids' interest.
- Conclude practice with the most popular drill to end the session on a high note.

Sample One-Hour Practice

Note: See Chapters 12 and 13 for specific drills to use.

- 10 minutes: Warm-up period
- 20 minutes: Individual and team hitting drills
- 5 minutes: Base running and situational drills
- 10 minutes: Team defense and situational drills
- 10 minutes: Position-specific defensive drills
- 5 minutes: Cool-down time and team meeting

Building Players Up

- Use the "sandwich" method for giving feedback to players by placing a critical remark between two encouraging comments.
- Always keep in mind that making mistakes is part of the learning process.
- Give kids high-fives and pats on the back to reinforce that their efforts are appreciated.
- Set realistic goals for the kids so they will gain a real sense of satisfaction upon reaching them.
- Never allow your tone of voice or body language to reveal disappointment in a child's performance or ability.

For Dummies: Bestselling Book Series for Beginners

Coaching Baseball For Dummies®

Cheat Sheet

Offensive Practice Drills

Note: See Chapters 12 and 13 for specifics on the following drills:

- Individual toss
- T-ball target
- Speed hitting
- Progression hitting off the tee
- Mixed speeds
- Mystery bases
- Extra-base challenge
- Get low
- Swiping bases

Defensive Practice Drills

Note: See Chapters 12 and 13 for specifics on the following drills:

- Strike challenge
- Bunt bonanza
- Slow roller
- Quick mystery throws
- Crazy-angle throws
- Double play starter
- Base throw challenge
- Ground ball mania
- Target throws

Responsibilities of First Base Coach

- Encouraging batter to hustle down first base line on infield hits
- Reminding runners of the number of outs
- Instructing runner when to take extra base and when to round first base but hold up
- Telling runners how far to go on pop flies

Responsibilities of Third Base Coach

- Sending runners home or holding them up at third base
- Letting runners know whether to slide into third base or come in standing up
- Assisting runners when tagging up by letting them know when to run
- Reminding runners of the number of outs

Delivering the Pre-Game Talk

- Meet with the team away from any distractions.
- Keep the meeting short.
- Focus on just a couple of main points.
- Stress to the kids the importance of being good sports — no matter what happens on the field — and to show respect toward the umpires.
- Exude confidence in their abilities.
- Avoid using unfamiliar terms or introducing new strategies.
- Conclude your talk by reminding players to have fun.

Delivering the Post-Game Talk

- Be upbeat and applaud the effort everyone put forth.
- Point out the positives and recognize the displays of good sportsmanship.
- Don't allow the scoreboard to dictate how you talk to your players.
- Wrap up the talk on a high note, conclude with a team cheer, and send the kids home with a smile.

For Dummies: Bestselling Book Series for Beginners

Coaching
Baseball
FOR
DUMMIES®

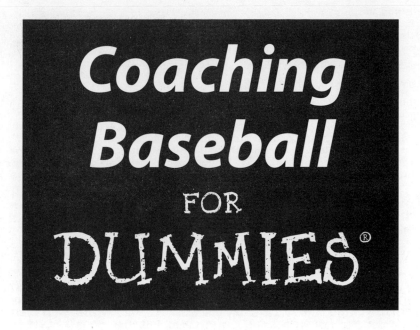

by National Alliance For Youth Sports
with Greg Bach

1807
WILEY
2007

Wiley Publishing, Inc.

Coaching Baseball For Dummies®

Published by
Wiley Publishing, Inc.
111 River St.
Hoboken, NJ 07030-5774
www.wiley.com

Copyright © 2007 by Wiley Publishing, Inc., Indianapolis, Indiana

Published simultaneously in Canada

For general information on our other products and services, please contact our Customer Care Department within the U.S. at 800-762-2974, outside the U.S. at 317-572-3993, or fax 317-572-4002.

For technical support, please visit www.wiley.com/techsupport.

Wiley also publishes its books in a variety of electronic formats. Some content that appears in print may not be available in electronic books.

Library of Congress Control Number: 2007920011

ISBN: 978-0-470-08960-6

Manufactured in the United States of America

10 9 8 7 6 5 4 3 2 1

WILEY

About the Authors

Greg Bach is the communications director for the National Alliance For Youth Sports, a position he has held since 1993. Before joining NAYS, he worked as the sports editor of the Huron Daily Tribune in Bad Axe, Michigan, where he captured numerous writing awards from the Associated Press, Michigan Press Association, and the Hearst Corporation. He has a journalism degree from Michigan State University, which he earned in 1989, and spends a lot of his free time during football and basketball season cheering for his beloved Spartans. He's also the author of *Coaching Soccer For Dummies* and *Coaching Football For Dummies*.

The **National Alliance For Youth Sports** has been America's leading advocate for positive and safe sports for children for the past 25 years. It serves volunteer coaches, parents with children involved in organized sports, game officials, youth sports administrators, league directors, and the youngsters who participate in organized sports. The Alliance's programs are utilized in more than 3,000 communities nationwide by parks and recreation departments, Boys & Girls Clubs, Police Athletic Leagues, YMCAs/YWCAs, and various independent youth service groups, as well as on military installations worldwide. For more information on the Alliance's programs, which are listed below, visit www.nays.org.

National Youth Sports Coaches Association — More than 2 million volunteer coaches have been trained through NYSCA, which provides training, support, and continuing education.

Parents Association for Youth Sports — Parents gain a clear understanding of their roles and responsibilities in youth sports through this sportsmanship training program, which is utilized in more than 500 communities nationwide.

Academy for Youth Sports Administrators — More than 1,500 administrators worldwide have gone through the Academy, which is a 20-hour certification program that raises the professionalism of those delivering youth sport services. A professional faculty presents the information, and participants earn Continuing Education Units (CEUs).

National Youth Sports Administrators Association — The program provides training, information, and resources for volunteer administrators responsible for the planning and implementation of out-of-school sports programs.

National Youth Sports Officials Association — Officials who go through this certification program gain valuable knowledge on skills, fundamentals, and the characteristics that every good official must possess.

Start Smart Sports Development Program — This proven instructional program prepares children for the world of organized sports without the threat of competition or the fear of getting hurt through an innovative approach that promotes parent-child bonding.

Hook A Kid On Golf — Thousands of children of all ages and skill levels tee it up every year in the nation's most comprehensive junior golf development program, which features an array of instructional clinics and tournaments to choose from.

Game On! Youth Sports — This worldwide effort introduces children to actual game experience by giving them the freedom to create and play on their own.

Dedication

From National Alliance For Youth Sports: This book is dedicated to all the volunteer baseball and softball coaches who give up countless hours of their free time to work with children and ensure that they have positive, safe, and rewarding experiences. We applaud their efforts and commend them for making a difference in the lives of youngsters everywhere.

From Greg Bach: This one is for Gram and Grandpa Coltson, and Grandma and Grandpa Bach, for all the great times and special memories they've given me through the years.

Author's Acknowledgments

A successful youth baseball program doesn't just happen. It takes a real commitment from not only dedicated volunteer coaches, but parents who understand their roles and responsibilities, and league directors and administrators who know what it takes to ensure that every child who steps on the baseball field in their community has a safe, fun, and rewarding experience. Baseball plays an important role in the lives of millions of children and provides them with the opportunity to not only learn the skills of the game, but the chance to develop both emotionally and physically as individuals. The National Alliance For Youth Sports extends a heartfelt thank you to every person who makes a positive difference through baseball in the life of a child.

This book is the result of a lot of hours of hard work from a lot of talented people at Wiley, and a huge thank you goes out to project editor Darren Meiss and copy editor Josh Dials, a duo whose creative touch and knowledge of the game made an incredible difference in the quality of the book you are holding right now; Stacy Kennedy, the acquisitions editor, whose efforts behind the scenes working with the National Alliance For Youth Sports has resulted in this being the third book in a series for youth coaches; and the fabulous efforts of the illustrators — whose work will be great references as you teach your team all sorts of baseball skills.

Publisher's Acknowledgments

We're proud of this book; please send us your comments through our Dummies online registration form located at www.dummies.com/register/.

Some of the people who helped bring this book to market include the following:

Acquisitions, Editorial, and Media Development

Project Editors: Mike Baker, Darren Meiss

Acquisitions Editor: Stacy Kennedy

Copy Editor: Josh Dials

Technical Editor: Michael Fremion

Editorial Managers: Michelle Hacker, Carmen Krikorian

Editorial Assistants: Erin Calligan Mooney, Joe Niesen, Leann Harney

Cover Photos: ©Lori Adamski Peek/ Tony Stone/Getty Images

Cartoons: Rich Tennant (www.the5thwave.com)

Composition Services

Project Coordinator: Erin Smith

Layout and Graphics: Carl Byers, Joyce Haughey, Shane Johnson, Laura Pence

Anniversary Logo Design: Richard Pacifico

Proofreaders: Aptara, Christine Pingleton, Brian H. Walls

Indexer: Aptara

Publishing and Editorial for Consumer Dummies

    Diane Graves Steele, Vice President and Publisher, Consumer Dummies

    Joyce Pepple, Acquisitions Director, Consumer Dummies

    Kristin A. Cocks, Product Development Director, Consumer Dummies

    Michael Spring, Vice President and Publisher, Travel

    Kelly Regan, Editorial Director, Travel

Publishing for Technology Dummies

    Andy Cummings, Vice President and Publisher, Dummies Technology/General User

Composition Services

    Gerry Fahey, Vice President of Production Services

    Debbie Stailey, Director of Composition Services

Contents at a Glance

Drills at a Glance

Table of Contents

Introduction

Welcome to *Coaching Baseball For Dummies,* a book dedicated to helping and teaching all the wonderful volunteer coaches who sign up to introduce kids to this magnificent sport that is played and enjoyed by millions around the world. Youngsters love the thrill of putting on the colorful uniform on game day, exchanging high-fives with teammates and coaches after making great catches and delivering clutch hits, and collecting grass stains diving for ground balls and sliding into second base. As a coach, you'll forge friendships with players, parents, and opposing coaches as you help youngsters build confidence, enhance skills, become good sports, and most importantly, have barrels of fun along the way.

You'll find this book informative, entertaining, and — most important of all — useful in your quest to guide the youngsters on your team to a fun, safe, and rewarding experience. Your kids, and you, will remember this season for years to come!

About This Book

We wrote this book so that it can help two different types of readers: first-time volunteer youth baseball coaches who are looking for some guidance before they take the field, and coaches who've been involved in baseball for a season or two and want to gain some more insight into different areas of the game. If you're new to coaching youth baseball, or the game in general, you probably feel a bit apprehensive about your ability to teach the kids about the many different aspects of the game. Don't worry, these feelings are natural. You should know that the book you're holding provides the essential information you need to know to do a great job and be a big hit — excuse the pun — with your players. We pack each chapter with great information that you can use to make a difference in your players' development — from offense, to defense, to just having fun. The more chapters you read, the more knowledgeable and confident you'll become, which will help you have a bigger impact on your team.

For those coaches who are accustomed to spending their free time at local fields around players and parents, we provide plenty of in-depth advice. In addition to all the basics, we cover drills you can use to raise players' skills at the plate, in the field, and on the bases, and we discuss strategies you can employ with a more veteran team.

And for those of you who have chosen to coach softball, you can apply most of the information presented in these pages to the beginning levels of this sport, too.

Conventions Used in This Book

To help guide you through this book, we use the following conventions:

- *Italic* text for emphasis and to highlight new words or phrases that we define in the text

- **Boldfaced** text to indicate keywords in bulleted lists or the action parts of numbered steps

- Sidebars — the shaded gray boxes that you see sprinkling the chapters — to present information that's interesting to know but not critical to your understanding of the chapter or topic

Mixed genders — he and she — are interchanged throughout this book while discussing everything from techniques to drills that you're teaching your players. Also, when you encounter "we," that refers to the National Alliance For Youth Sports' voice, which is America's leading advocate for positive and safe sports for kids.

What You're Not to Read

In our humble opinion, every page of this book is filled with valuable information that you don't want to miss out on. But, we have to share a little secret with you: You don't have to read every single word. For instance, the shaded boxes you come across from time to time — called *sidebars* — feature interesting, but ultimately skippable, information.

Foolish Assumptions

The following list presents some things that we assume about you, our reader:

- You know that players use bats, balls, and gloves to play baseball.

- You're a novice or fairly new baseball or softball coach who's looking for information on how to manage a youth team.

- ✔ You have a child who wants to play baseball or softball this season, but you're not sure how to go about teaching him or her the game.

- ✔ You don't have an interest in coaching at the high school or collegiate ranks anytime soon.

- ✔ You want to know how to interact with the kids and their parents, what to do at the first practice of the season, and how to figure out who plays where.

If any of these descriptions are on target, you've come to the right place.

How This Book Is Organized

This book is divided into parts, and each part pertains to a specific aspect of coaching a youth baseball team. The following sections give you a quick rundown.

Part 1: Child's Play: Beginning Your Coaching Career

Taking the proper preparatory steps before your kids take the field can make the difference between a season filled with non-stop fun and one that dissolves into disappointment. The first part presents everything you need to know to get the season off to a fun-filled start — and keep it there. You get insight on creating a coaching philosophy that fits the kids' needs. You take a look at the rules and terms you need know. And you find out why a preseason parents meeting is so important.

Part II: Building Your Baseball Coaching Skills

Gathering the kids for practices and games and seeing the excitement in their eyes as they take the field is what makes coaching youth baseball so rewarding. But before you run those practices and coach in those games, you need to answer some questions, such as the following:

- ✔ How do I determine who plays where?

- ✔ How do I plan practices that are fun and that enhance my kids' skills?

✔ How can I help all the kids — from the uncoordinated to the super-talented — learn and develop skills?

✔ How do I prepare my kids before a game, and what do I do during the game?

✔ How do I know if my coaching is making a difference, and when do I need to adjust my approach?

You find the answers to these questions and more in Part II.

Part III: Working on the Fundamentals of the Game

Teaching kids how to hit, field, and run the bases — the basic elements of the game — is a vital part of a coach's job. The good news is, your kids will have a lot of fun learning these skills. This part presents the fundamentals of offense, infield and outfield defense, and pitching and catching. We also offer a wide selection of fun drills that will help your kids develop in all areas of the game. Plus, when your players have a pretty good handle on the basic fundamentals, you can head to Chapter 13, which is devoted to advanced drills that upgrade your players' skills.

Part IV: Playing Sound Situational Baseball

Once your players have a firm grasp on basic baseball skills, they'll be ready for a look into the strategic aspects of the game. We've filled Part IV with strategies for generating runs on offense and preventing them on defense. We cover everything from situational hitting to backing up on defense in these pages.

Part V: The Extra Innings

Hopefully, you won't have to spend any time this season dealing with injuries or discipline problems with your players or parents, but if any issues arise, this part offers some valuable input for handling them. Part V lets you know how to keep your players healthy, and it shares the many challenges you may face as a youth baseball coach. We also include some tips on pre- and post-game nutrition that you can share with your players.

Part VI: The Part of Tens

A fixture of all *For Dummies* books is the Part of Tens. Here, you find ten things to help relax and focus your players before a game. We include ten innovative ideas that will make your season memorable. And we present ten ways to end your season on a high note and keep the kids coming back for more baseball.

Icons Used in This Book

This icon puts the bat signal on valuable tips that can save you time and frustration and really enhance your coaching skills. If time permits you to only scan a chapter, you should take a moment to read these tips when you come across them. You — and your players — will be glad you did.

A lot of effort and time go into coaching a youth baseball team, so it helps to have the most important facts and reminders in easy-to-find places. This icon alerts you to key information that's worth revisiting after you close this book and take the field.

Take heed when you come across this icon, which puts the spotlight on dangerous or risky situations.

Where to Go from Here

One of the best things about this book is that you can jump to any chapter to gain the specific insight you're looking for. You aren't bound by a cover-to-cover rule here. Each chapter is divided into easy-to-navigate sections, and each section contains all the information you need to know about a specific topic regarding coaching baseball.

If this is your first time guiding a youth baseball team, you probably have questions swirling around in your head about how to conduct a practice or what to do on game day. Your best bet may be to settle in with the chapters of Part I. If you've met your team and want to find out how to evaluate them and hold fun, action-packed practices, Part II is your cup of tea. If you want specific drills for your practices, look no further than Chapters 12 and 13. The possibilities are endless.

Take comfort in knowing that you can quickly find answers to your most pressing questions by simply checking out the Table of Contents or Index — tools that will point you in the right direction. Whatever approach you take, be sure to sit back, relax, and soak up the information that will lead to your players having a safe, fun, and rewarding season.

Part I
Child's Play: Beginning Your Coaching Career

The 5th Wave   By Rich Tennant

"The first thing you need to know about coaching Little League is that it takes patience, understanding their limitations, and allowing them to feel like they're participating. And that's just the parents..."

In this part . . .

In order to steer your season in the right direction before you hit the field with the kids, you need to do your fair share of preparation. You have to become familiar with the basic rules of the game, and the rules of your league. You need to determine what type of approach you want to take when coaching your team. And you have to conduct a meeting with the parents to put everyone on the same page. This part covers all this vital information and much more.

Chapter 1

Teaching Baseball to Children

In This Chapter

▶ Handling your behind-the-scenes duties

▶ Hitting the field for practices and games

▶ Balancing your role as a coach and parent

▶ Taking on coaching challenges

*1*f you've recently agreed to coach a youth baseball team, congratulations! You deserve credit for taking on the special role of volunteer baseball coach. You're about to embark on a one-of-a-kind journey that you and your players will remember for the rest of your lives. Your season will be packed with many special moments, coming from your midweek practices and your weekend games. If you're still pondering the decision on whether to coach, we hope that the picture we paint of youth baseball will make it enticing enough to prompt a commitment.

Before you step on the field with the kids, though, please be aware that you're assuming a position that will have a far-reaching impact on their lives. Your approach to the season — from the goals you put in place to how you interact with the kids during practices and games — impacts how your players will feel about themselves, the sport of baseball, and you. You can use your many job responsibilities to help the kids develop an unquenchable passion for the game. However, if you neglect or mishandle your responsibilities, you may smother their interest in ever swinging a bat again.

What you need to get your season headed in the right direction — and to keep it on course — is some quality information on all the different aspects of the game.

In this chapter, we spell out what it takes to build solid relationships with parents to get them working with you rather than against you, and we take a peek at the rules and terms that are a big part of the game. Equally important, we share some of the secrets of running fun-filled practices and managing the game-day coaching basics, shed some light on managing the complex role of coaching your own child, and tip you off about some of the challenges you'll likely face.

Acknowledging Your Behind-the-Scenes Responsibilities

Chances are you volunteered to coach this season because you want to spend more time with your child; you want to be right there on the field introducing him to the great game of baseball. Or, maybe your local league is struggling to find coaches, and you came forward to help out because you love the game. Or, perhaps you just love working with kids, and you want to give coaching baseball a shot with the free time you have. Whatever your reasons, we applaud your enthusiasm and willingness to devote your time and energy to teaching kids.

Allow us to make the assumption that the biggest things on your mind are how to relate to your players, make them like you, and teach them the skills of the game. But before any youngster takes the field for his first practice under your direction, you have plenty of behind-the-scenes work to do — work that will ensure that the season gets off to a smooth start. In the following sections, we discuss the relationship you'll develop with your players' parents, and we explain the importance of knowing the rules and terminology of the game and the requirements of your league.

Working with parents

When coaching your players, you'll stress the importance of working together as a team. The same approach applies to dealing with parents. When coaches and parents find ways to work together — the adult form of teamwork — you provide the formula that fuels a fun-filled season, in which the kids reap countless benefits. Most parents of children involved in youth baseball programs are wonderful, supportive, and caring and only want the best for their kids.

Of course, some parents can turn out to be sources of season-long aggravation who'll have you reaching for the aspirin. Disagreements over playing time, batting orders, or game strategy, for example, cast a negative shadow over the entire team. Being prepared to deal with all types of parents is the only remedy for preventing issues from detracting from the kids' enjoyment of the season. You can dodge many potential problems by gathering the parents before you begin working with their kids so you can all get on the same page (see Chapter 4 for more on holding the preseason parents meeting).

Getting off on the right foot with the parents can be the springboard to a problem-free season. Keep the following tips in mind to help maintain order in your little baseball universe:

- ✔ **Outline your expectations.** Outlining your expectations for the parents and their kids, as well as going over your coaching methods, puts the season in focus and cuts down on the chance of a misunderstanding causing a major disruption. Keep in mind that many parents may be new to organized baseball; those in unfamiliar territory will appreciate the valuable information you share with them. During your preseason discussion, highlight what you want everyone to take away from the experience.

  You can find advice for developing your all-important coaching philosophy in Chapter 2. We also stress the importance of knowing your league's policies and rules so that you can communicate them to the parents.

- ✔ **Include the parents.** Parents invest a lot of time and money in their child's baseball experience, and the experience will be much more enjoyable for them and their youngster if you can find ways to include them on your season-long journey. They can do so much more than bring snacks and drinks to games. Do what you can to incorporate them into your practices, and recruit suitable parents to assist you on game day. Chapter 4 offers a variety of tips on boosting parental involvement, and Chapter 6 provides ideas for getting parents involved in the action on the field during practices.

- ✔ **Give them regular updates.** You should keep the lines of communication open all season long. Find time to talk to the parents about their child's progress; share your thoughts on areas of the game where the player is really making improvements; offer suggestions for things the parents can do to help their youngster's development; and check in to make sure the child is having fun playing for you. Including parents in all facets of the season is the right thing to do, the smart thing to do, and the best way to ensure positive experiences for all involved.

The key to diffusing negative situations with parents is to always remain in control of your emotions, regardless of how out of control the upset parent may be. Do your best to prevent situations from escalating. In Chapter 17, we present some of the more common problems that youth baseball coaches must deal with, and we offer the best approaches for solving them before they leave a negative imprint on the season.

Getting a handle on the rules and terminology

Not only do you need a good grasp of the basics of baseball, but you also have to be comfortable enough with them to be able to explain all the rules, popular terms, and strategies to your players. Relaying this information isn't as complicated as it may seem — especially for younger kids or even kids with a lot of experience — but it may require a quick refresher on your part to get up to speed on all the different areas that make up the great game of baseball.

We devote the bulk of Chapter 3 to helping you with all the different rules and options the game has in place for batting, running the bases, and playing in the field. We run down the key skills, techniques, and strategies that you need to pass along to your players throughout Parts III and IV of this book. If you're new to the game, or if you simply want a quick review before you jump into coaching a beginning-level team, we have you covered. If you need more detailed information for working with a group of skilled kids who have played the game for years, you've picked up the right book; we include plenty of information to help you be an effective advanced-league coach, too.

You also need to know any special rules that your league has in place. The rules your league utilizes may vary from the rules you know, depending on the age and experience level of the players. Every detail, from the size of the field to what types of rules are enforced, can change from community to community. Knowing these rules — and being able to share them with your players and their parents — makes a tremendous difference in how smoothly your season runs. Check out Chapter 2 for more info on league-specific rules, and head to Chapter 4 to find out how to present the rules to your kids' parents.

Stepping onto the Field

Seeing the looks on your players' faces after they get pretty good at fielding ground balls, hitting fastballs or laying down bunts during practice is part of what makes coaching youth baseball so much fun. The more players learn from you during practice, the more they can transfer over to the field on game day. The following sections introduce how you can plan great practices and get you and your players ready for game day.

Keep in mind that what you say, and how you say it, has a significant impact on your players' development — from day one until the end of the season. You want to fuel the kids' passion and have them excited to get started when they arrive at practices or at games. Smiles, laughter, and enthusiasm are the signals that you're teaching the right way.

Planning and executing fun and effective practices

The practices you design influence how much learning takes place under your watch and how much fun your kids have playing for you. Constant movement, challenging drills, and positive feedback due to your fun style are the hallmarks of a well-structured practice.

Make sure you lay out your practice schedule well in advance, including which drills you want to run, the order in which you want to run them, and how much time you plan on devoting to each part of practice. If you throw a practice together while sitting in your car before the players arrive, your session probably won't be much fun for the players or very effective in developing their skills. Chapter 6 has the scoop on preparing and running great practice sessions.

When selecting drills for your practices, always go with exercises that keep the kids moving and pose enough of a challenge to hold their interest. Drills that force the players to stand in line awaiting turns are boring, and they slice into the amount of learning taking place. Kids learn and develop by playing and getting plenty of repetitions, not by listening to you talk or standing in line. You can find a wide range of drills for hitting, fielding, and base running in Chapters 12 and 13; these exercises should challenge and excite beginning and intermediate players.

You can squeeze the most fun and productivity out of every practice session by keeping these additional tips in mind:

> ✔ **Use your position to be a positive influence on your players' lives.** Yes, you volunteered to coach kids the game of baseball and all the skills that go along with playing it. What you may not have given much thought to is the tremendous impact you'll have on these young lives in areas outside the game. Your position gives you the opportunity to make a significant difference. For example, when your kids are warming up (see Chapter 16), you can take the time to talk to them about the importance of doing well

in school. You also can speak to them about the importance of staying away from tobacco, alcohol, and drugs. For more on dealing with all kinds of personalities on your team, check out Chapter 5.

✔ **Conduct stress-free practices.** Allow your youngsters to make mistakes without the fear of criticism or embarrassment. Before your first practice of the season, make it a point to let the kids (and their parents; see Chapter 4) know that mistakes are part of learning how to play the game. All you should ask of them is that they listen to your instructions and try their best every time.

Taking your coaching out to the old ballgame

Being a youth baseball coach requires you to adapt to ever-changing conditions — from game to game and from inning to inning. You'll be challenged to make all sorts of decisions, without the luxury of time to think about them, while dealing with multiple responsibilities and countless distractions. You have

✔ Playing time to monitor

✔ Defensive adjustments to make

✔ Plays to call

✔ Pep talks to give

✔ Energy levels and enthusiasm to keep high

Yes, a pretty hefty list of responsibilities accompanies game day, but don't just sit there and reach for the antacid tablets. In Chapter 7, you get the skinny on all you need to help game day go smoothly.

Besides giving kids the chance to wear colorful uniforms and put all their skills to use against opposing teams, game day gives you all sorts of teachable moments. Reinforce the important points you brought up during practice, such as the following:

✔ Working together as a team

✔ Displaying good sportsmanship

✔ Abiding by the rules

✔ Doing your best at all times

✔ Having fun, regardless of what the scoreboard reads

Succeeding in the Dual Role of Coach and Parent

We certainly don't have to tell you that being a parent is an enormously difficult job. But we should tell you that handling the dual role of parent and coach to your child can present its share of unique challenges — many of which you haven't even thought about. In Chapter 2, we prepare you to deal with the issues that may materialize after you step on the field and your child steps into the batter's box. Being prepared for the issues, and knowing what to do when they pop up, enables you to create memorable experiences for you and your youngster.

Don't allow yourself to view your position as coach as an opportunity to control your child's destiny. Your coaching title isn't a vehicle that can steer your child to a spot on an All-Star team or secure a college scholarship for him down the road. If you take this unhealthy approach, you'll compromise your youngster's experience, because you'll push him harder than the other kids, demand more from him, and criticize him when he doesn't fulfill your unfair expectations. All you may do is drain his interest in learning and playing the game in the coming years.

Conquering Coaching Challenges

Being a youth baseball coach requires more than the ability to teach batting grips and throwing fundamentals. You also need to handle all the unique challenges that appear throughout the season. Having the knowledge and the confidence to steer your team around these obstacles — so they don't sabotage the fun and cut into the learning — is vital.

Working with all the different types of kids you'll find on your roster — ranging from the super shy and the nonstop talker to the athletically gifted and clumsy — is one of the most exciting and challenging aspects of coaching any sport. Sure, the smorgasbord of personalities will test your patience, communication skills, and ability to connect with each individual to meet their constantly changing needs, but we're confident that you're up for the task. Chapter 17 provides plenty of advice for dealing with potential discipline issues you'll encounter (as well as a number of other common coaching challenges).

Regardless of the skill level of your players, and whether this is their first venture into organized baseball or they have been collecting grass stains diving for ground balls for several seasons, one of your top priorities is keeping them as safe as possible during practices and games. Although making any season injury-free is nearly impossible, you can strive for safety by teaching only proper techniques, preparing for emergency situations and knowing how to handle them, and having a properly stocked first-aid kit on hand at all practices and games. You can find tips and advice for keeping kids safe in Chapter 16.

Chapter 2

Preparing for a Successful Season

*I*f you want to be a youth baseball coach who teaches kids skills, puts smiles on their faces, and makes them feel good about themselves, you have plenty of behind-the-scenes preparation on your plate before you ever get to the field. Much like hosting a successful dinner party, coaching a youth baseball team requires many ingredients.

So before you break out the bats and balls, dig into this chapter. We provide a helping hand on the easily overlooked aspects of coaching a youth team — aspects that can get lost in the excitement of playing ball. In this chapter, you find a rundown on crafting a coaching philosophy that fits the needs of your players. We explain what you can expect from kids at different ages and how you can motivate, build teamwork, and create a positive atmosphere. We cover the basic steps you need to take before the season: becoming familiar with your league and preparing the necessary equipment. And, if your son or daughter is on your team, we include information to help the two of you have a truly rewarding experience. The information here will help you achieve your goal of being a coach that kids look up to, learn from, and want to play for.

Developing a Coaching Philosophy

Putting your coaching philosophy in place before you start the season is important to your success both on and off the field. It's like the road map you use when you take the family on a vacation to a new destination. Without one, your chances of getting lost are much greater. A coaching philosophy doesn't have anything to do with hitting fastballs or turning double plays; it centers on how you relate to the kids and what you want them to take away from their experience of playing for you.

Developing your philosophy is the easy part, however. The hard part is sticking to it game after game. Others will challenge your philosophy. You may have Sandra's dad questioning why she isn't playing more, because she's the best player on the team. Cameron's mother may wonder why he isn't playing more innings at shortstop. (In Chapter 4, we cover the importance of explaining your coaching philosophy to the parents.)

Build your philosophy around coaches you admire. Think of a coach from your childhood who stands out in your mind for the way he or she made you feel special and taught you to be a good sport. Borrowing the best strategies from the coaches you've played for — or who have coached your kids in the past — is a great way to establish a sound philosophy.

Keep in mind that a sound coaching philosophy — one that's child-friendly, fun, and safety oriented — keeps you and your team on track as you maneuver through the season. In this section, we introduce the various components that should go into crafting your philosophy, including sportsmanship, skill development, safety, and fun.

Tailoring your philosophy to your age group

You want your kids to take the field with the right-sized gloves and bats; having the correct equipment increases their chances of success. The same goes for your coaching philosophy. You need to make sure that your philosophy is the right fit for the age and experience level of the players on your team. The talent level of your team will be all over the map, but age dictates some general characteristics, to a large extent. The following sections outline some of the general characteristics of the different age groups.

Relating to your players — regardless of their age — is paramount for being successful as a coach. The more you get to know your kids on a personal level, the more comfortable and happy they'll be with you. Talk to them about anything appropriate to forge a coach-player bond. Hit on topics such as their favorite baseball players or teams or their favorite subjects in school.

Ages 6 and under

Many kids in the 6-and-under age bracket — besides having an attention span that is measured in seconds — have no clue how to hold or swing a bat, how to use their gloves to scoop up ground balls, or how to run the bases. As a coach for these kids, you're in the unique position of introducing them to the wonderful game of baseball. How you go about teaching the fundamentals of the game can spell the difference between whether your kids want to continuing playing or look elsewhere for other interesting activities.

Because kids in the 6-and-under age group are newcomers to baseball and will be limited to T-ball and coach's pitch, your mission is to zero in on the most basic elements of the game. You want to build a solid foundation that other coaches can add to as the kids continue on with the sport. Youngsters at this age usually have very little to no experience with organized teams, so they won't be comparing how their skills measure up to others on the team. These kids get excited about wearing cool uniforms, hanging out with their friends, and chasing the occasional butterfly. Because of this, many beginning baseball programs, like T-ball, don't keep score.

Ages 7 to 9

Children in the 7-to-9 age range — particularly kids who have been playing baseball for a couple years now — begin becoming more interested in various aspects of the sport. They observe how their teammates perform certain skills — how hard they can hit the ball and how proficient they are at catching pop ups — and want to compare how they stack up. Some of these kids show an interest in competition, and they want to showcase how well they can perform certain skills, for any number of reasons. Maybe they thoroughly enjoy the sport and simply want to keep progressing, or maybe they've watched older brothers or sisters play and now want to receive the same approving looks and applause for playing well.

With this age group, coach-pitch is the predominant program for kids, though some programs allow youngsters to pitch, too. With kids in this age bracket, your philosophy should be focused on really honing in on the fundamentals of the game. If kids don't have a solid foundation to work from, their chances of progressing in the sport are greatly diminished.

Ages 10 to 12

For many youngsters, the 10-to-12 age range is the time when sports start taking on defining roles in their lives. Many kids have posters of their favorite players on their bedroom walls; they can recite their heroes' stats as quickly as the alphabet; and they closely watch the moves of the players on their favorite teams and try emulating them when they step on the field.

As a coach for these kids, your mission is to continue fueling their interest by helping them build on their skills so they're able to enjoy learning and improving. The majority of 10- to 12-year-olds have been involved with baseball for several years, and they've really taken a liking to it. Winning and losing takes on more prominence for them. They anxiously look forward to competition and to displaying their skills during games and honing them during practice. Each kid wants to play a role in his or her team's success.

Most of your kids at this level will have a decent handle on most of the game's basics, and they'll rely on you to help propel them to higher levels.

Ages 13 to 14

Although the baseball field isn't nearly as challenging for a coach as teenage issues are for a parent, coaching teenagers requires a special touch on your part. Kids ages 13 to 14 are often on a journey of self-discovery. Some may tune out your instructions because they think they know the game well enough by now. Making matters even trickier is that you'll also be competing with lots of other things that will grab your players' attention, such as boyfriends and girlfriends.

For this age group, your mission is to continue the fun and learning, while also finding the right positions on the field for each player that give the team the best chance of performing up to its ability.

Emphasizing teamwork

With team sports like baseball, the more your kids can work together, the more success they're likely to enjoy on the field. The true essence of teamwork comes out when players understand the benefits of working together and actively want to do so. As the coach, the responsibility of bringing the team together falls on your shoulders. Teamwork should be part of the foundation of your coaching philosophy. The following list provides some pointers for fostering teamwork:

- ✔ **Applaud all components of a successful play.** Cheering success seems pretty simple, but many coaches neglect this aspect without even realizing it. For example, say your shortstop makes a nice backhanded grab on a ground ball and makes an off-balance throw to first base that hits the dirt in front of the bag but still gets the runner out by a half-step. Naturally, you should applaud the shortstop's effort, but don't overlook the first baseman. Maybe his scoop made the difference in the play.

- ✔ **Encourage enthusiasm in the dugout.** A dugout with players continually supporting one another is the best indicator of team camaraderie. Encourage your kids to keep their focus on the game, and let them know that when they cheer for their teammates, they'll get the same treatment when the roles are reversed. Also, make sure you give as much praise to a kid who never gets on base as you do a player with a rocket arm and a quick bat.

- ✔ **Spread the captain's role around.** You don't need to have team captains, but if you want to go that route to build self-esteem and enthusiasm, be sure that all your kids get the opportunity — particularly if you're coaching younger kids (see the previous section). (At the more advanced levels, you can feel more comfortable with the team captains serving in that role all season long.) Giving kids the chance to lead practice warm-ups or to demonstrate a particular drill puts everyone on equal footing, reducing the likelihood that certain kids will feel less important than some of their teammates.

✔ **Build team bonds.** Organizing team activities is a great way to build team chemistry. Chapters 19 and 20 offer some cool suggestions.

Motivating your players

Chances are, you volunteered to coach this season (or applied for the job) because you love the game and want to help young kids learn and enjoy the game. The reasons the kids show up to play for you, however, usually aren't quite so clear. Youngsters may play baseball for all sorts of reasons. Some players want to try something new; some play because they love the game; and others sign up because their parents want them to be stars, just like they were. You need to tailor the motivational portion of your coaching philosophy to the different personalities on your team.

Here are some tips to keep in mind to squeeze the most out of your players' ability and to help them fully enjoy their season:

✔ **Be enthusiastic.** Enthusiasm is contagious — if you show passion and genuine love for teaching the game of baseball, your infectious attitude will rub off on your players.

✔ **Dangle goals that the kids can reach.** Create goals that your kids can realistically attain, which keeps them working hard. If your goals are too far out of reach, they'll become more of a burden than a motivator.

✔ **Teach winning.** Let your players know that the scoreboard doesn't define winners. Winners are players who always give their best effort, whether your team is winning a close game or trailing by ten runs in the bottom of the last inning. For example, if your team is losing by ten, but your players keep hustling out ground balls and cheering for each other in the dugout, make a big deal of this after the game. If you instill this trait in your kids, it can spill over into all other aspects of their lives.

✔ **Downplay wins and losses.** At the younger levels, coaches must learn to ignore the scoreboard and focus on teaching and making the game fun. If you're constantly worried about the score, your players will notice. If you downplay the score — regardless if you're up or trailing by a bunch of runs — your players will follow suit.

✔ **Make a big deal about the good stuff.** You'll spend time during practice correcting players who perform skills the wrong way. This task is important, but be sure to give equal time to all the good things that happen during practice, too. When a player uses the proper form to backhand a ball — even if he doesn't throw the runner out at first base — let him know what a nice play he made.

✔ **Throw out the threats.** Create an environment in which your kids understand that making mistakes is part of baseball and that you won't punish them for the slightest slip-up. You want your players to learn from their mistakes, not be humiliated because of them. If a child works hard but can't seem to pick up a skill, you need to find another approach that helps him get it down while always offering encouragement.

Fostering a positive atmosphere

Employees do their best work, with the motivation to give their best efforts every day, when they feel that their companies value their contributions and appreciate their efforts. The most effective leaders create work environments in which people enjoy coming to work every day.

A similar approach is applicable in the baseball-coaching ranks. Establishing an environment where your players feel comfortable and like they're part of something special allows plenty of learning and skill development to take place. A vital part of your coaching philosophy is building team bonds between you and your players and between your players and their teammates.

The following list presents a couple approaches that will help you carve out an atmosphere that promotes team spirit and rewards players who give 100 percent at all times:

✔ **Perform a team cheer.** This gives you an opportunity to bring your team together before you take the field. Belting out a simple cheer is a great reminder to your kids to play together and support one another. You can solicit input from your players if you want to get really creative with your cheer. If not, a basic cheer — such as "one, two, three, team!" or "one, two, three, together!" — does the job.

✔ **Call attention to great effort.** Kids need constant reminders that putting forth their best effort — even if it results in mistakes — is okay. Praising a player's effort, while providing positive feedback to correct any mistakes, is a much more effective coaching technique than simply criticizing a miscue. If you follow this technique, your players will have more fun learning, because they won't worry that if they make a mistake, you'll yell at them or remove them from the game.

Keeping lines of communication open

The most effective coaches establish special bonds with their players, in which coach-player conversations involve so much more than how the player should bend his knees to field a ground ball. Besides being a coach, you should be a mentor and confidant — someone that your players are comfortable coming to for any reason, whether they have problems or want to share personal successes.

It's up to you to create these lines of communication. You can fuel conversations by talking about subjects that have nothing to do with baseball. While you're playing catch before practice, walk around to different players to find out if they have any brothers or sisters, what kinds of pets they have, or what they like doing away from the field.

When dealing with really shy kids, patience is more than a virtue, it's paramount for making any progress. Instead of pressing the child to talk, continually make positive comments to him at every practice to try to gradually get him to open up a bit. Early in the season, sprinkle your comments to him with yes-and-no questions that don't put much pressure on the child to talk, and eventually you can build up to asking him questions that require more than one-word answers.

Keep up an active dialog with your kids' parents as well, a topic we discuss in much more detail in Chapter 4.

Focusing on fun and skill development

As you embark on the season, you need to set your sights on making sure your kids acquire a variety of skills and have fun doing so. The true measure of your effectiveness as a coach is whether your kids learned skills — safely — and had big smiles on their faces the entire time.

However, winning and losing is part of the youth baseball puzzle, too, and you shouldn't overlook it. After all, kids will experience various forms of wins and losses in everything they do — from taking tests in school, to applying for jobs, to going head-to-head against business competitors — and one of your jobs as coach is to prepare the kids for life off the field.

When you define the importance of winning with younger kids, proceed as carefully as you would through a minefield. Kids are highly impressionable. If they sense that, deep down, winning is what really matters to you, fun and skill development will take a back seat, and they may not give you a chance. The younger and less experienced the children are, the less emphasis you should place on wins and losses. Focus on teaching skills and, even if your team fails to score a run, praise them for their efforts and make sure they had a good time. When you don't pay attention to the score, your players are less likely to worry about it.

A team goal board is a great tool for shifting the focus away from the score-board and toward developing and improving as players and as a team. The goals you create should give the kids something to strive for during the game. You can keep the goals basic for the younger kids, such as running hard to first base every time. For kids on a more advanced team, you can challenge them to limit the number of extra-base hits by the opposition. (For more on setting goals, see the earlier section "Motivating your players".)

Modeling good sportsmanship

A not-quite-so-obvious aspect of coaching youth baseball — but one that's equally important as teaching infielders how to handle ground balls and out-fielders how to catch pop flies — is teaching good sportsmanship. Because television bombards youngsters with images of poor sportsmanship in both the professional and collegiate ranks, you need to make a committed effort to encourage them to be good sports.

Good sportsmanship starts and ends with you; you are the model for your kids to follow. The following list presents some ways you can put a respectful roster on the field:

- ✔ **Talk about sportsmanship all the time.** Anytime you have a chance to slip in a comment about being a good sport, be sure to take advantage of it. If a big game on TV featured a great display of good sportsmanship, casually talk to the kids about it while they loosen up before practice. Take every opportunity to establish a mode of behavior that earns respect and admiration from opponents, parents, and fans.

- ✔ **Always practice what you preach.** Talking to your team about the importance of being a good sport and then arguing with an opposing coach or umpire during a game sends a pretty distorted message to your kids. Chances are good that the kids will behave exactly like you over just listening to what you said.

- ✔ **Make a big deal about your good sports.** Acknowledging displays of good sportsmanship is a nice reminder to your players that their behavior before, during, and after games is important.

- ✔ **Shake hands with the opposition.** Whether you win the game by a run or got clobbered by a dozen, you and your players should always line up to shake hands with the opposing team after the game. Another classy move is to shake the umpire's hand and/or say "thank you" afterward.

- ✔ **Never allow problems to linger.** Hopefully, you'll have few encounters with out-of-control parents or coaches who spend entire games yelling at umpires. In Chapter 17, we present tips on how to handle this type of inappropriate behavior, which has no place in youth baseball.

Understanding How Your League Operates

Youth baseball programs vary from community to community all around the country — from the operations rules to the type of league itself. The basics of the game itself are the same for the most part, but each league tweaks or modifies the rules to fit the needs of its community. Some programs stick to the official rules of baseball and youth sports as closely as gum sticks to a shoe, but the majority of youth programs make alterations to tailor to the age and experience level of the kids. A big part of your job as a coach is to understand the league you work in and to be able to communicate the rules of the league to players and parents. In the following sections, we outline the factors you must consider — league rules, the rainout policy, rescheduling issues, practice time, and the competitiveness of the league.

Throwing the book at 'em: Your league's rules

Even if you played high school or college baseball and know the rules of the game inside and out, make sure you scan through your league's rulebook anyway as a refresher, paying special attention to any rules that have been tweaked to fit the age or experience level of the kids. Your league may use some rules that you never learned when you played as a youngster, or some basic rules may be drastically changed to fit the program you're coaching in. To be a complete coach and a good teacher of the game, you have to know the rules of the game *and* the special rules your league will enforce this season. If you don't know and understand the rules that have been modified to accommodate the needs of your players, your players probably won't either.

Even if you'll be coaching older players, don't jump to conclusions and assume that everyone on the team knows all the rules. You don't want to overwhelm kids with a lengthy discussion on the different rules in place in this league, so introducing a couple of them during each practice is usually a pretty good way to allow them to get comfortable with all of them. In the parent packets that you distribute during your preseason parents meeting, which we cover in Chapter 4, include a rundown of the rules that have been modified for your league. This helps eliminate any confusion among the parents and is another great way to show them that you care about making everyone's experience this season an enjoyable one.

Blame it on the rain: Makeup games

Sometimes, Mother Nature won't let your players take the field. Some leagues also exert some power by shutting down access to fields, even for practices, later because of slippery conditions that pose a liability risk. When your league cancels games because of rain or other bad weather, you need to know what steps the league takes next and what to tell your players. Some leagues set aside days in the schedule for makeup games, and others simply instruct teams to move forward without making up games. Knowing your league's policy regarding makeup games and communicating this policy cuts down on any confusion among parents when bad weather hits. (See Chapter 4 for more info on handling the scheduling and rescheduling of games and practices.)

The job of youth baseball coach comes with many responsibilities, but being a meteorologist isn't one of them. However, you must constantly be aware of your surroundings and changing weather conditions in your area. Waiting for the first sign of lightning before you cancel practice or stop a game so you can squeeze in some baseball is a risk not worth taking — ever. Get your players off the field before weather threatens the area. If conditions become dangerous during a game, you don't have to wait for the umpire or a league official to make the call. Step up to the plate, so to speak, and get your kids off the field right away.

Age is the only number: Practices, practices, practices

The age of the players on your team usually determines how often you get to practice each week:

- ✔ In most beginner leagues (ages 5 to 8), you can have only one practice and one game a week.

- ✔ In most intermediate leagues (ages 9 to 12), you're typically allowed one to two practices a week, with a game mixed in.

- ✔ In most advanced leagues (ages 13 and above), you often play a couple games a week, as well as practice once or twice a week, too.

Make sure you're aware of your league's policy before you start planning your practices and before your initial parents meeting (see Chapter 4).

Sometimes, leagues take the burden of planning practices off the coaches' shoulders by scheduling the entire season based on the number of fields available. So, before your season gets underway, find out if this is the case. You may discover that your team will be practicing every Tuesday from 6 to 7 p.m. on Field 2, for example.

Two teams enter, one team practices: Rescheduling policies

Occasionally, you may show up for practice only to find another team already on the field. Therefore, you should get to know your league's policies for scheduling practices before the season. Usually, the league takes care of all the scheduling and assigns your team to a specific field and time each week.

Other times — often at the more advanced levels of play — the responsibility falls on the coach to reserve fields at the league's facility for practice. With older kids, you need to schedule practice around the league's tournament or travel schedule. Knowing your league's policy saves you the embarrassment of showing up at the facility with nowhere to play.

For fun or for first place?

You're most likely coaching in one of two types of youth baseball programs: A recreational league or a competitive league. Each league requires a different coaching approach, so you need to know what you're getting yourself (and your players) into from the start.

Make sure you find out what type of league you're coaching in prior to agreeing to volunteer to coach. You need to know if the opportunity is the right fit for you. Simply check with the recreation director to find out.

Recreational leagues

Most first-time baseball coaches or coaches who have limited experience are involved in recreational leagues. Recreational programs center on helping the kids learn the fundamentals of the game while having a lot of fun.

A recreational youth league has many unique characteristics that you must consider when you sign up and begin preparing for the season:

✔ Most recreational leagues have rules in place regarding equal playing time. This makes your job somewhat easier because the focus is on making sure all the kids get fair chances to play a variety of positions. (See Chapter 5 for info on evaluating your team.)

✔ Usually, the smaller the kids, the smaller the playing field when it comes to rec leagues.

✔ Rec leagues feature slightly altered rules to meet the needs of the age and experience level of the kids.

T-ball is the perfect example. Because the players are so young — usually five years old — they hit off a tee because at this age, kids don't have the coordination to hit a pitched ball. Many rec leagues are *coach's pitch,* where the coach of the team that's batting pitches to his or her players. Coach's pitch ensures that the kids get a chance to hit the ball.

✔ Rec leagues are also popular among kids ages 9 to 14. These leagues, while focusing on equal playing time in many programs, are also competitive. These leagues allow the kids the chance to test their skills against others their age in a less stressful environment than in the more advanced programs.

If you're coaching in a coach's pitch league, make sure that you spend time during practices pitching to the kids from the distance that's allowed in the games. Also, try pitching from one knee so that the pitches don't have such a steep trajectory, which gives kids better pitches to hit. (Use a foam pad, such as the type gardeners use, to ease the strain on your knees.) Practicing in this manner get the kids accustomed to hitting pitches they'll see in games, and it's also good practice for you. The last thing you want is to get into a game situation where you can't deliver the ball over the plate for the kids to hit!

Competitive leagues

For many kids, their passion and love for the game is so great that they want to practice more and play more games than their local recreational leagues offer. Luckily for these go-getters, many communities offer competitive programs, which are often referred to as *All-Star teams,* or *travel teams.*

Travel teams aren't for every child, just as they aren't for every coach. Kids that play on these teams have more advanced skills and enjoy the chance to compete against players of similar ability. As the name suggests, these teams often travel to compete in statewide and national tournaments. Some of the kids on these teams have their eyes on long-term advancement in the sport, such as securing college scholarships. So, tread carefully if you want to venture into the waters of this highly competitive environment.

Travel-team and All-Star coaches have vastly different responsibilities compared to recreational league coaches:

✔ You may have to conduct tryouts.

✔ You may have to make difficult decisions on what players to add to the team and who to cut.

✔ You have to run multiple practices during the week, which come between a pretty heavy load of games.

✔ You have to deal with all the travel (and the expense that comes with it), particularly if your team fares well at local and regional tournaments and keeps advancing to higher levels of competition.

For these reasons, All-Star or travel teams are usually coached by individuals who have plenty of experience coaching youth baseball and who are knowledgeable about all areas of the game.

Try coaching for a season or two to prepare yourself to coach in a league with more advanced players and with more intense parents. Or, offer your services as an assistant coach on a travel team and get a season or two of experience there before taking the reins of a travel team yourself. If you sign up for a travel team only to find yourself in over your head, notify the league director immediately. Tell him that you prefer coaching a less-experienced team in a less-competitive league.

From Helmet to Cleats: Gathering the Necessary Gear

One of the many great aspects of the sport of baseball is that it doesn't require a ton of equipment to play like football or hockey. That's why you can drive by any vacant lot in the summer and see kids out hitting balls and playing catch. Plus, most youth programs provide some basic equipment, leaving it up to the players to take care of only a few items. The following sections give you a rundown of what your players need to provide and what the league will provide. Make sure to make it clear to parents what they need to provide (see Chapter 4). We also give you some pointers on checking equipment to make sure it meets safety standards.

What the player is responsible for

In most leagues, youngsters are responsible for providing the following pieces of equipment:

- **Glove:** A glove is a highly personal piece of equipment. It must fit the child's hand and feel comfortable. Using a glove that's too big or too small compromises the child's effectiveness in the field.

  Softball gloves are larger, because, after all, the ball is larger. Gloves should be specifically labeled for use as baseball or softball gloves.

  At the more advanced levels of play, where kids typically play a specific position all season long, you may want to encourage them to get a glove that is appropriate for where they play in the field. Many gloves are made for specific positions, so a youngster playing the outfield is going to be more successful using a glove designed for outfielders. Follow the manufacturer's guidelines on age and glove size.

- **Bat:** Bats come in a variety of lengths and weights. Recommend to the parents of your players that they have their kids swing several bats before making their selections. At the beginning levels bats are usually provided by the league, but some youngsters may be more comfortable having their own.

  Baseball and softball bats differ, too. At the youngest ages, the differences are negligible, but make sure you examine bats you're thinking of purchasing to see if they're made for softball or baseball use.

- **Shoes:** At the beginning levels, like T-ball, regular athletic shoes work just fine for the kids. At the more advanced levels, kids opt for cleats for better traction at the plate and in the field. Leagues often have policies in place regarding what types of cleats are allowed; be sure to check on this prior to your preseason parents' meeting (see Chapter 4).

✔ **Socks:** Regular socks work fine at the younger levels of play. At the more advanced levels kids will opt for baseball socks. Many programs also provide the players with socks that match the uniform.

Have all your players bring an extra set of laces for their cleats. Put the laces in a bag with their names on it, and store the bag in your first-aid kit or equipment bag. Broken shoelaces can wreak havoc if you don't have a spare set.

✔ **Baseball pants:** Much like a pair of jeans, fit is the most important aspect of a pair of baseball pants. The pants must be comfortable and provide plenty of room so that they don't hinder the child's ability to run the bases or to chase down balls in the field.

✔ **Cup and jock strap:** This combo is an important piece of equipment — particularly for catchers, who have to deal with balls that batters foul off the plate. Players can find cups and jock straps at sporting-goods stores, usually placed together. These pieces of equipment aren't needed at the younger levels since kids rotate around to a variety of positions.

✔ **Batting gloves:** Players wear batting gloves to get a better grip on the bat. Kids love looking like Major Leaguers, and Major Leaguers love to wear batting gloves.

✔ **Mouth guards:** Many programs require that kids wear mouth guards whenever they are at bat or playing in the field. You can even encourage your players to all wear the same color to help promote team unity.

During your preseason parents meeting, let parents know that if the cost of the equipment is a financial burden that they should check out what is available at a used equipment store; or perhaps the league has a surplus of equipment that it can loan out.

What the league is responsible for

Most youth baseball leagues provide the following pieces of equipment for their players:

✔ **Batting helmets:** No child should ever stand at home plate without a batting helmet — in practices or in games. A properly fitting helmet is the key to protection and comfort, so your league should provide many helmets of varying sizes. In many leagues, the helmet must include a face guard to protect the child's eyes and face from errant pitches.

Teach your players to treat the helmets as the valuable pieces of safety gear they are. Don't allow them to throw or slam the helmets in anger or to otherwise damage them.

✔ **Team shirts:** The jerseys usually have the team name on the front. Some leagues base their team names on the major league teams, and others have sponsors that pay for the cost of the shirts.

✔ **Caps or visors:** Players wear hats to help shield their eyes from the sun and to proudly display their team colors off the field.

Outfitting a catcher with safety equipment

Catchers look like they're going into battle with all the gear that they wear. However, they aren't just showing off to intimidate opponents; every piece of equipment plays an important role in providing protection. Here's a rundown of what a catcher should have on before he squats behind the plate, including how you can ensure that the equipment fits properly:

✔ **Mask/helmet:** Many leagues mandate that catchers must wear hockey-style goalie helmets. Regardless of the helmet style, make sure the helmet has some sort of throat protection. Most of today's masks are made with an extended throat guard. The helmet should fit securely, but it shouldn't be so tight that the child can't easily remove it when he's attempting to catch a foul ball or throw to a base.

✔ **Chest protector:** This piece of equipment protects the shoulders, chest, clavicles, and heart. Measure the youngster from his clavicle bone to his belly button to determine the required length. The straps should be adjusted until the protector fits firmly; it shouldn't move around on the catcher's body as he performs his duties. Also, he shouldn't feel any space between any part of his body and the chest protector while he's in the squatting position, and the protector shouldn't fold up on him. Some protectors provide shoulder guards for extra protection.

Softball-specific chest protectors feature a full-body design for youth-league use.

✔ **Shin guards:** Shin guards protect the child's knees, ankles, and shins. Different manufacturers use different measurements for their models, so you (or your league) can check with them (often on their Web sites) to determine how they establish their measurements. Some common measurements go from the top of the leg guard to the ankle or from the center of the kneecap to the ankle. To ensure a proper fit, have your catcher take his normal squatting position, as well as run, with the gear on. His knees should be covered within the leg guard, and his anklebone shouldn't be exposed. The toe plate should cover the top of the child's foot, but it shouldn't extend past the player's toes.

✔ **Cup:** This provides the youngster with protection from foul balls, as well as collisions with opposing players sliding into home plate.

✔ **Catcher's glove:** At the advanced levels youngsters use a special glove designed for the position. It features extra padding to protect the catcher's hand as he receives pitches.

✓ **Bats and balls:** Some leagues provide each coach with used bats and balls. If your league does this, let your parents know ahead of time (see Chapter 4). This way, their kids can experiment with the bats you have during practice to find out if you have bats they like; if not, they can look into buying different models.

✓ **Catcher's equipment.** The league generally provides all the gear for the youngster behind the plate, which includes a face mask with throat guard, chest protector, and leg guards that protect the knees, shins, and feet. See the sidebar "Outfitting a catcher with safety equipment" for specific info on catcher's gear.

Inspecting equipment to ensure that it meets safety standards

A piece of safety equipment can do what it's designed to do only when you and your players properly maintain it and inspect it regularly. Anytime you're about to give a youngster a piece of equipment, be sure to inspect it for any problems or signs of wear that can hamper its effectiveness. For example, check batting helmets to make sure they don't have any cracks or loose screws. Also, look inside the helmets to ensure that the foam padding is in good condition and isn't loose. Also, you should always read the manufacturer's instructions for caring for a piece of equipment to make sure that you're properly maintaining it.

If you notice that a piece of equipment provided by the league is defective, remove it right away and contact the league director to secure a replacement. If a player brings equipment to the field that isn't in good condition, don't allow him to use it. Let the parents know that it isn't safe and either needs to be repaired or replaced.

Calling Coach Dad! Tips for Coaching Your Own Child

If your child has an interest in playing youth baseball, and you have an interest in coaching the sport, you should have a chat with him to get a sense of how he feels about you running his team this season. Remember, the sport of youth baseball is all about your child and ensuring that he, along with his teammates, has the most rewarding experience possible. If you don't find out how he feels right away, you risk starting the season off on a poor note.

Roughly 85 percent of volunteer baseball coaches have their own children on the team. If you fit into this category, you've ventured into common parenting territory. Take this to heart and talk to other parents you are friends or acquaintances with who have coached their own children. These coaches can be great sources of information and can give you advice on how to make the situation work. If you're new to your community, check with your local recreation director for the names of some parents who would be great contacts to get feedback and insight from.

Focusing on all in the family

If you and your child agree that coaching his team sounds good to the both of you, keep these tips in mind as you go through the season to help ensure that you both enjoy the experience:

- **You're not just the coach, you're also the parent.** Regardless if your child knocks in the game-winning run or strikes out in the bottom of the last inning, assume your parenting role on the car ride home from the game. That means asking him whether he had fun and piling on the praise for doing his best and displaying good sportsmanship.

- **Communicate.** In order to know how your child feels about you, your coaching, and the season in general, make sure he clearly understands that he can come to you with a concern or problem at any time. Just because you're the coach doesn't mean certain topics regarding the team are now off-limits.

- **Don't force practice sessions at home.** If you sense he's really interested, casually ask if he'd like to spend some time working on a certain skill at home. If he is, that's great, and you two can spend some quality time together working on his game. But if not, let it go. Pushing your child to perform extra repetitions can drain his interest in the sport.

- **Never make comparisons.** All kids learn skills at different rates, so be sure to give your child room to develop at his own pace. Don't burden him with expectations to perform like an older or younger sibling. This type of pressure is unreasonable and unfair, and it can crush self-esteem, destroy confidence, and often drive kids away from the field.

- **Pile on the praise.** Your child deserves a lot of credit for sharing you with a group of other kids and you should let him know that you appreciate his willingness to do so.

Walking the parenting-coaching tightrope

Coaching your own child can be a great experience for both of you, though it isn't always easy. You may feel like you're riding a roller coaster of emotions as you wrestle with finding a balance between providing preferential treatment or going too far out of the way in the other direction to make sure you're not. Ideally, your behavior should fit somewhere between these two extremes. If not, take a look at the consequences that you may face:

- **Providing preferential treatment:** Coaches naturally have to fight the tendency of showing preferential treatment for their own children. This special treatment can be in the form of extra playing time, the chance to play the best positions, team-captain designation, or a lopsided amount of praise during practices and games. Do your best not to play favorites because it pushes your child into an uncomfortable position with his teammates and weakens team camaraderie.

- **Overcompensating to avoid the preferential treatment label:** Coaches can also go too far in their efforts to ensure that no one thinks their children are getting preferential treatment. What happens is they actually reduce their child's playing time or give him less attention or instruction during practices, which obviously isn't fair.

Chapter 3

Covering the Baseball Basics

Chances are, if you're interested in coaching a youth baseball team, you played baseball as a child growing up, you enjoy watching the game on television, and you may even attend major league games to cheer on your favorite team. Regardless of your playing background or how passionate you are about baseball, though, being a coach who kids love playing for and learning from requires having a thorough knowledge of the basics of the game.

One of your many coaching responsibilities is not only knowing all the rules — both general and league-specific — but also being able to explain them to your players. You need to be able to identify every area on the playing field. You also must have a grasp on all the offensive and defensive skills kids need to have to be successful. Plus, the kids will learn a lot about the game and have a good time if you can teach them some baseball lingo. All that valuable information and more is at your fingertips in this chapter.

Surveying the Playing Field

No view in sports is quite like the sight of a freshly mowed and raked baseball field. Of course, if you're new to the game and only see it on television occasionally, all those chalk lines and markings may seem a little intimidating — but no need to worry. In this section, we give you a quick rundown of what you'll find when you step on the field with your players. After taking our tour — both inside and outside the lines on the field — we're confident that you'll have an even greater appreciation for the game.

Inside the lines

One of the coolest characteristics of a baseball field is that every marking within the playing area serves a distinct purpose that's integral to the game. Most of the action occurs within the white lines that divide fair and foul territory, so your tour of the playing field begins here (see Figure 3-1 for a visual representation of the markings in the following list):

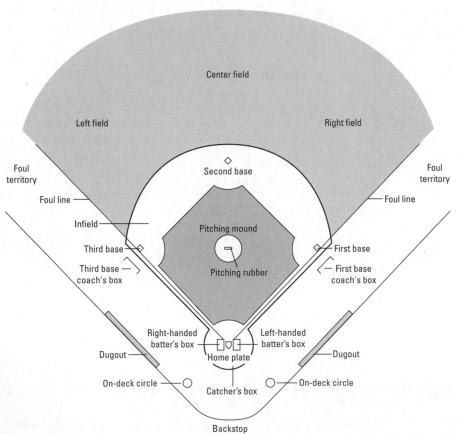

Figure 3-1:
The setup of a baseball field.

- **Foul lines:** These lines, marked by white chalk, extend from home plate to the outfield fence along the first and third base paths. The bottom portion of home plate — the two diagonal lines coming to a point — serves as the starting point for both lines.

  Foul lines are there to determine if a batted ball is fair (in play) or foul (out of play, counting as a strike [unless the batter has two strikes, in which case the at-bat continues]). Any ball that lands on a foul line, to the left of the first-base line, to the right of the third-base line, or that hits first or third base is considered fair. Balls that land outside the foul lines are foul balls.

- **Bases:** A baseball infield is shaped like a big diamond, with the bases placed at the four corners of the diamond. Moving counterclockwise from home plate around the infield, which is what a base runner must do, you have first base, second base, and then third base.

- **Base lines:** These lines, also marked by white chalk, extend from home plate to both first and third base. When players run outside these lines they can be called out for being too far outside the base paths. The base lines that run from first to second base and second to third base aren't marked.

- **Batter's boxes:** The chalked rectangles to the left and right of home plate. A batter stands in one of the boxes during his at-bat — a right-handed hitter in the left box, and a left-handed hitter in the right.

- **Catcher's box:** At the younger levels, some programs use chalk to create a catcher's box to give the catcher a better sense of where he should position himself. Advanced programs don't mark off this area.

- **Infield:** This refers to the entire playing area surrounding first, second, and third base. It also includes the areas around the pitcher's mound and home plate. The infield isn't necessarily "marked," but you can consider it contained on most fields by the foul lines and the outfield grass that starts where the infield dirt ends. (For more on teaching infield play, see Chapter 10.)

- **Outfield:** The grassy area beyond the infield, in front of the fence, and in between the foul lines where the left fielder, right fielder, and center fielder play. (For more on teaching outfield play, see Chapter 10.)

- **Pitcher's mound:** The dirt hill located in the center of the diamond, where the pitcher stands to deliver pitches. Many programs simply designate the pitching area with the pitching rubber (see the following bullet) and don't have mounds, and others may scale down the size of the mound.

- **Pitching rubber:** A white slab of rubber located on the pitcher's mound. The pitcher must touch the rubber with his foot while delivering a pitch to a batter. (For more on a pitcher's foot placement, see Chapter 11.)

Outside the lines

Beyond the playing field exist several markings and areas that coaches need to be aware of, too. The following list gives you a glimpse at several important features of a playing field that rest outside the foul lines:

- **Backstop:** A fence behind the home plate area that protects spectators from foul balls. The backstop also corrals wild pitches and throws to home plate that get past the catcher.

- **Coaching boxes:** These areas, which sit by first and third base in foul territory, give coaches a place to stand during the action to provide their players with instruction when their team is up to bat. Some beginner leagues allow coaches of the fielding team to actually stand in the field of play to offer guidance to the youngsters (and to keep them from chasing bugs).

- **Dugouts:** These enclosed areas along the first- and third-base sides of the field give players a safe place to sit when their team is up to bat or when they must go to the bench while the team is on defense. Most leagues prohibit youngsters from hanging around open areas of the dugout during play.

- **On-deck circles:** These circles, often formed by dirt or in the grass with chalk or paint outlines, rest behind and off to the side of home plate. The next player to hit in the lineup after the child currently at-bat is known as the *on-deck hitter.* This hitter uses the on-deck circle for a couple of purposes:

  - To loosen up before his at-bat

  - To scout the pitcher to gauge the types of pitches he throws and how hard he throws them

Scouting League-Specific Rules

One of the many great aspects of the game of baseball is that the people who run a league can easily modify the rules to fit the age, experience, and skill level of the youngsters who step onto the field. At the beginning levels of youth baseball, from T-ball to coach-pitch, the focus should be on introducing the kids to the basics of the game. At these younger levels, you don't have to stick to the rulebook, because all your attention should center on teaching the kids the fundamentals of the game in a fun environment. Even as the kids get older and more skilled, the rules continue to evolve; as a coach, you have to evolve as well, and you have to know the rules that govern your age group. In the following sections, we outline ways that your league may tweak the rules, or make its own unique modifications, to ensure that all the kids get the most out of their participation.

Making adjustments for the really young

All youth programs at the youngest levels have special rules in place to ensure the kids' safety, ensure fair play, and keep the games moving (for the kids' and parents' sakes). This section details some of the ways your league may modify the rules to meet the youngest kids' needs.

Reduced field size

In youth baseball, the younger the kids are, the smaller the field will be. You can't expect a 6-year-old and his small legs to cover the same amount of terri-tory as a 15-year-old player. After all, the bases appear to be a time zone away! Putting youngsters on a regulation-size field before their bodies are ready leads to frustration and disenchantment with the sport. Keeping begin-ning players on a scaled-down playing area allows them to stay involved in the action and feel like real parts of the game. As players get older, bigger, and stronger, the fields will get bigger, too.

On a regulation field, the bases are 90 feet apart, and the pitcher stands on the pitching mound 60 feet, 6 inches away from home plate. Many youth fields are set up with the bases 60 feet apart and the pitcher standing 46 feet away from home plate. (At the youngest levels, the kids hit off a tee, so the pitcher serves as an additional infielder.)

Of course, field sizes vary from community to community. Factors such as much space is available and how many youngsters are involved in the pro-gram often dictate field size. Find out the size of the field you'll be playing on before getting together with the kids for the season's first practice. You can check with the league supervisor or, better yet, visit the playing field to check it out yourself.

Placement of kids on the field

Many youth games at the youngest levels don't come close to resembling the traditional setup of a pitcher, catcher, four infielders, and three outfielders. The goal of the youngest age levels is to introduce kids to baseball by giving them plenty of chances to field the ball, swing the bat, and get dirty on the base paths — which won't happen with a traditional setup. Just imagine the boredom of a child who's forced to stand way out in center field during a T-ball game. At this level, the kid swinging the bat simply doesn't have the strength to hit the ball into the deep part of the outfield. And in the infield, with only four players, the game would be never ending.

Depending on the number of kids who sign up for your program, you'll have to make adjustments to the norm. You may want to put 10 or 11 players around the field, from the closest part of the outfield in, to make sure that everyone gets an equal amount of playing time and to keep the kids involved. For example, you can line up four players at their infield positions, as well as put three players in the outfield. If you're coaching in a T-ball or beginner league, you may have different options at your disposal because the league doesn't use pitchers and catchers. You may be able to put a player on each side of the pitching area, or position one player in the pitching area and an extra player in the infield or outfield. If you happen to be working with a small roster, you'll have fewer kids spread around the field, but they'll get more opportunities to make plays.

Other rule modifications for beginning-level leagues

At the T-ball level and in other beginner leagues, additional rules are put in place to maximize safety and to keep the kids entertained. The following list presents some of the rules you may encounter:

- **Using different balls and bats:** Most leagues start young kids with a much softer ball than the older kids use so they won't get hurt — or be afraid of getting hurt — when fielding a ground ball or attempting a catch.

 Bats come in a variety of models, and (usually) the younger the player, the lighter the bat. Also, many programs have rules in place on what type of bats are allowed (typically expressed by a length-minus-weight number; for example, a 26-inch, 15-ounce bat is a –11 [spoken as *minus eleven*]). T-ball and younger leagues generally don't have many bat restrictions; older and more competitive leagues may limit bats to –3 or above.

- **Allowing everyone to bat:** To ensure that the kids get an equal number of swings at the plate, some programs require that coaches give each player a chance to bat each inning.

- **Finding the pitcher for outs:** One rule, popular in the T-ball ranks, allows infielders to throw the ball to the "pitcher" rather than first base to get a runner out before he reaches the base. Most young players don't have the coordination or strength to make throws all the way to first base. Usually, the field has a designated circle that the pitcher must stand in for the out.

- **Banning strikeouts:** Many beginner leagues, especially at the T-ball level, allow kids as many swings as they need to put the ball in play.

- **Encouraging on-the-field coaching:** In many leagues, coaches can be on the field to provide firsthand instruction to their players. Maybe you'll want to make sure your kids are positioned properly and that they understand what to do if the batter hits the ball in their direction. The coach remains on the field during the actual play to closely monitor what takes place.

✔ **Shortening games:** Beginners-league games are usually based on a set period of time — about an hour — rather than innings. Many T-ball programs use two-out innings, in which an inning is over when the defensive team records two outs.

✔ **Making unlimited substitutions:** To ensure equal playing time for all the kids, most leagues allow coaches to make unlimited substitutions. This also gives a coach the freedom to let his or her kids experience playing a variety of positions.

Modifying the rules as the kids get older

As kids turn seven and eight years old, many of the rules a league puts in place to protect and help entertain younger players get relaxed a bit or removed altogether. The following rules — sometimes with slight variations — now become important to you. These rules still protect the youngsters you coach beyond the T-ball levels:

✔ **Automatic third-strike outs:** Even if a catcher drops the ball on a third strike, the batter is called out, and the youngster behind the plate doesn't have to make a throw down to first base for the out like he does at more advanced levels of play.

✔ **Coaches as pitchers:** After T-ball beginner's leagues, the next step often is a coach-pitch league. In this type of league, the coach of the team that comes up to bat acts as the pitcher. This format allows the players to enjoy the excitement of hitting pitches and fielding batted balls, and it keeps the game moving.

✔ **Fastballs only:** Many youth programs don't allow youngsters to throw breaking balls or other specialized pitches to protect their arms from injury. The most common pitch on the banned list is the curveball; throwing this pitch places tremendous strain on a youngster's still-developing bones and tendons.

✔ **Limited innings:** As the kids get older, games become structured by innings. Five-inning games are commonplace for kids ages 10 to 12; the older and more advanced levels of play offer games that go seven innings.

✔ **Mercy rules:** If a team scores a set number of runs, determined by the league, during an inning, the team is done batting in that half of the inning. Other variations exist; for example, games may be called if one team leads the other by ten runs or more after five innings.

✔ **No sliding headfirst:** In order to reduce the chance of serious injury, youth leagues often impose rules against players sliding headfirst into bases.

✔ **No stealing:** A common rule at younger age levels is that players can't steal bases. In most leagues, a base runner must have at least one foot on the base until the batter makes contact with the ball. Another option that some leagues prefer is to allow a base runner to take a set number of steps off the base after the ball leaves the pitcher's hand.

✓ **Pitching limitations:** To help young pitchers avoid arm problems, leagues often impose a pitch count, which stipulates that a youngster can throw only a set number of pitches — or innings — in a game before the coach must replace him with another pitcher.

Differences between softball and baseball leagues

Baseball and softball are nearly identical in many respects, but you'll notice a few major differences between the two sports when you begin to compare. You need to know the differences if you're planning to coach beginning-level softball, especially if all your experience has been in baseball. The following list gives you a glimpse at some of the more glaring distinctions:

✓ **Pitching area:** Youth baseball programs, particularly at the advanced levels, feature a pitching mound that the pitcher throws from (the younger levels may call for hitters to hit off a tee or from a ball pitched from their coach). That isn't the case in softball — at any level. The pitcher delivers balls on level ground with the batter. The other major pitching difference is that softball pitchers deliver the ball in an underhand motion; baseball pitchers can throw overhand or even sidearm if they choose.

✓ **Distance from the pitcher's area to home plate:** The game of fast-pitch softball puts a greater emphasis on pitching, because the pitcher throws from a distance much closer to home plate than in baseball. At the beginning levels of youth softball, pitchers generally deliver pitches about 35 feet from home plate. At the higher levels of play, pitchers throw balls from 40 feet.

✓ **Base paths:** The base paths in softball are several feet shorter than those in baseball. When pitchers throw from 35 feet, the bases typically are 55 feet apart; when pitchers deliver balls from 40 feet, the bases usually are 60 feet apart. The smaller base paths in turn create a smaller infield area, which affects the defense of the infielders (see Chapter 10 for more on teaching infield defense).

✓ **Field size:** Outfield measurements vary greatly. A common distance from home plate to the outfield fence in softball is 150 feet for the younger kids, while for the older kids it extends to 225 to 250 feet.

✓ **Size of the ball:** A regulation softball is significantly larger than a regulation baseball. A softball measures between 11.88 and 12.13 inches in circumference and weighs between 6.25 and 7.00 ounces; a baseball measures between 9.00 and 9.25 inches in circumference and weighs between 5.00 and 5.25 ounces.

Sometimes, leagues for the youngest softball players use smaller and softer softballs, because a girl's hand at the beginning levels of play isn't big enough to grip and throw a regulation softball.

✓ **Bats:** At the youth level, bats used for baseball and softball are interchangeable. At the advanced levels of play, players use softball-specific bats, which come in a variety of different materials, such as graphite, carbon, Kevlar, and liquid metal, to name a few. Many softball programs only allow specific types of bats to be used.

Poring Over the Rules of the Game

The game of baseball, in the most basic sense, boils down to the team at bat trying to move runners around the bases and score runs while the team in the field tries to make three outs. Of course, the game can be much more complex than that at the more advanced levels, and at all levels, some of the rules that govern the game can be more confusing than calculus. No need to worry, though, because we have you covered! This section covers the basic aspects of the game; knowing this information makes baseball easier to understand and teach to your youngsters.

Reviewing the structure of the game

Most youth baseball leagues follow the same game structure, with a few variations here and there. Grasping the structure of a game allows you to prepare better and let the kids and parents know what to expect. The following list outlines the basics of what takes place before and during a baseball game (for more on rules variations your league may have, see the earlier section "Scouting League-Specific Rules").

✔ Before the game begins, you must fill out a lineup card. You create the batting order for your team, decide who starts the game on the bench, and assign a position to each youngster who's playing. You must follow the batting order throughout the game, unless you decide to make a substitution at some point. An incoming player takes the same place in the batting order as the player he's replacing.

✔ At the youth league level, games range from two or three innings at the beginning leagues to seven innings at the more advanced levels. Each team gets one turn to bat each inning. When the first team to bat makes three outs (or two if your leagues stipulates), its half of the inning is over. The players grab their gear and take the field, and the opposing team gets to bat.

The team that bats first in the inning is said to bat in the *top half* of the inning, and the team that bats second hits in the *bottom half* of the inning. The team designated as the *visitor* bats in the top half, and the *home team* bats in the bottom half. Most leagues use a simple flip of the coin to determine who bats first.

In the more advanced leagues, you may not have to complete the final inning based on the score. For example, say you coach in a league that plays five-inning games, and your team bats in the bottom half of the innings. If you're leading after the top half of the fifth inning, you don't need to continue, because your team has already won the game!

Batter up! Scoring runs and making outs

A baseball game begins when the umpire yells "Play ball!" and the pitcher toes the pitching rubber on the mound. When he's ready, he delivers a pitch to the opposing batter. The pitcher's goal is to throw the ball in the *strike zone* — an imaginary rectangle as wide as home plate that extends from the batter's armpits to his knees.

In the youngest leagues, games begin differently. In T-ball, play starts after the umpire (or the coach if your league doesn't use umpires yet) sets the ball on the tee and the defensive coach helps his player get positioned. In coach-pitch, the inning gets underway when the umpire signals to the coach that he can deliver a pitch for his player to swing at.

The pitcher can achieve his goal of throwing a strike in different ways:

✔ If the batter swings and misses the pitch.

✔ If the batter doesn't swing at the pitch, but the umpire thinks the ball went through the strike zone.

✔ If the batter hits the ball, but it lands in foul territory.

If the batter already has two strikes against him, he can't make an out for a third strike on a foul ball. It isn't uncommon for a hitter with two strikes to foul off several pitches, keeping his turn at bat going.

Alas, much like batters and umpires, pitchers aren't perfect, which means they'll throw balls on occasion. If the umpire thinks a pitch is outside the strike zone and the batter doesn't swing at it, he calls it a ball. If a batter gets four balls before three strikes, he takes a *walk* and gets a free pass to first base.

A walk is only one of the ways to get on base, however. A batter can reach base and put himself in a position to score in multiple ways; unfortunately, he can also get himself out in many ways. You can find out how in the sections that follow.

No player should ever step out of the dugout without a properly fitting batting helmet so he's protected against foul balls and wild throws. For the scoop on all the different safety equipment, check out Chapter 2.

Getting on base

The goal of every hitter is to get on base or do his part to advance other runners. With either, his team gets closer to its main objective: scoring runs. The following list, though, outlines how a batter can reach base safely:

- ✔ **Hit:** A batter gets a *hit* when he hits the ball and reaches first base without a fielder catching the ball or throwing him out. Getting a hit is the most common route for reaching first base safely. A hit can be any one of the following varieties:

    - **Single:** reaching first base

    - **Double:** rounding first and reaching second base

    - **Triple:** rounding first and second and reaching third base

    - **Home run:** A batted ball that goes over the outfield fence in the air

- ✔ **Error:** Occurs when a fielder misplays a batted ball. An infielder can let a grounder roll under his glove, for example, or toss a ball over the first baseman's head.

- ✔ **Hit by pitch:** When a batter is hit by a pitch without swinging his bat (as long as his feet remain inside the batter's box), he gets to head down to first base.

- ✔ **Catcher's interference:** When the catcher disrupts a batter's swing, often by contacting the player or the bat with his glove, he's called for catcher's interference, and the umpire awards the batter first base.

- ✔ **Fielder's choice:** When a defensive player opts to get another base runner out rather than the batter, the batter reaches base due to a *fielder's choice.* For example, if a batter hits a ground ball to the shortstop with a runner on first base, and the shortstop doesn't have a chance at the double play, he may be satisfied with getting the runner out at second base.

When a batter hits a triple, all the previous base runners score in front of him. With a home run, the player who hits the ball and all runners on base score. With singles and doubles, previous runners may score, but they also can stop at second or third base. For all the other on-base methods, scoring depends on how many runners are on base and how aggressive the base runners are.

Making an out

Batters at all levels do their level best to get on base and avoid making outs, but even the best hitters in the world get out 70 percent of the time. The following list details the many ways that hitters make outs:

- ✔ **Ground out:** When a batted ball rolls along the ground to an infielder, who picks it up and throws it to first base before the batter gets there

- ✔ **Fly out:** When a batted ball flies into the air and is caught by an opposing player before it hits the ground (also known as a *pop out* on balls not hit to the outfield, or a *line out* when the ball is hit sharply)

- ✔ **Foul out:** When a batted ball flies into foul territory and is caught by an opposing player

- ✔ **Strikeout:** When a batter with two strikes swings and misses the pitch; makes contact with a part of the ball (a *foul tip*), but the catcher manages to catch it; bunts the ball foul; or takes the pitch and the umpire calls strike three

- ✔ **Double hit:** When a batter makes contact with the ball, putting it into fair territory, and then touches the ball with any part of his body or bat

- ✔ **Batting out of turn:** When a player doesn't follow the set batting order and goes up to the plate during another player's at-bat (usually not strictly enforced at the beginning levels of play)

- ✔ **Stepping outside the batter's box:** When the batter sticks a foot outside the batter's box while putting a ball into play

Plenty of rules govern the base paths, too — rules that enforce an out for certain actions. You need to make your players aware of what they can and can't do while running from base to base, because base running will be very important to your team's success and your players' development. The following list presents some important bits about the bases:

- ✔ **Going outside the base lines:** The lanes connecting the bases are referred to as the *base paths,* and players must stay within them when running, much like staying between the lines when coloring or driving. If a base runner takes several steps to his right or left to avoid a tag and winds up out of the base path, the umpire can call him out.

- ✔ **Getting tagged out:** A base runner is out if a fielder has the ball in his glove and touches the runner when the runner has no part of his body touching the appropriate base.

    The tag out doesn't apply when a batter runs through first base after touching it — as long as he immediately returns to the base without making any type of move toward second base.

- ✔ **Getting forced out:** A *force out* occurs when a ball hit on the ground forces a base runner to advance to the next base, and an opposing player touches the base with the ball in his possession, before the runner gets there, to record the out.

- ✔ **Touching the ball:** A base runner who touches a batted ball in the field of play costs his team an out. For example, if a runner is going from second to third on a ground ball, and the ball hits his foot mid-stride, he's out.

✔ **Obstructing a player:** A base runner can't interfere with a fielder making a play on a ball. For example, a runner can't bump into a fielder trying to make a catch on a pop fly.

✔ **Passing another base runner:** The base paths are a no-passing zone on the baseball field. A runner who passes a teammate on the bases earns an out and a trip to the dugout.

✔ **Sharing bases:** Although we all know the virtues of sharing and want our kids to share bats and balls, you don't want your base runners sharing bases. Two players can't occupy the same base when a ball is in play; if the defense catches two players in this situation, it can tag out the following runner.

✔ **Missing a base:** A runner must touch each base on his way around the diamond or risk being called out. For example, if a player hits a sure double but fails to touch first base on his way to second, the opposing team can *appeal* the play to the umpire if its players or coaches notice the error. A player (often the pitcher) simply throws the ball to the first baseman, who touches the bag. If the umpire agrees that the runner didn't touch first base, he calls him out.

Navigating the base paths

When players get on base, via a base hit, walk, fielding miscue, or other manner, their job is only partly done. Now they have to navigate their way around the bases. The goal for every base runner is to reach home plate, score a run for the team, and receive high-fives and congratulations from coaches and teammates in the dugout. Running the bases is a tactical part of the game for coaches; you can choose to have your players be aggressive and take more chances — like challenging an outfielder's arm by trying to turn a base hit into a double — or take a more conservative approach and advance one base at a time on hits. Chapter 7 shows you the basic signals that your base coaches use to help guide the runners around the bases.

No matter your approach, you need to make your players aware of a couple base-running rules, which we present here:

✔ Whenever a runner is touching a base, he can't be tagged out by the opposition.

✔ When a ball is in play, runners can try to advance as many bases as possible. For example, when a runner is on first base and the batter hits a base hit into the outfield, the runner may choose to advance to second base and stop; he may want to be more aggressive and try reaching third base; or, if the outfielder misplays the ball, the runner may try to go all the way home (as long as he doesn't pass any teammates along the way or allow the ball to touch him; see the earlier section "Making an out").

✔ When a player is on first base, or stands on another base with the bases behind him full, he must advance to the next base on a ground ball.

✔ When a defender catches a fly ball or a line drive, a base runner must tag up before advancing a base or the umpire will call him out. *Tagging up* means the runner stays on the bag until the defensive player catches the ball; at that point, he can take off for the next base or stay put.

When a runner is about to be a part of a close play at a base, he can gain an advantage by executing a slide to avoid a tag. A *slide* simply means the base runner uses the momentum he has built up by running to drop to the ground and slide into the base. A runner can use several types of slides, but the most common have a player's foot making contact with the base first. For details on teaching your kids sliding techniques, check out Chapter 9.

Taking Positions in the Field

Much like each component of a car engine serves a specific and important purpose, each position on the baseball field contributes in a various ways to a team's success or failure. Each position has a set of unique responsibilities that impact the overall effectiveness of your team's defense. In this way, the positions you must fill are as different as the kids under your care.

Most leagues call for you to have nine players on defense (see Figure 3-2). A basic defense consists of a pitcher, catcher, first baseman, second baseman, shortstop, third baseman, center fielder, left fielder, and right fielder, broken down into the following categories:

✔ **Battery:** Pitcher and catcher

✔ **Infield:** First baseman, second baseman, shortstop, and third baseman

✔ **Outfield:** Left fielder, center fielder, and right fielder

Many beginner's leagues allow more players on the field and arrange for unique setups (see the earlier section "Scouting League-Specific Rules" for more).

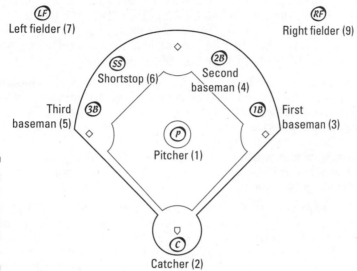

Some positions require players to carry out certain responsibilities if they want to enjoy the positions and play them well. The following list presents the responsibilities that come with each of the positions on a baseball field:

✔ **Pitcher:** The ball rests in the pitcher's hands at the beginning of each play. A pitcher's top priority is to focus on getting the hitter out. Secondary responsibilities include fielding bunts and ground balls, covering first base when the first baseman fields a ground ball, and backing up other infielders during plays at the bases.

✔ **Catcher:** The catcher works closely with the pitcher to get hitters out. Because of the squatting position the catcher takes right behind a hitter, he's covered in protective equipment from head to toe (see Chapter 2 for more on a catcher's equipment).

At the advanced levels of play, a catcher may be in charge of signaling the pitches he wants thrown, as well as where he wants them located, and backing up first base on ground balls. At most every level of play, he's responsible for blocking wild pitches to prevent base runners from advancing, catching foul balls behind home plate, throwing out would-be base stealers, tagging out runners at home plate, and determining whether infielders need to cut off throws from the outfield to home plate when opposing players attempt to score.

✔ **First baseman:** The youngster handling this position is on the receiving end of the majority of the throws other infielders make, including pick-off throws from the pitcher. His responsibility is to catch the ball and make the out — whether the throw is high, off to one side, or bouncing in the dirt. He also must field ground balls and bunts hit his way and catch foul balls on the right side of the infield.

✔ **Second baseman:** The second baseman is in charge of handling ground balls between second and first base and making accurate throws to first and second base (most of the time). He must catch pop ups to the right side of the infield and shallow right and center field. He must field throws from the catcher trying to catch a base stealer and from outfielders at second base or when he serves as the cutoff man. He covers first base on bunt plays. He also executes double plays on ground balls hit to the left side of the infield.

✔ **Shortstop:** The shortstop is responsible for cleanly handling ground balls between second and third base and making accurate throws all over the diamond. He fields throws from the catcher trying to nab a base stealer and from outfielders at second base or as the cutoff man. He covers third base when a third baseman charges a bunt. He tracks down pop ups on the left side of the infield and in shallow parts of the outfield. He also executes double plays on ground balls hit to him and to the right side of the infield.

✔ **Third baseman:** The third baseman must knock down and field ground balls and make long, accurate throws to first and second base. He may serve as a cutoff man for the left fielder, and he receives throws from all the outfielders at third base. He also fields most bunts to the left side of the infield and catches foul balls on the left side of the infield.

✔ **Outfielders:** Outfielders track down and catch fly balls and line drives hit to their specific areas of the field. They scoop up base hits that make their way to the outfield. They're responsible for quickly and accurately throwing the ball back to the infielders. And in advanced leagues, they back up throws made around the infield in case errors are made.

As the coach, you can arrange your players in the field in ways that maximize your team's strengths and take advantage of the other team's weaknesses. For example, if most of your infielders have strong arms, you can have them play farther back than normal to prevent more balls from getting to the outfield. Or, if you play against a team that tends to pull the ball, you may want to shift your infield to the batter's pull side to take away his strength. You can jump to Chapters 5 and 15 for more information on assigning defensive positions based on your players' strengths and using different defensive strategies.

Batting Around Some Baseball Lingo

Baseball has a unique language all its own. The professional game dates back to the 19th century, which makes it one of our oldest sports. Over the years, the game has developed a vocabulary that makes it both intriguing for scholars and fun for kids! The following list presents some of the more common terms and phrases that shape the sport.

Take the time to go over these terms with your young players before you begin using them during practices and games.

At bat: When a player takes a turn hitting at the plate and doesn't record a base on balls or get hit by a pitch.

Bag: A reference to first, second, or third base.

Base on balls: A batter is awarded first base when the pitcher throws four balls (pitches that the umpire deems to be out of the strike zone) before throwing three strikes or inducing the batter into making contact. A base on balls is also known as a *walk*.

Base hit: When a batter hits a pitched ball into fair territory and reaches a base safely without the opposing team committing an error on the play.

Batting average: A figure calculated by dividing the number of base hits a batter has by his number of official at-bats. Batting average is displayed as a number with three decimal places (for example, 0.327).

Corner: A pitch that just barely enters the strike zone is said to be "on the corner," as in "that pitch was just over the inside corner."

Count: The number of balls and strikes on a hitter during an at-bat. When reciting the count, you say the number of balls before the number of strikes. For example, if a batter has one strike and two balls against him, the count is 2 and 1. A batter has a *full count* when the pitcher has thrown three balls and two strikes (3 and 2).

Cutoff man: A player, most often an infielder, who positions himself between an outfielder and the player occupying a base so that he can "cut off," or catch, a long throw and relay the ball to the intended base.

Double play: When a defense gets two players out on one play.

Error: When a defensive player makes a mistake, such as a tossing a wild throw or misplaying a routine ground ball, that allows a batter to reach base safely or a base runner to advance.

Fielder's choice: When a defensive player chooses to attempt getting a base runner out rather than the batter, which allows the batter to reach base safely.

Foul ball: A batted ball that lands on the grass outside the foul lines or goes out of the field of play.

Gap: Also known as the *alleys,* the gaps are the areas of the outfield between the center fielder and left fielder and between the center fielder and right fielder.

Ground-rule double: This occurs when a batter hits a ball that lands in fair territory and bounces out of play, such as over a fence or into the stands, and the umpire awards the batter second base.

Intentional walk: Occurs when a pitcher purposely delivers four pitches well outside the strike zone to walk a batter. Coaches often call for an intentional walk when it's advantageous to the defense to face the next batter or create a different situation on the base paths.

In the hole: A batter who's due up to hit after the on-deck hitter is said to be in the hole.

Line drive: A ball hit sharply in the air, approximately four to eight feet off the ground.

Out of play: A ball hit (or thrown) beyond the fence bordering foul territory (or a designated area if your field doesn't have fences) is out of play.

Passed ball: A pitch — not wildly thrown — that gets past the catcher and rolls to the backstop, allowing the base runners to advance.

Pinch hitter: A player on the bench who enters the game to hit in place of a teammate.

Pinch runner: A player on the bench who enters the game to run in place of a teammate who's on base.

Putout: When a defensive player makes a play that results in a batter or base runner being called out.

Relay: When an infielder (known as the cutoff man) takes a throw from an outfielder and throws the ball to another base.

Run batted in: When a batter delivers a hit, or executes a sacrifice, that allows a base runner to score.

Rundown: Occurs when a base runner gets caught by fielders between two bases, and the fielders try to "run him down" to make the out. A rundown also is called a *pickle.*

Sacrifice: When a batter records an out on purpose in order to advance a base runner. For example, a batter may hit a fly ball to the outfield with a runner on third base, which allows the runner to advance to home after he tags up.

Stolen base: When a base runner swipes a base, usually by taking off for the next base after a pitch crosses the plate. (Rules vary widely for stolen bases; check your league's rules for specifics on stolen bases.)

Baseball by the book

Keeping a scorebook can be a great way to improve your coaching skills at the more advanced levels of play. A *scorebook* is basically a chart that recaps what happens during the game. The chart allows you to look back at how events unfolded and evaluate areas where your team requires a little more practice time. You also can use a scorebook to keep track of who played, how much they played, and where they played. (The scorebook is a good way to generate stats for the team, which your kids will love.) Consider asking an assistant coach or an interested parent to keep the scorebook for you during games so you can focus on your coaching duties.

If you have a good handle on the numbering system for each position (check out Figure 3-2 for a refresher), and when you master some abbreviations common to the game, you're well on your way to having a useful coaching aid at your disposal. Every kind of baseball play has an abbreviation that can appear in your scorebook. The following list gives you a rundown of the important abbreviations:

- ✔ BB: base on balls (walk)
- ✔ DP: double play
- ✔ E: error
- ✔ F: fly ball
- ✔ FC: fielder's choice
- ✔ H: hit

- ✔ HP: hit by pitch
- ✔ K: strikeout
- ✔ L: line drive
- ✔ PB: passed ball
- ✔ RBI: run batted in
- ✔ Sac: sacrifice
- ✔ SB: stolen base
- ✔ WP: wild pitch

Each time a hitter steps to the plate, the scorebook keeper documents what happens by using the numbering system and abbreviations in the previous list. For example, if a batter hits a ground ball to the third baseman and makes an out, the play goes down in the scorebook as 5-3, indicating that the third baseman (5) fielded a ground ball and threw to the first baseman (3) for the out. Use the small diamond in each box to indicate the progress of each base runner. Fill in the diamond when a base runner scores. By keeping track of the other team's batters, too, you'll be able to look back after the game and evaluate how your defense performed.

Keep in mind that you can devise your own symbols, or make your own notations, to keep track of what goes on, too. The scorebook is just another tool you can use to help your players learn and develop in all areas of the game.

Tag up: This refers to base runners advancing on a fly ball. In order to do so, they must touch the base they began on before the pitch and remain there until the ball is touched by a defensive player before attempting to advance to the next base.

Take: To *take* a pitch means to not swing at it.

Triple play: A rare occurrence when the defense gets three players out during one play.

Chapter 4

Meet the Parents

. . . .

In This Chapter

▶ Preparing the preseason meeting (and preparing yourself for the meeting)

▶ Relaying your coaching philosophy

▶ Shuffling the necessary (and helpful) paperwork

▶ Casting parents for supporting roles

▶ Embracing kids with special needs

▶ Fielding questions during and after the meeting

. . . .

*O*ne thing is for certain this season: You're going to be coaching a wide variety of kids and, in turn, meeting a diverse group of parents. Regardless of whether this is their first experience with organized baseball or they're veterans of the bleachers, parents will arrive at the field with their own hopes, ideas, and motivations — many of which will be vastly different than your own. But here's another thing that's for certain: How well you get along with the moms and dads makes a big difference in whether the season runs smoothly or gets derailed by squabbles and complaints.

On deck in this chapter is the preseason parents meeting, which is just as important for you as bats and gloves are for your players. We'll let you know what should you cover during the meeting and give you tips for explaining your coaching philosophy, sharing your goals, and running down your team policies. We'll also prepare you for all the paperwork that gets shuffled your way, and give you the inside scoop on recruiting the right parents for participation in key jobs both on and away from the field.

Let Me Introduce Myself. . .

Whether you're meeting your future in-laws for the first time, a professional for whom you desperately want to work, or the parents of your new players, you only get one chance to make a great, and lasting, first impression. You're on your own with the first two, but when it comes to — excuse the pun — hitting a home run with your players' parents, we're here to help. Holding a preseason meeting can earn you big bonus points right off the bat (okay, enough's enough).

The preseason parents meeting serves multiple purposes. The meeting opens critical lines of communication and sends the all-important message that you value your relationship with the kids and want to work closely with all the parents to ensure that their children have a rewarding season. It's the chance for parents to get to know who their children will be spending time with this season. And it gives you an opportunity to go through important information about how the season will run so parents don't have any unpleasant surprises along the way.

Planning the meeting

Putting the parents at ease before the season starts and creating a comfort zone for them sets the stage for a positive coach-parent-athlete relationship. When you plan your meeting, keep the following key points in mind; they should help the meeting go smoothly:

- ✔ **Plan the meeting right away.** Most parents juggle chaotic schedules, so the more notice you give them about the meeting, the greater the chance that they'll attend. When you get your hands on your team roster, contact each child's parents to introduce yourself and let them know the date, time, and location for your meeting.

- ✔ **Pick a convenient location.** The most convenient meeting spot may be at the recreation department that runs the league. You want to make it as easy as possible on the parents, and most should be familiar with this location because the department is where they signed up their children to participate. Informing the league or recreation director that you want to use the department to meet with your team members' parents is all it usually takes to reserve a room.

  If the recreation department doesn't have the available space, check with a common public place like your local library.

  Anytime you're forced to choose an alternate meeting spot, make sure you provide accurate directions to ensure that parents have no confusion when getting there.

- ✔ **Choose a convenient time.** You want a time that's convenient for the majority of the parents. A meeting at 5 p.m. on a Wednesday is next to impossible for working parents to attend. Your best bet is a 7:30 p.m. meeting sometime during the week.

✔ **Encourage attendance.** During your conversations with the parents, stress the importance of attending the meeting because of all the important information that you'll be sharing.

✔ **Have a backup plan.** Chances are good that not every parent will be able to make the meeting. If you have parents that can't attend, make arrangements to meet with them separately to go over everything you cover during the preseason meeting.

Now that you've set up the meeting and prepared the parents with time, location, and directions, you need to take time to prepare yourself to conduct an efficient, informative, and even entertaining meeting. You want parents to feel at ease when turning their children over to you. Here are some tips for preparing yourself for the preseason meeting:

✔ **Determine what to cover.** Ask yourself what you'd want to know if you were turning your child over to a coach you didn't know for a full season. Some of the questions that immediately come to mind include

- How often will the team be practicing?

- How do you determine playing time?

- How do you assign positions?

- What is our level of involvement?

Use questions such as these as starting points for what you want to talk about, and take it from there. Of course, we spend about a dozen more pages in this chapter helping you with this task!

✔ **Practice your presentation.** You want your players to get better at hitting, fielding, and throwing this season by practicing, so you should expect the same of yourself when it comes to your meeting. The more you practice what you want to say, the more comfortable you'll be. Comfort translates into a smooth-running meeting that will really impress the parents.

Because this meeting carries a lot of significance, approach it with the same enthusiasm and preparation you'd demand when giving an important presentation to a boss. Don't worry, no one expects you to be a professional speaker. However, you should be able to clearly explain your thoughts on the topics you want to cover. This demonstrates how deeply you care about the upcoming season and reinforces your commitment to each child on the team. In the days leading up to the meeting, stand in front of a mirror and practice what you'll say, or rehearse in front of your spouse or a friend.

✔ **Use notes.** Jot down the main topics you want to cover on a notepad, and use the pad during the meeting as a reference. Don't go overboard and read a short novel word-for-word; you don't want to bore the parents and cause them to worry about how much fun their children will have playing for you this season.

Implementing effective meeting strategies

We spend the rest of this chapter detailing the ins and outs of what you should cover during your parents meeting, but keep the following tips in mind when conducting (and when planning) your meeting:

- ✔ **Start with an introduction.** Share with the group why you're coaching the team. You don't need to get carried away with your life story, but a few nuggets of information will be appreciated. Maybe you have a child on the team, or maybe you've coached before and fell in love with it. Show the parents your enthusiasm; it gives you even more credibility when it comes to working with kids.

- ✔ **Transition with an icebreaker.** A good icebreaker, after you introduced yourself, is to have the parents introduce themselves and share the names of their children. The parents will be seeing quite a bit of each other during the season, so they may want to begin getting comfortable with one another.

- ✔ **Distribute handouts.** Pass out any paperwork you have at the conclusion of your meeting (see the "Putting Together the Paperwork" section later in the chapter for information on what to include here). You don't want parents to read through the material during the meeting, causing them to miss important points.

- ✔ **Wrap it up.** Don't subject the parents to a long, drawn-out meeting that has them squirming in their seats and wondering if it's too late to pull their children out and request a different coach. Present your information clearly and concisely without dragging the meeting out. Plan on spending between 30 minutes and one hour — and no more.

Conclude the meeting by asking if anyone has any questions. Also, let parents know that you'll be available immediately afterward if they prefer speaking to you one-on-one.

Presenting Your Coaching Philosophy

Presenting your coaching philosophy to parents doesn't necessarily make you a baseball philosopher, but it does make you an approachable and likeable coach. Let the parents know before the first practice how you're approaching the season and what you want your focus to be. This reduces the chance of having misunderstandings that can sabotage the season and smother the fun. After all, some of your players' parents may be looking at the season from a point of view entirely different than your own. You should concentrate on your stance on three particular issues: playing time, positions, and winning — the foundation of your coaching philosophy. We concentrate on these issues in this section.

Determining playing time through the ages

The issue of how much time players get in the field accounts for the most disagreements and misunderstandings between coaches and parents. Several factors should dictate the amount of playing time kids receive — most notably what type of league you're coaching in and the age of the players. Your job is to explain your process for delegating playing time well in advance of stepping on the field to reduce the chance of problems arising.

You can enter the season with a general plan in place regarding playing time. Putting together a policy that outlines the number of innings each player will play is almost impossible. For example, if the majority of your games are one-run affairs that require your best players on the field, the backups won't see quite as much playing time as they may have thought. Try to outline your policy in general terms so everyone understands what you're aiming to achieve.

Sometimes you have to deliver news that won't go over well with parents. Let them know that you understand the disappointment and hurt feelings and that although they may disagree with you, they need to maintain their composure, control their emotions, and accept your decision as the coach. It's your job to determine who plays where and how often kids get into the lineup.

Be sure parents know that you're always available to speak to them in private about any decisions you make regarding their child. Having an open-door policy in place before the season gets started signals that you're willing to do everything possible to work with parents every step of the way.

Rotating the rookies

Parents who sign up their children for a beginning-level program have a right to expect that the coach will spread out the playing time evenly among all the kids on the team. You should reinforce this goal during the preseason meeting so that every parent understands how you plan to run things on game day. Of course, after the season gets going, some parents may forget your discussion as soon as they see their child taking a turn on the bench, and they may have some difficulty adjusting to that sight. (Jump to Chapter 17 to get the scoop on how to handle these situations.)

Let your parents know that giving kids an equal opportunity to play, have fun, and learn the basics of the game is what the beginning level is all about. Relegating certain kids to the bench or getting them into the game for only an inning or two will quickly drain their interest in the sport. Inform parents that you will carefully track each player's number of innings on the field so that they are evenly distributed as fairly as possible, and that you'll do your best to give kids an equal amount of time at all of the different positions on the field.

If you decide to institute a policy that states the kids who regularly attend practice will share the bulk of the playing time — and you should — make sure you explain the policy clearly during your meeting. It's simply not fair to the kids who show up for every practice to have to share coveted playing time with teammates who show up only on game day. You can get specific and let parents know that missed practices will result in the child sitting on the bench for a set number of innings. For example, your policy can state that if a youngster misses a practice, he'll sit on the bench for two innings during the next game before you work him into the rotation. If parents have legitimate excuses, such as doctor appointments, for why their child missed practice, your best approach is to be reasonable and allow the child to participate.

Fielding the veterans

If you're coaching a team that features kids ages 12 and older, your policies on playing time may be much different. At advanced levels, playing time is more often tied directly to ability, though lots of other areas also dictate how much time the child gets on the field. For example, a talented player who doesn't show up for practice, work hard, or support his teammates shouldn't be put on the field simply because he's a good batter or fielder. Parental eyes are extremely prejudiced — and with good reason — and most parents view their child as the better player when he's competing against another kid for a specific position.

Share with your parents that you understand how they feel and that you realize they won't always agree with you. Speak from the heart that delegating playing time is one of the most difficult aspects of your job because you're put in the position of judging the abilities of these kids. Stress to the parents that you'll always be honest and fair in any decisions you make.

Creating your lineup: Who plays where (and why)

Some parents, when signing up their youngster to play baseball, are already envisioning where they think he should play in the field. Mom and dad were catchers in their heydays, so Junior should be a catcher, too, right? Naturally, the assigning of positions often doesn't play out as they'd hoped, particularly when half a dozen dads think their sons should be playing shortstop. The preseason meeting is the time to set the record straight. Where a child plays depends on his age, his interests, and his abilities. Some kids' skills may be best suited to excel at third base, though they may have had their sights set on playing in the outfield. It'll be up to you, through your practice observations, to evaluate all of your players, assess their skills, and fit them into the right spots to mold a team together.

Your mission, at the youngest age levels, is to give the kids a taste of as many different positions as possible so they get a thorough introduction to the game. Let parents know that your plan is to do your best to let the kids play a variety of positions. With the short amount of time you generally have with the younger age group, though, letting them experience every position may not be possible. At the very least, make sure each child gets to play a couple different spots in the infield and outfield. Most parents will appreciate your efforts.

During the meeting, make the parents aware that they shouldn't be disappointed or express disappointment to their child over the issue of position. Let them know that they may be pleasantly surprised to see their child excel at a position they never gave much thought to him playing. They may find out that he has an interest in playing another position and discover that he has the talent to play it quite well.

At the more advanced age levels, figuring out where kids are best suited to play takes on more importance and plays a significant role in how much success a team enjoys in terms of wins and losses. You may have several kids who want to be the team's starting center fielder, and your job is to figure out which player has the talent to best handle that position and the responsibilities that accompany it.

Let parents know what your plans are for evaluating the kids and that you'll make your decisions based on what's best for the team. If you have a time frame in mind to announce the starters — after the tenth practice, for example — be sure to share it with the parents and kids so they fully understand the process. (In Chapter 5, we provide additional information on evaluating players and assigning positions.)

Emphasizing the importance of model behavior in the stands

Sometimes the childish behavior at youth baseball games around the country doesn't take place on the field; it takes place in the stands, with parents as the culprits. Crazy parent behavior may make for entertainment in the movies, but in real life, it only leaves the children embarrassed.

Be very clear and straightforward during the meeting about how you expect parents to behave during games and practice. Emphasize that parents need to be models of good sportsmanship before, during, and after games, regardless of who wins or loses or what transpires on the field.

Teaching players the importance of good sportsmanship requires the parents working with you and not against you. Your youngsters should be following in their footsteps (and yours). If the kids receive mixed signals from what you say and how their parents behave, your message gets lost. Parents don't talk to their child about the dangers of smoking while cigarettes dangle out of their mouths!

Let the parents know that children are easily distracted and don't perform as well — or have nearly as much fun — when faced with negativity from the stands. Make it clear that you won't tolerate the following actions:

- **Yelling at umpires:** Teenagers frequently umpire games, especially for the younger age groups. These kids are probably going to make mistakes simply because of their lack of experience. Umpiring mistakes should be understandable; they're part of the game of baseball, from T-ball to the professional game. Parents must know that heckling umpires, no matter how awful the calls may seem, is totally unacceptable under *any* circumstance.

- **Shouting instructions:** You want parents to refrain from shouting instructions to the kids during games. Hearing all sorts of instructions can be confusing to the kids. As the coach, instructing is your job, along with your assistants.

- **Arguing with coaches:** Devising and implementing strategies falls under the coach's responsibilities, not the parents'. You know what is best for the players because you're working closely with them at every practice. Encourage parents to keep their strategic "tips" to themselves during games, as well as refrain from commenting about the opposing coach's game-day tactics, too.

- **Criticizing players:** You want the parents' comments to players to be positive, encouraging, and uplifting. And when a player from the opposing team makes a diving catch in the field, encourage parents and players to show good sportsmanship by applauding the play. These are all kids, and they all deserve support and praise — regardless of the uniform they're wearing.

Your players' parents need to know that although you never want a situation to deteriorate to the point where you have to have them removed from the stands, you won't hesitate to do so. Many leagues have policies in place for the removal of spectators, and you should be aware of what steps are required for removal. When discussing this topic, don't be condescending in your tone; hammer home the point that this season is about the kids and making sure they have fun learning and playing the game. You can't achieve these goals when the parents are being disruptive influences in the stands. (Chapter 17 has for more information on dealing with unruly parents.)

Putting Together the Paperwork

Now comes the part of the program everyone is sure to love: paperwork. (Make sure any secretaries or accountants coming straight from work don't try to run away.) Most organized baseball programs require parents' signatures on forms — authorization to participate and medical evaluation are the most common — before their child can lace up his spikes and slip on the batting gloves. Parents may need to take care of their paperwork during the registration process, but sometimes the responsibility falls in your lap. Although the content and style varies from league to league, the purpose is generally the same.

Beyond any forms the league requires, you may want to put together information packets for the parents. You can include everything from a team roster with phone numbers to a practice and game schedule. You can even go a step further and include details on any special rules the league features (maybe it has a ten-run mercy rule that states when a team leads by more than ten runs after five innings, the game is stopped).

You can also win some parents' hearts by including some basic information on baseball itself, which can be a handy reference for any parents who aren't knowledgeable about the sport.

Like a good office-supply store, this section covers all your paperwork needs.

Filing the league paperwork

Parents (and physicians) need to ink their John Hancocks on a variety of forms before their youngsters can step on the field. The following sections give you a rundown of some of the more common types of forms and information.

Consent forms

A consent form states that the parents understand the risk that their child may be injured during practices or games and that the league isn't responsible for any injuries. Most programs have insurance policies in place for protection. Be sure to inquire about the league's coverage and what the coach's status is under the policy. The National Youth Sports Coaches Association, a program of the National Alliance For Youth Sports, provides coverage to coaches who complete its training program, for example.

Medical evaluation forms

The medical form, signed by the child's physician, states that the youngster is physically healthy and able to participate in the sport. Any conditions the child has, such as asthma or diabetes, should be listed on the form.

Emergency treatment authorization forms

You can never be too safe or prepared, which is why having an emergency treatment authorization form on file is a good idea. Have a child's parent or guardian provide the names and phone numbers of three people who you or the league should contact in the event of an emergency where the child requires emergency medical treatment. The form gives you or other league personnel the authority to seek medical treatment for the child if you can't reach the parents or guardians.

Passing out personal packets

Anytime you put in extra effort to make sure that you include the parents every step of the way, you're likely to gain their respect, admiration, and assistance. One great way to earn some bonus points with parents — and provide them with valuable information in the process — is by distributing a team packet. You can pack these tomes with all types of important information that parents can easily access throughout the season. The following sections give you some options for information to include in a packet.

You have a busy season ahead of you. You have to put in the hours outside of game time planning practices and outlining drills. Therefore, you don't need to turn your packet construction into an all-night affair. You don't need a fancy cover sheet, binders, or colorful paper. Just include a few pages, stapled together, that cover the important information. The packet won't be going on many coffee tables as an accessory; it will most likely end up in an office next to the bills.

A rules primer

Chances are good that most of your parents played baseball or softball growing up or are at least somewhat familiar with the game; however, you have to account for the possibility that not everyone has a baseball background. But you simply don't have enough time to go over the game in a lot of detail without dragging the preseason meeting into all hours of the night. A rules primer can be a valuable reference tool for parents who aren't knowledgeable about the game or who can use a little refresher; after all, it's probably been awhile since they last swung a bat or ran the bases. (Check out our discussion of the rules of the game in Chapter 3.)

If you're coaching in a league that tweaks some of the rules of the game to fit the age and skill level of the players, be sure to provide parents with the information. For example, most youth leagues don't allow base runners to steal until after the pitch crosses the plate. Pointing out all special modifications during your meeting — and detailing them in your packet — helps eliminate any confusion during the course of the season.

Phone lists and contact information

A listing with all the parents' names along with the kids' names and telephone numbers is handy for everyone. At some point during the season, a parent may need to contact another parent to arrange a ride to practice.

When Mother Nature decides to hit your field with a light drizzle an hour before practice, she can create real confusion among all the parents. Calling every parent to let him or her know you're canceling practice would be enormously time-consuming. Therefore, you can create a phone tree with the list of contact information you provide. Ask for a parent to volunteer to head the tree at the meeting; the parent you pick will be the person you call to spread information to the group. For example, in the event that weather forces you to postpone practice, you let your telephone-tree coordinator know, and that person takes it from there. Usually, the coordinator calls two parents on the phone list, those two parents each call two parents, and so on. (See the section "Searching for support" later in this chapter for more jobs parents can sign up for.)

Practice and game schedules

The league sets the schedule for the season weeks or months in advance of the first game, so be sure parents get copies of the schedule so they can plan accordingly. Also, if the league specifies the days and times your team is allowed to use the field for practice, make sure you include that information as well.

Equipment

You should give parents a list of what equipment their children are responsible for bringing and what the league provides so they don't have to jet from store to store, purchasing unnecessary items. In Chapter 2, we outline what equipment most leagues take care of.

Assembling Your Parent Posse

The more you can get the parents of your kids involved — whether you ask them to coach first base during games, help with a bunting drill during practice, or organize the post-game snack schedule — the more satisfying the entire experience will be for the youngsters. Most of the time, you'll find that the parents of your players are more than happy to help out in any number of ways; most parents just want a little direction from you on how they can be of assistance. During your meeting, let parents know that the more they're involved in their child's baseball experience, the more enjoyable it will be for everyone. Give them a rundown of all the different areas they can help out in and gauge their interest in taking part.

Granted, some parents are guilty of using practices as baby-sitting services while they run errands, but they may keep their distance simply because their child's previous coaches never asked them to stick around or made any effort to include them. Making the effort can ease your coaching burden and make everyone feel as if they have a stake in the outcome of the games. The following sections show you the way.

Seeking assistant coaches

Coaching a youth baseball team, regardless of the skill level or age of the kids, always goes a lot smoother when reliable and competent assistants help out along the way. Conducting practices alone can be challenging because you can't be everywhere on the field at once. If you want to run a hitting drill at home plate and a fielding drill in the outfield, for example, you need some assistants to lend a hand, provide instruction, and ensure the safety of the youngsters. Your assistant coaches can handle all sorts of other responsibilities on game day, too, such as

- ✔ Overseeing warm-ups to make sure the kids stretch properly
- ✔ Conducting pre-game batting practice and fielding drills while you meet with the opposing coach and umpires

Recruiting your assistants

Let your parents know at the preseason meeting that after the season gets rolling, you'll seek volunteers to serve as assistants. Ask them to let you know if they're interested in helping you out. This way, you can keep an eye on parents that express interest to see how they behave and interact with their child and others.

You probably won't know most of your players' parents at the start of the season, so don't rush to fill your assistant positions. Take some time to get to know the prospective parents during the first few practices to get a sense of who makes the best candidates. Watch how they interact with their children, and gauge their interest and enthusiasm for the sport, as well as their knowledge. Conducting these "observational interviews" helps ensure that you select parents whose demeanor and approach best match the fun and learning you want to stress.

The following are characteristics you — and your players — would like to see in your assistant coaches:

✔ Knowledgeable

✔ Enthusiastic

✔ Patient

✔ Positive

✔ Friendly and non-intimidating

✔ Funny

✔ Motivational

If you have outside friends who are willing to help, you may want to enlist their help if no parents seem fit for the job. Make sure your friends share the same coaching philosophy and that you're really comfortable working with them.

Avoiding unhealthy assistant situations

Sometimes parents who serve as assistant coaches can lose focus on what their roles are and on what's really best for the kids. These parents wind up imposing their own philosophies and techniques on the youngsters. Other seemingly fit parents may not be comfortable working with a group of youngsters and require so much mentoring and assistance from you that they actually detract from valuable practice time. You don't want to be stuck in an unhealthy situation, which is why choosing parents based on one brief conversation with them at your preseason parents meeting can backfire. Keep in mind that a dad who appears laid-back at the meeting may turn out to be a yeller with no patience for mistakes when he steps on the field.

If you have an assistant coach who you have to relieve of his duties, arrange to speak with him in private. Be sincere in thanking him for his time but let him know that how he's working with the kids doesn't quite fit with your coaching philosophy and that he'll have to step down. If you have parents who you know aren't good fits to help out, but they keep pressing you to serve as assistants, continually thank them for their interest but let them know in a friendly tone that they're not quite what you have in mind.

Searching for support

Some parents may not be interested in stepping on the field for an assistant role, but that doesn't mean you can't utilize them to fill any number of other roles. Most parents are happy to lend a hand; they just need some direction on where you need them most. Here's a roster of some of the jobs that parents can fill to ease your workload; feel free to bring these up at the preseason meeting:

- ✔ **Team parent:** Gathering the team after games for healthy snacks and beverages is a great way to conclude the fun days of baseball. Parents who take on the role of team parent are in charge of putting together a schedule that assigns different parents to specific games they're responsible for. The team-parent responsibility can also include organizing an end-of-season party or team banquet.

- ✔ **Concession-stand worker:** If your league runs a concession stand at the diamond, it may require its teams to take turns providing parents to help out. If so, check with the league director to find out which dates need filling, and find out which parents are willing to step forward at those times.

- ✔ **Photo coordinator:** Team photos make great keepsakes. Your league may work directly with a local photography company, but some leagues put the photo responsibilities on the coaches. If the burden falls on you, having a parent fill the position and make the necessary arrangements is helpful. The photo coordinator can also arrange for a photographer to come out for a game or two to take action shots of all the kids, which can make great end-of-season gifts. (You can find a rundown of fun ways to conclude the season in Chapter 20.) Because the parents split the costs of photos, make sure you have everyone's approval before moving forward.

- ✔ **Team trainer:** Children suffer the occasional bumps, bruises, scrapes, and abrasions during the season. If you have a parent who has first-aid training and is experienced in handling injuries, recruit his or her help. Even though all coaches should be trained in CPR and know basic first aid, having a skilled parent is pretty comforting for all involved.

- ✔ **Trophy coordinator:** Most youth baseball leagues hand out some awards to teams at the end of the season. At the beginning levels, every player may get a participation trophy, medal, or certificate; at the more advanced levels, leagues may distribute trophies to only the top teams. Sometimes, leagues don't have the financial resources to provide anything extra, which means it's up to you and the parents to decide if you want to do something for the kids. Put it to a team vote and see if the parents are interested in chipping in to cover the cost of arranging awards. If so, a trophy coordinator can arrange to have trophies or some other type of keepsake made for the team.

> ✔ **Parent umpires:** Many leagues don't have the financial resources to pay for umpires at the beginning levels of baseball, so parents from both teams may be recruited to help out. If your league operates under this policy, be sure to mention it during the parents meeting and find out which parents are willing to take the field if needed. You have too much to worry about on game day to go through the bleachers trying to corral a parent to work third base.

During the preseason meeting, circulate a list of responsibilities that you need filled and have parents sign up for duties they want to help out with. If several parents show interest in the same role, have them work together as a committee or take turns each week. If certain responsibilities go unclaimed, find out if any parents who signed up for a crowded duty would be willing to switch.

Meeting Your Players' Special Needs

Much like teachers who work with various types of kids in the classroom, coaches must teach varying kids on the field. Some kids will surprise you with how proficient they are with certain aspects of the game; others will challenge you to find ways to help them get a handle on the mere basics of the game. You may also have special-needs kids on your team, needs that range from a hearing or vision problem to a learning disability or physical impairment.

During your preseason meeting, find out whether any of the children under your care have conditions that you should be aware of before you take the field. Many times, parents aren't comfortable divulging this type of personal information in front of all the other parents, which is why you should set aside time at the end of the meeting for private discussions with each family. Make inquiring about special needs a standard question for all parents, because some conditions may not be obvious. For those that are, simply ask how you can best care for the child. For more details on meeting kids' special needs, check out Chapter 5.

Emceeing a Follow-Up Q and A

Hopefully you'll have active participation and interest in what you're saying during your preseason meeting. Don't be thrown off by questions during the your presentation of information. Anytime a parent has a question or needs clarification on something you say, take it as a good sign that they want to ensure that their child has a fun and rewarding season. You should allow some time after presenting a specific topic for parents to ask any questions they may have. Holding a small question-and-answer session lets parents know that you want to make sure what you've said is clear, and it opens the way for parents who may have questions but are reluctant to interrupt.

Always make yourself available at the end of the meeting for any parents who may be more comfortable speaking to you one-on-one. Let parents know that you're happy to speak with them afterward or over the phone at a time that's convenient for both parties. Also, make sure to jot down any questions you can't answer at the meeting and let parents know that you'll find the answers as soon as possible and get back to them as quickly as possible.

Part II
Building Your Baseball Coaching Skills

The 5th Wave   By Rich Tennant

"Let's see – I'll need some children's aspirin for my players and some sedatives for their parents."

In this part . . .

Teaching your players how to hit and catch is one of the main reasons you're coaching, but this task is meaningless if you don't understand what it takes to plan practices and oversee game day. You can find everything you need to know about conducting practices and handling all your game-day responsibilities in this part. In addition to these topics, we give you advice for evaluating your team and its many personalities, and we let you know when it may be time to adjust your coaching philosophy to meet your team's needs.

Chapter 5

Evaluating Your Team

. . . .

In This Chapter

▶ Evaluating skills

▶ Creating a lineup

▶ Coaching different types of kids

. . . .

Successful leaders — regardless of their professions — know the importance of evaluating skills and making accurate decisions on where their people have the best chances of flourishing. Understanding the strengths and weaknesses of your team, and determining which positions are right for your youngsters, are two responsibilities you take on. The decisions you make determine whether your season is packed with fun or stained by disappointment.

How proficient you are in the art of evaluating skills is determined by your ability to understand, communicate with, and bond with all your kids. In this chapter, we explore how you can assess your players' skills, assign fielding positions, and put together a batting order. Your goal in making these evaluations is to put your players in a position where everyone works together as a team. We also give you a rundown on how to work with the many different types of kids you'll have on your team — ranging from the shy and super-talented to the outgoing and clumsy.

Practicing the Art of Evaluation

The ability to accurately gauge the skills of your players during your first couple of practices is a key factor in getting the season off to a solid start. Recognizing the areas of the game that your team has a pretty good grasp of, and identifying the skills that your players need some additional work with, clears the way for you to maximize your practice time (see Chapter 6 for tips on running a good practice). This evaluation also reduces the chances of your players being overwhelmed by drills that are too difficult or being bored by drills that fall short of their skill level.

The time to evaluate your team is right from the start of your first practice of the season. Everything you learn from evaluating the players during those first couple of practices dictates your practice planning and helps determine specific areas of the game that you may need to devote extra attention to.

In the following sections, we take you through the process of evaluating your players' skills and identifying your team's strengths and weaknesses.

Evaluating your players' skills

Properly assessing a player's skills is necessary for determining where he's best suited to play in the field and bat in the lineup. You may find that some kids really enjoy wearing all the cool equipment that's required to play catcher (see Chapter 2) and love being behind the plate; some kids may have the quick reactions needed to play third base and hit leadoff; and others savor the challenge of covering large amounts of territory in the outfield. Finding positions for all the players on your team — while balancing their abilities with the needs of the team — is one of your most important responsibilities. In the "Using Your Evaluations to Help Fill Out the Lineup Card " section, we delve more into positioning your players.

You have many evaluating tools at your disposal to gauge the ability levels of your players at the start of the season. The following are a few ways to help get the most out of your evaluations:

- ✔ **Observe warm-ups.** You can get a pretty good sense of a child's throwing and catching skills simply by observing them playing catch before practice. Watch to see if they're using proper fundamentals and if their throws are on target, as well as how they fare moving in different directions to make catches.

- ✔ **Contact past coaches.** If you have time, you may want to put in a quick phone call to the coaches your players played for last season to gain some insight on their strengths and weaknesses.

- ✔ **Rotate players around.** During your initial practices, move players around to lots of different positions to see how they handle playing in the infield and outfield. Watch how comfortable they are fielding ground balls and fly balls and how strong and accurate their throwing arms are.

- ✔ **Use lots of different drills.** Run the kids through a variety of drills covering base running, hitting, fielding grounders, and catching fly balls so you can obtain an accurate gauge of their overall abilities.

Talk to your players to find out what positions they're interested in playing. Although you can't make any promises that they'll get to play where they want — especially if several kids have their eyes on playing shortstop, for example — you'll get a leg up on piecing together your defense.

Identifying strengths and weaknesses

In order to start your team out in the right direction, you need to get a good read on its strengths and weaknesses, and you need to devote extra attention in your practices to the areas that can use some upgrading. When you recognize the areas of the game where your team needs additional work, you can attack those areas enthusiastically and creatively during practice. (See Chapter 8 for more on making adjustments when the season hits its midway point.) Of course, don't neglect your strengths either — keep the kids sharp by fitting in some work on their best skills, too.

Monitor your initial practices closely. If you have assistant coaches, count on them to do the same. If you notice that many of your players are bobbling ground balls during your drills, scrimmages, or games, you may want to give them a refresher on the fundamentals of handling grounders at your next practice. (You also can consider position changes; see the section "Assigning fielding positions" later in this chapter.)

Your team is bound to encounter bumps — especially at the beginning of the season. Your team may suffer through a hitting drought for several games where you have trouble scoring runs. Players may suddenly have difficulty catching balls and making throws.

Never be afraid to ask for a little observational help if you need it. If you have an acquaintance who is a coach or has coached baseball, ask the person to come watch one of your practices. Another set of eyes can provide fresh observations and valuable feedback on areas of the game where your team may need some work or shows great skill. This coach also may be able to suggest some helpful drills for you to try. Having assistant coaches on your team can be a big help in this regard.

Using Your Evaluations to Help Fill Out the Lineup Card

Have you ever seen the classic Abbott and Costello skit "Who's on First"? Well, as a youth baseball coach, that's one of the many questions you'll be answering before each practice and game — along with who's batting first. Coaching a youth baseball team requires a never-ending string of decisions on your part. Two of the bigger ones you'll make are determining who plays where in the field and who bats where in your lineup. The good news? You have the luxury of mixing up your batting order from game to game (and in practice), as well as rotating players to different positions during each game, to provide your players with a complete baseball experience.

In the following sections, we provide you with tips on using the evaluations you've made (see the previous sections) to field players at positions at which they can succeed and have fun, and we aid you in creating a batting lineup that will be fun for the kids and functional for your team.

Assigning fielding positions

Your primary objective when coaching at the beginning levels of baseball is simply introducing all the kids to the basic elements of the game. In T-Ball and other beginning-level programs (such as coach's pitch; see Chapter 2), positioning players takes a back seat to simply getting them out on the field and involved in the action. Be sure to expose the kids to a variety of positions. Assigning a player to one position at the start of the season — and confining him there all season — detracts from his experience. Your young players will have more fun if they get the chance to try out several positions.

For beginning-level players, rotate them around to different positions throughout the season so they get a chance to experience as much of the game as possible. For example, don't stick a child at third base all season long when he may be wondering what it's like to play in the outfield. Keep close track of where you play the kids each game so you can refer to your notes to make sure everyone is getting a fair shot at playing all over the field.

As kids gain experience and advance to the higher and more competitive levels of baseball, selecting positions for them takes on greater importance. If you're coaching older kids, you need to determine what positions best match each player's talents and what fielding arrangement works best for the team. In the following sections, we give you tips on assigning fielding positions for your pitcher and catcher, infielders, and outfielders. (Chapters 10, 11, and 12 give you more info on teaching the fundamentals for each position.)

Never assign players to positions based strictly on their physical appearances. What we're saying is that you shouldn't automatically tab youngsters who are slightly overweight to play catcher (even if some of the best catchers in the world are nicknamed "Pudge") or tall, slender kids to be pitchers. A pudgy or tall child may possess wonderful hand-eye coordination, which can make him a great shortstop or center fielder, but he won't get to show off his skills if you shuttle him into one position based on his appearance.

When you assign positions to players, let each player know that you've chosen him for that spot because of the special skills and abilities that he's shown during practice. You want the player to feel confident in your decision, even if he isn't. After the season gets going, you may recognize that a player you have in right field is better suited for third base. Just because you pencil in a player at a certain position at the start of the season doesn't mean you can't move him around throughout the season. (We discuss making mid-season adjustments in Chapter 8.)

Charging your battery: Pitcher and catcher

The battery is where the action is — the pitcher and catcher are involved in every single part of a baseball game. For both positions, having a strong, accurate throwing arm is an obvious plus. The following list gives you some more traits and skills common to these positions:

- **Pitcher:** Kids that seem fearless and have confidence in their abilities — and are able to keep their focus and concentration — generally fare better as pitchers, because all eyes are on the pitcher on every play. Possessing a calm and relaxed demeanor also helps — especially when the game isn't going the pitcher's way. Endurance is another plus.

- **Catcher:** Even though some of the most famous catchers in history have been nicknamed "Pudge," don't automatically put the heavyset youngster behind home plate, which many coaches do. Fearlessness and toughness are great traits for youngsters who want to play catcher. A catcher has to deal with hitters swinging bats right in front of him (sometimes wildly), foul balls deflecting off his mask and chest protector, pitches bouncing in front of him, and runners sliding into him on plays at the plate — all while wearing cumbersome protective gear (see Chapter 2). Catchers also need good hand-eye coordination in order to handle the incoming pitches while the bat goes through their field of vision.

  At the advanced levels of play, the catcher is the leader of the defense and is often entrusted with calling the pitches, making trips to the mound to discuss strategy with the pitcher and infielders, and calling out the play on cutoff throws from the outfield. (See Chapter 15 for more on cutoff throws and positioning.)

Playing in the dirt: The infield

Skill at fielding ground balls is an obvious advantage for your potential infielders. Second basemen, shortstops, and third basemen, in particular, benefit from having quick, nimble feet. Strong throwing arms for shortstops and third basemen are important because of the longer throws and the limited amount of time to make a play. The following list gives you a breakdown of handy skills unique to each infield position:

- **First baseman:** A first basemen must be able to shift out of his stance quickly (whether in fielding position or when holding runners on at first base, often straddling the bag; see Chapter 10) and get into position to receive throws from the other infielders or to field ground balls. The ability to consistently handle throws — whether they come in high, low, or as one-hoppers in the dirt — is vital for success at this position.

  Left-handers often are preferred for the first-base position. Because the glove is on a lefty's right hand, and the majority of balls he fields are to his right, he can more easily field balls moving in that direction. Taller players can be a defensive bonus because they provide bigger targets for infielders' throws, plus they can stretch farther to snare errant throws. Kids who don't have the quickest feet can often get comfortable at this position, too, because they're not required to cover nearly as much territory as the other infielders.

✔ **Second baseman:** Good coordination, quickness, and footwork are good skills for a second basemen, especially for making (or *turning*) double plays. During a double play, the second basemen has to handle a throw from another infielder (most everyone except for first basemen), step on second base, and pivot and throw to first base while a base runner is sliding into him. Given the short throw to first base, throwing power isn't quite as critical as it is for shortstops and third basemen.

✔ **Shortstop:** By far the most difficult position in the infield to play. A coach usually fills this position with one of the team's most athletic players. Playing shortstop requires covering a lot of territory — to both the left and right, as well as in toward the plate (on softly hit dribblers) and out into the outfield (on pop flies). Shortstops also need to be able to field grounders cleanly.

The shortstop is the other half of the double-play combo at second base (along with the second basemen). He shares the same double-play duties, with the exception of receiving the throw from different fielders. A shortstop also performs a double play on his own more often, which requires quickness and athleticism.

✔ **Third baseman:** Playing third base requires especially quick reflexes, because the player doesn't have much time to react to hard-hit balls — both on the ground and in the air. For this reason, toughness (and maybe a bit of craziness) is a plus. Because a third basemen has the longest infield throw to first base, a strong throwing arm is most useful here. A third basemen should be able to move his feet well, too, because he needs to charge forward on bunts and soft dribblers.

Peppering the grass: The outfield

Being able to snare fly balls is a clear plus for outfielders. A skill within this skill is the ability to *read* the ball off the bat — to quickly judge its trajectory and distance. Being proficient in this area is a great advantage for outfielders. Strong throwing arms are always beneficial for outfielders, too, along with the willingness to charge ground balls and line drives. And it doesn't hurt to have outfielders who are willing to dive for balls — as long as you teach them when it's safe to do so (not near fences, preferably).

The following list presents some other things to look for, by position:

✔ **Right fielder:** A common misconception is that right field is where the team's weakest player should be positioned — especially at the beginning levels. But plenty of balls find their way to right field. Right field is actually more difficult to play than left field, because a right fielder needs a stronger arm to make long — and accurate — throws to third base. (The throw from left field to third base is much shorter.)

✔ **Center fielder:** Out of the three outfielders, the player who mans center field usually is the best athlete. The center fielder is responsible for covering more territory than anyone on the field, so good foot speed is advantageous. He also must be aggressive in his pursuit of fly balls and willing to exercise his vocal chords when necessary, like when he's charging in on a short fly ball and needs to let the infielder backpedaling toward him know to move out of the way. (See Chapter 15 for more on proper defense on short fly balls, as well as a number of other scenarios.)

✔ **Left fielder:** Left field often sees the most fly balls out of any outfield position, so being able to consistently handle the action is critical for playing here.

Choosing a batting order

After your first several practices, you'll start to get a good sense of each player's abilities at the plate. You'll know which players make pretty good contact on a consistent basis, which players possess the most power, and which players struggle to get the ball out of the infield.

At the beginning levels of youth baseball, you should concentrate on letting your players hit from different spots in the order. The goal is for the kids to have fun, not to win games. At the more advanced levels, you need to put more thought into your batting order, because it takes on more prominence — in terms of the outcome of games and in how players view their places on the team. Your batting lineup directly impacts your game strategy and how your team will attempt to generate runs. The list in this section gives you some general guidelines for establishing your batting order.

When filling out batting orders at a beginning level of youth baseball, be sure to change the rotation every game so that your players aren't stuck in the same spots all season long. Batting last in the order all season can be pretty disheartening to a child. An easy way to mix up the order is to slide every player down a notch for the second game of the season. In other words, the player who batted last gets to hit leadoff, the first hitter slides down to bat second, and so on. Continue this trend for the subsequent games as well.

For the T-ballers and younger kids, you can base your batting order on the kids' uniform numbers, going from lowest to highest. This easy-to-follow order helps them remember when they're up because they know they follow the uniform number before theirs. For each game you can slide everyone down a notch so that during the course of the season everyone gets an equal chance to bat at the top, middle, and bottom of the order.

Number 1 hitter: The first hitter, referred to as the *leadoff hitter,* is pretty proficient at getting on base, whether by base hit or a walk. Getting your leadoff and number 2 hitters on base leads to good scoring opportunities provided by your big bats (numbers 3, 4, and 5 hitters). Your team also has an advantage if the leadoff hitter is fast and can steal bases (see Chapter 14).

Number 2 hitter: This player is good at making contact with the ball and getting on base a lot. If the leadoff hitter sets the tone, the second hitter carries the tune so the big hitters can drive home runs. You also have an advantage if your second hitter is a good bunter so you can rely on him to execute sacrifice bunts to move the runners along. (See Chapters 9 and 14 for more on sacrifices.)

Number 3 hitter: This spot usually is occupied by your team's best hitter because if the number 1 and number 2 hitters are good at getting on base he has lots of opportunities to drive in runs. Plus, because the hitters in the top portion of the lineup typically get more at bats than those at the bottom of the lineup, you want to have good hitters occupying these slots.

Number 4 hitter: The player in this spot is referred to as the *cleanup hitter.* He's the one who "cleans up" the bases by getting big hits and scoring the players who hit ahead of him and got on base. You want this hitter to have the most power of anyone on the team, because having power in this position is the most beneficial for scoring runs.

Number 5 hitter: The next best power hitter on the team usually goes in the fifth slot. You rely on him to drive in runs if the fourth hitter fails. He also should be a good contact hitter so he can start rallies after the cleanup hitter cleans the bases.

Number 6 hitter: The player in the 6 spot usually is somewhat similar in ability to the Number 2 hitter. He should be able to continue rallies and start new ones.

Number 7 hitter: A player in this position may not be the most consistent hitter, but he still has the ability to make things happen.

Number 8 hitter: A player with decent speed who's pretty good at making contact often winds up here.

Number 9 hitter: The final hitter is just as important as anyone else in the lineup. He should have the ability to bunt well, and he should possess decent speed on the bases. At this point in the lineup, you want to get runners on base for the first few hitters in the lineup to drive home.

Understanding All Kinds of Kids

What your youth-league roster consists of, for the most part, is a nice group of kids who share the following characteristics:

✔ They enjoy the game of baseball.

✔ They want to have fun.

✔ They want to learn from you.

✔ They want to be with their friends.

However, one of the most interesting — and challenging — aspects of coaching a youth baseball team is that every child on your team is different in all sorts of ways. How you interact with all your players, and how you handle the smorgasbord of personalities on your squad, significantly impacts how much learning takes place and how much fun the kids have in the process.

Your players' athletic ability, physical development, and emotional maturity will be all over the map. The following sections give you a glimpse at some of the more common types of kids you may be coaching this season. Along the way, we include tips for coaching a variety of different personality types and blending them together into a cohesive unit.

The shy child

Chances are good that if you get a call from the IRS, it won't be good news; in youth baseball, chances are just as good that you'll have to coach kids who are shy — some painfully so. Some kids are just naturally shy in most situations, and others may just be more reserved at the start of the season as they get accustomed to the other players, their coaches, and the sport.

You'll soon discover that your shy players put a lot of effort into blending into the background. During practices, they frequently avoid asking for help, try to avoid eye contact, and move from drill to drill in the back of lines and in silence.

All you need to lure youngsters out of their protective shells is a mixture of patience and understanding. Your team's warm-up period before practices and games provides a great opportunity to help shy kids get a little more comfortable with the rest of the team. Select a shy child, along with a couple of outgoing players, to lead the stretching in front of the team. (You should rotate the kids at each practice and game so that everyone has the same opportunities.) Because the shy child is in front of the team with other players, he's less likely to feel isolated or uncomfortable.

Here's another subtle action you can take: During your drills, give a shy player a pat on the back after he performs a technique well. He may not be ready for a verbal acknowledgment that draws attention, but small gestures on your part can make a big difference in slowly drawing him out of his shell.

The uncoordinated child

Hitting a baseball isn't easy. Fielding ground balls and catching pop ups is pretty difficult, too. Toss in the fact that many kids on your team are grappling with the basics of coordination at the younger age levels, and adjusting to their ever-changing bodies at the older levels, and you can quickly see how many youngsters fall — excuse the pun — into this category. Some of these kids are really going to struggle with even the most basic fundamentals of the game, such as running down the first-base line without stumbling over their own feet or tripping on the base.

Adding to the difficulty of your job will be that some children just aren't athletically inclined, and never will be. Don't give up on these kids, though. Helping a child work on his coordination takes lots of practice — and patience. Although he may never excel at the game, you can help him gradually become a little more proficient at some of the basics. Here are a few tips to help get him there:

- ✔ **Camouflage your frustration.** Repeatedly demonstrating specific skills sometimes doesn't yield the desired results. Choose your words carefully, and never allow a frustrated tone to creep into your voice or negativity to be revealed in your body language.

- ✔ **Give constant praise.** Kids who wrestle with coordination issues that their teammates have mastered are likely to become disappointed in themselves. Constantly praising effort and applauding even the slightest improvements reinforces that they're making progress.

- ✔ **Encourage positive parenting.** Turn to the child's parents for assistance. Encourage them to spend a few minutes each week working on different baseball skills. Stress the importance of keeping it fun. Gradually, the kids will begin noticing a difference in their skills, which will snowball into more confidence and increased development.

The child with a short attention span

Short attention spans are as common with kids as skinned knees and runny noses. The younger the child, the shorter his attention span is likely to be — and the more patience you're going to need to keep your blood pressure from skyrocketing. Since you'll be outdoors coaching baseball you'll be competing for their attention with all sorts of things you never imagined. Butterflies, airplanes, or a pal on the next field over may all be more interesting to them than what you are saying or demonstrating.

As we discuss in Chapter 6, focus on constructing practices and devising drills that continually capture the kids' attention and keep their interest and excitement level high. With younger kids, if you're going against a big, multicolored bird you're going to need a really fun drill to win over their attention.

The quickest route to losing a child's attention on the baseball field is spending large chunks of time talking instead of keeping him moving and actively involved in different types of drills.

The athletically gifted child

Just about every youth baseball team seems to have that one child whose talent and ability surpasses everyone else's by a whopping margin. After just a handful of practices his teammates will recognize that he's the best player on the team, and you and many of the parents of the other kids will notice it right away, too.

One of the trickiest aspects of coaching the athletically gifted is providing drills that enable him to enhance his skills while not compromising or isolating the rest of the team in the process. Use your creativity to devise clever ways to help *all* kids derive benefits at the same time. For example, if you've got a star outfielder and a youngster who is struggling to catch fly balls, you can tweak a basic drill to meet the needs of both players. When hitting fly balls to the talented child, you can hit them higher than you do to a struggling youngster, as well as force him to move several more steps in all directions to make a play on the ball. If you come across that situation with infielders, deliver grounders with more pace, as well as farther out of his range, to the gifted player. Chapters 12 and 13 provide all sorts of drills that will meet the needs of players of all different abilities.

Make sure you keep your emotions in check and refrain from going overboard with admiration and praise for the best athletes on your team. Throwing too many accolades their direction can have adverse effects, such as the following:

- ✔ **Added pressure for the "star":** Some kids may translate the extra attention to extra pressure, which can sabotage their performance and smother their enjoyment of playing the game.

- ✔ **Resentment and hurt feelings among the others:** Some youngsters on the team may be hurt by your constant praise of this one particular child and may feel as though they aren't as valued or appreciated.

By all means, however, enjoy your time coaching athletically gifted youngsters. When these players possess good attitudes and aren't critical or condescending to their teammates, they can be wonderful team leaders and positive role models. Just remember that these players are only one piece of the team puzzle and that you have a responsibility to help, support, and guide every youngster on your team.

The disinterested child

No matter how creative your practices are or how much fun you are to be around, there's always the chance that you'll have kids on your team who simply don't want to be involved. The following list details some potential reasons for their non-interest:

- **Burnout:** Perhaps they've played for several years now and simply need a break from the game.

- **Previous bad experience:** They may be carrying over an unpleasant experience that occurred last season. They may have been treated poorly or embarrassed by the coach or maybe picked on by a teammate.

- **Discovery that baseball really isn't for him:** The only way kids can find out what sports they enjoy is by trying a variety of them. Some kids are going to discover that baseball isn't for them, and that's perfectly okay.

You'll have to reach into your bag of coaching tricks to spark interest with a disinterested child. Here are a few things you may want to pull out:

- **Issue challenges.** See how many pop flies or ground balls he can field in a row, or how many times in succession he can swing the bat without missing the ball.

- **Go one-on-one.** Before practice, have contests between the two of you to see who can throw a ball the farthest or who can come closest to hitting a specific target.

- **Have chats.** Discuss how he can apply certain skills he learns on the baseball field to other sports or activities that he's interested in.

All too often, parents force their kids into playing a particular sport, and sometimes the youngster's enthusiasm for participating doesn't match the adults'. Let the parents know — tactfully, of course — that you've noticed that their youngster really isn't all that interested in baseball and would prefer doing something else. If this chat doesn't get you anywhere, try to find ways to make the game as enjoyable and interesting as possible for that youngster.

The disruptive child

Sometimes kids are more interested in seeing how far they can push you, and what they can get away with, than learning batting skills and improving on fielding techniques. So, you'll need to be prepared to deal with those that may test your authority, ignore your team rules, and try your patience.

When handling disruptive youngsters, don't sacrifice discipline just so that the kids will like you; and on the other hand, don't be overly unforgiving and hand out punishment too quickly. Explain to players what type of behavior you expect from them during practices and games, and anytime players cross the line, address the situation right away so that it doesn't happen again.

Don't embarrass a youngster the first time he misbehaves. Instead, speak to him privately and make it clear that what he's done is unacceptable and out-line his punishment. Anytime you're forced to speak to a player regarding a behavior or discipline issue, be sure to let the parents know about it right away as well. Keeping them in the dark only creates unwanted problems for you down the road.

Also, be aware that anytime you allow the team's best player to get away with inappropriate behavior without suffering the consequences, you're sending a disturbing message that the team rules don't apply to him simply because he's a better player than his teammates. Reacting this way actually elevates this player to a position more powerful than yours. Failing to hand out pun-ishment evenly to all players usually occurs when coaches operate under a win-at-all-costs mentality, and they turn their backs on any problems that can hinder how many wins their team collects. The bottom line is that you must have a system of consequences in place from the beginning of the season that apply equally to everyone.

The child with special needs

No child should ever be deprived of the chance to play, regardless whether he has special needs ranging from hearing loss and vision impairment to medical conditions such as diabetes or epilepsy. Even kids who have physical conditions in which they don't have full use of their arms or legs fall into this category. Sure, you may have some reservations about your qualifications of working with a child with special needs and that's completely normal. But there's no reason to doubt that you can do the job. It's really no different than working with a child who has no coordination or is super shy: Handle each child on an individual basis and figure out what's going to work best for him.

In Chapter 4, we introduce the preseason parents meeting and the importance of finding out whether any players have conditions you need to be aware of. If any do, be sure to talk to the family before the season gets going about their hopes and expectations so that you can determine the best approach that benefits everyone. This season may be the parents' first foray into organized sports, and they may be apprehensive about having their child participate. In fact, they may be counting on you for all the answers. Figure out ways that this youngster can be included and be a valued and contributing member of the team.

Regardless of the age or skill level of your team, having a child with special needs on the squad can also be enormously beneficial for other players. Youngsters get a firsthand lesson on developing understanding, compassion, and patience for their teammates while also learning to accept everyone's differences.

If you're coaching an older team, ask players for their thoughts and ideas on how players with special needs can be included. They can be great resources for you, and they may surprise you with their creative suggestions on how to ensure that everyone gets to be a part of the action.

Prior to each game, meet with the opposing coach (and the umpires) to share any information regarding children on your team who have special needs, and find out whether any players on his team have special needs as well. Quite often, the league director goes over this type of information with all the coaches at a preseason meeting so that everyone is aware, well in advance, of any accommodations that need to be made.

The bully

While growing up, most of us can recall the unpleasant memories of dealing with a bully. As a coach now, you may find yourself in the position of dealing with a bully who brings his bat, glove, and troublesome behavior to your team. Bullies crave attention and find satisfaction in upsetting others. There's no room for bullies and their intimidating tactics on your team.

Kids who are tormented by bullies usually stay quiet and endure the harassing. Typically they remain silent out of fear of having the situation escalate into something even worse.

It's up to you to police what's going on at all times. Keep a close eye on how the kids interact not only during practice but also before and after your sessions, too. Bullies wreak the most havoc when adults aren't around or are preoccupied with other matters. Don't allow horseplay that often unfolds before practice, because that's a prime time when bullies strike, use physical force, and intimidate.

If you've got a child that's bullying teammates, speak with him — in a friendly yet firm fashion — away from the team, and let him know that this type of behavior won't be tolerated and must stop immediately. Stress that he should be encouraging and supporting teammates rather than picking on them or making fun of them.

The inexperienced child

If you're coaching a T-Ball team, or a beginning-level team, all the kids are pretty much going to be in the same boat when it comes to playing experience. As you progress to older and more advanced levels of coaching you'll likely encounter a pretty big discrepancy between playing abilities and playing experience. Sometimes kids get a late start in baseball. For example, if you're coaching a 12-and-under team, you may have a player that has never played a season of organized baseball before while the rest of his teammates have been involved for several years. With the relatively short amount of time you have with your team each week, getting the inexperienced child caught up to the skill level of his teammates simply isn't going to be possible. After all, you can't cram several seasons' worth of practices, drills, and game experience into a month or two. But you can still help the youngster develop skills and be a valued and contributing member of the team.

If you sense that the child is uncomfortable knowing that he's behind in a lot of the skills, singling him out for some one-on-one work with you while his teammates go about their drills may have negative effects and make him even more uneasy about his decision to play baseball this season. However, if the child seems receptive to your offer and you spend this time wisely it can help fuel his progress. You may also want to mention to the parents some things they can do together at home to work on certain aspects of the game, whether it's fielding grounders, catching pop ups, or executing bunts.

The scared child

Getting plunked with a hard baseball isn't fun. Neither is having a ground ball ricochet off a shin or shoulder. Some kids, regardless of their age, skill level, or experience playing the game, will harbor fears of being hurt. A youngster new to the game of baseball may have seen an older sibling get hurt and can be concerned that it's going to happen to him, too; or an experienced player may be struggling to shove memories of a previous injury out of his mind.

Fear can potentially suffocate a child's ability to perform and chase him away from future participation, so you must work with him to conquer these feelings. Play detective and uncover the source of the fear — and then commit to helping him move past it.

For example, fear of being hit by a pitch is perfectly understandable and quite common. This concern is usually easily overcome, for example, by pitching tennis balls to the youngster to help him get comfortable at the plate. Then, mix in some wild pitches that he has to dodge — and which won't hurt if they happen to hit him. He'll gradually learn the proper techniques for moving out of the way and protecting himself. Tennis balls also work great for helping youngsters learn how to field ground balls and fly balls, because kids won't flinch from — or be hurt by — crazy bounces.

Chapter 6

Preparing for and Running a Great Practice

*O*ne of the secrets of being a youth baseball coach that kids want to play for — and learn from — is running practices that are fun and entertaining. All kids have fun during games — that is, after all, why they signed up in the first place — but practice is where the work and improving take place. You'll likely spend more time with your kids during practice, so practices that the kids look forward to attending, and participating in, are the foundation for a fun-filled and rewarding season.

In this chapter, we give you the rundown on what it takes to create and run creative practices that help your players learn and develop skills more quickly than you ever imagined. We give you the inside scoop on how to ensure that the first practices of the season run smoothly, how to avoid common mistakes right off the bat (excuse the bad pun), and how to make sure all your kids feel good about themselves during and after every practice.

The Big Picture: Creating Your Practice Plan

Every leader must be prepared if he or she expects to enjoy success; without preparation, followers will lose faith in their leader. As a youth baseball coach, you must prepare your practice plans (for a glance at some sample practice outlines, jump to Chapters 12 and 13) and then carry them out to have success with the kids on the field. You need to map out the skills you want to teach during the season (often depending on the age and ability level of your kids; see Chapter 2), and based on how many practices you can have with the kids this season, you need to determine which areas you can cover in each practice and how much time you can devote to each area.

The following sections help you map out a great practice plan for your season. From the planning stages, to the drilling stages, to the adjustments you need to make, we cover the big picture of planning for a youth baseball practice.

Setting practice frequency and duration

Most youth baseball leagues, particularly at the younger age levels, have specific policies in place regarding practice time. Your league may limit how long your practices can run and how often you can get together with your team. Before you can begin creating your practice plans, you need to know your league's rules. (Check out Chapter 2 for more advice on checking out your league's rules before the season.) Here's a breakdown of the typical practice allotments for different youth leagues:

- ✔ At the younger age levels — T-ball and coach's pitch — you typically get a one-hour practice with your team once a week, along with one game per week.

- ✔ For the middle age groups — ages 9 to 12 — you're typically allowed one to two practices a week, with a game mixed in.

- ✔ For the older kids — ages 13 and above — you often play a couple games a week, as well as hit the practice field once, and sometimes twice, a week, too.

If you coach in an advanced league that leaves it up to the coaches' discretion as to how often teams practice, use your best judgment when devising your team's practice schedule. Don't go overboard and monopolize the kids' time by cramming the calendar with practices. However, they can probably handle a couple of practices a week if you play only one game per week. Anytime your schedule features more than one game for the week, be sure to modify your practices accordingly so that you don't overwhelm your kids.

Through preparation, you can accomplish plenty in an hour, so stick to that time frame. Only at very advanced levels should your practices run any longer than an hour.

Distribute your practice schedule during your preseason parents meeting, which we cover in Chapter 4. The parents will appreciate the advanced notice, and players will likely miss less practice time because parents have time to alter their schedules.

Putting plan to paper

Remember writing papers in school when your teachers made you put together an outline first before plunging ahead so that your paper had a logical flow to it? Well, the same approach applies for creating practice plans that build on one another and follow the proper sequence. Putting your ideas down on paper helps organize your thoughts and translates into better results on the field.

If you have friends, co-workers, or neighbors who have coached youth baseball before, don't hesitate to get their input during this process. These people can be great resources for planning great practices and sharing with you what types of approaches work and don't work with kids. Also, if your assistant coaches have been around the game a little bit, solicit their feedback on your plan because they'll probably have some suggestions to help you improve it. Here are some practice-planning pointers:

- **Write some notes about your ideal practices.** Jot down what skills you want to teach your players during those first few practices of the season. For example, with a beginning level team that doesn't know many of the basics, you'll probably want to split your practices up, with half the time devoted to the fundamentals of hitting and base running, and the other half focused on playing in the field. Also, write down your early-season goals for the team (see Chapter 8 for more about goal setting at mid-season). Getting some of your practice ideas down on paper helps you jump-start your thought process and begin to piece together effective plans.

    Don't think in terms of wins and losses when planning your practices; concentrate on more skill-oriented details, like gripping the bat properly or bending down the right way to handle a ground ball. Wins and losses should never be your motivation for teaching young kids. You want them to learn the game and have fun.

- **Break down the big picture into practice segments.** After you get some big-picture practice notes written down, take your planning a step further by breaking down your ideas into how much time you want to devote to each specific area in each practice. For example, if your league allows you to practice with your team for only one hour a week (see Chapter 2 for league rules info), a basic practice breakdown can be 10 minutes for warming up and stretching, 15 minutes for hitting, 15 minutes for fielding, 15 minutes for throwing, and 5 minutes for going over the practice and reminding players of when the next game or practice will take place.

✔ **Select some drills to fill your practice time.** You can dive even further into your practice projections by selecting some drills you want to use in practice. You certainly don't have to etch these drills in stone right away, but you can start to get a rough idea of the types of drills that you think your kids would like and find useful. For younger players, you may want to concentrate on the basics. For older players, you can throw in advanced drills to provide challenges and really improve skills. See Chapters 12 and 13 to find some drills that will suit your plan.

Always set aside practice time for plenty of water breaks. Also, make sure your players know that anytime they need water — even before a scheduled break — they can step out of a drill to get some. You should never withhold hydration from a child for any reason. If you think the child is using the break as an excuse to get out of a drill, have a chat with the child later, away from the other players.

When is scrimmaging a good idea?

A scrimmage is an informal game often done by breaking up your team into two smaller teams and having them play one another; or you can get together with another team for some fun. Holding a scrimmage is a good idea when your players have a pretty good grasp of the basics and can benefit from gaining some experience using them in a game-like setting. Scrimmages are also a good way to spice up your practices, especially if they're tweaked to make them interesting and challenging. For example, making each batter hit with two strikes on him, or only giving each team two outs to work with, is a fun approach that also is an effective way to build skills.

A scrimmage shouldn't just mirror the rules and length of a regular game in every way; if it does, you may lose your kids' interest. Use your creativity to bump up the energy and excitement for a scrimmage by changing the rules here and there. A rules change also can help your team learn and improve. For example, if your players are struggling to execute bunts (see Chapter 9), you can stipulate that anytime either side lays down a successful bunt, that side gets an extra out for that inning.

Although a scrimmage is a great tool to use on occasion to break up the monotony of a practice routine, don't fall into the trap of overusing scrimmages. Running too many scrimmages takes away from the individual teaching and instruction you can provide. Also, steer clear of using them early in the season. These practices are crucial for helping kids build skills through drills and repetition. Save the scrimmages for when they have learned some skills and can benefit from using them in game-like situations.

Ensuring plenty of repetitions for each child

Standing in line is acceptable at grocery stores, fancy restaurants on a Saturday night, and amusement parks during the summer, but your players won't find waiting in line to be acceptable on the baseball field. No child should ever have to stand in line during practice. Kids need to be running around, diving for balls, and collecting grass stains, not waiting to perform drills like little soldiers.

You can ensure plenty of repetitions for each player and slam the door on boredom by designing your practices so that several drills take place at one time all over the field. You want to keep everyone moving around and involved in some sort of action. When you map out a practice that involves several stations set up around the field, figure out how you can quickly transition the kids from one drill to another (for example, you can outlaw horseplay during rotations to maximize your time). Keep these tips in mind when scheming your practices at the beginning of the season and researching potential drills you may want to run during practice.

Letting kids help select practice drills

When your season hits full stride (after the first couple of practices, perhaps), you may want to devote a segment of your practice time for the players to choose their favorite drill to perform. Saving the last segment of your practice for this drill usually works well since it gives the kids something to look forward to. You introduce many drills at the beginning of the year; your kids will embrace some, others will generate less-than-enthusiastic responses.

In your practice planner, be sure to note which drills the kids enjoy and which drills inspire groans; you'll appreciate having this information for future seasons. You may need to devise ways to make the drills that the kids never pick more exciting (or you may simply dump them).

Older players may even have suggestions for tweaking current drills or introducing fun drills that they learned from previous coaches. Regardless of the source, you can always make room in your practices for fun drills that promote skill development.

Depending on how many players you coach and how many practices you have (see the earlier section "Setting practice frequency and duration"), you may be able to assign one player at each practice to choose one drill for the team. This tactic gives you a great way to include all the kids and make them really feel like they're a part of the team. Also, the drills they pick give you great feedback.

Setting the tone for practice

Take a moment to reflect back on your school memories and the classes that you enjoyed the most. More than likely, they were the ones in which the teachers made learning fun and interesting and kept you fully engrossed in the subject. Making that same type of connection with your players comes down to the tone you're able to set from the outset of the season. Build it around positive feedback, encouraging words, an upbeat approach, and a good sense of humor and you're on your way.

One of the big components of being an effective youth baseball coach is always exuding positive energy and enthusiasm — no matter how good or bad practice is going. Sure, we all have bad days, but you shouldn't show up for practice in a bad mood because your poor state of mind will interfere with what you can teach the kids. This is especially true early in the season. When your players see that you're in a good mood and happy to be at the field, they'll practice and play in the right frame of mind, too. You have to set the tone for each and every practice; build it around positive feedback, encouraging words, and a good sense of humor.

Just like the president of a company, you're in control of your team, which means that you're the one that your players will look up to. You can't rely on others to establish a positive tone. The more upbeat your attitude, the more joy and confidence your kids will have. When you're preparing your practices for the upcoming season, focus on setting a fun tone. If the kids don't look forward to attending your practices, you're probably not doing a very good job, and they're not learning many skills. So, as you're putting together your practice plans, ask yourself if the drills are fun and if you'd like participating in them.

Keeping your practices as consistent as possible

You have a limited amount of practice time with your kids each week, so if you can establish a practice routine as soon as possible, your sessions will be more efficient and effective. When your kids know what to expect when they get to the field, they can mentally prepare themselves and be ready to go. On the other hand, if you constantly change up your practices, you'll find that you waste valuable practice time because the kids will just stand around and listen to your constant instruction.

For example, you can change the drills you run from week to week, but you should try to hang onto a core group of drills that focus on the fundamentals of the game. You'll rely on these drills to really ingrain in the kids the basic elements of baseball.

Stick to the same warm-up and stretching routine at the start of each practice. Doing so sets a comfortable agenda for the kids before they jump into a session. Because some of your drills will change from week to week as you try to focus on different parts of the game, establishing and maintaining a routine at the outset of practice can set the stage for good productivity. Also, you want to have regularly scheduled water breaks throughout your practices so the kids understand that they'll have plenty of chances to get a drink. Anytime you're switching to a different drill, encourage the kids to grab some water.

Adjusting your practice plan as the season unfolds

As the season moves along, your players — if you're doing a good job — will be learning and developing skills. So you need to modify your practices accordingly to account for their progress. Relying on the same practice plan that you used the first week of the season is counterproductive several games into the season. Coaches must find ways to continually adjust their practices to meet the kids' needs so that learning and skill development continue moving forward. (For information on adjusting your goals and philosophy at the midway point, check out Chapter 8.)

- ✔ **Tweak your drills to account for strengths and weaknesses.** Your players may pleasantly surprise you with how quickly they pick up certain aspects of the game. However, their acumen forces you to make adjustments to your practice plans. For example, say your players have become really proficient at fielding ground balls, but they're lagging a little behind in the throwing department. In this case, you should spend a little more practice time on throwing, incorporating additional throwing drills, and scale back on the fielding drills.

- ✔ **Judge your drills based on their difficulty.** You may have to overhaul your practice plan if your drills turn out to be so easy that you aren't challenging your kids. Likewise, if the drills are so difficult that they're frustrating the kids and not helping them improve, you need to lighten up and work on some new ways to challenge your players.

- ✔ **Make changes based on upcoming opponent.** At the more advanced levels of play, you may want to adjust a particular practice based on the team that you are playing in an upcoming game. For example, if you know that the opposing pitcher throws really hard, you may want to devote the bulk of your practice to giving the kids extra repetitions batting in drills that emphasize hitting hard-thrown balls.

The First Practice: Kicking Off Your Season

Encountering a shark in the ocean, a rattlesnake in the grass, and an IRS agent at your front door are all terrifying experiences. However, you don't need to add "conducting your first baseball practice" to that list, too. If you've never coached a youth baseball team before, that first practice may weigh on your mind for weeks. Even if you have coached a season, your nerves are likely to be frazzled and excited before you meet your new players. You have a lot at stake when you step on the field to practice for the first time, because your first impression sets the tone for the season and provides your kids with a pretty good indication of what's in store.

Not to worry, we're here to guide you through this nerve-racking time. In the following sections, we explain how you should greet your team, introduce all the players and coaches, and run the remainder of your initial practice. Good luck!

Nothing sabotages a practice more quickly than kids arriving without the proper equipment. During your preseason parents meeting, which we cover in Chapter 4, emphasize what kids are responsible for bringing to the field.

Greeting your team for the first time

Making a great first impression is oh-so-important when greeting your players for the first practice of the season. Having positive contact with the kids before they even have a chance to earn their first grass stains helps put them at ease.

Here some tips to keep in mind to make sure that your initial greeting goes smoothly:

✔ **Beat the players to the field.** Make sure you're the first one to arrive. Greeting each player and his parents as they arrive sends a positive message that you're enthusiastic about getting started. If you pull up a few minutes before the practice is supposed to start, you give the impression that you're disorganized, too busy, and unprepared for all the responsibilities that coaching entails.

✔ **Make everyone feel comfortable.** As soon as the kids climb out of the cars and make their way to the field — probably with an anxious walk and nervous jitters — welcome them with a friendly smile and hello. Starting something new where you don't know a single person is uncomfortable for everyone. You don't want a child to stand off to the side, wondering whether he's at the right field or if anyone will talk to him or even say hello. The more relaxing you can make the atmosphere, the more enthusiastic the kids will be about getting started.

✔ **Chitchat.** You should begin establishing bonds right away. If time allows, talk briefly with each child to find out a little bit more about him. Ask him how long he's been playing baseball, what team he played for last season, and what positions he has played in the past. Taking a genuine interest in your players — which they'll recognize and appreciate — is the foundation for forging special relationships with them — one of the benefits of both playing and coaching organized baseball.

Introducing everyone

Formally introduce yourself and any assistant coaches you have at the start of practice once everyone has arrived. The introduction helps to alleviate your players' anxiety and makes them more comfortable. You can do it in the infield or gather the kids in the dugout, whatever is most comfortable for you.

During your intro, share some quick tidbits about yourself, including the following:

✔ Whether you prefer being called "Coach," "Coach Brad," or any other moniker. (Feel free to use any funny nickname you may have that will get a chuckle out of the kids.)

✔ How long you've coached and where.

✔ Details about your coaching and playing background.

✔ If you have a child on the team.

✔ Your favorite major league team or player.

After the coach introductions, you can have each child stand up and introduce himself to the rest of the team. Ask him to relay the following information:

✔ Name

✔ Age

✔ Favorite team

Keep the player introductions short and to the point. Some kids are going to be overly shy and the last thing you want to do is traumatize them before the practice has even begun.

You may have more than a dozen kids on your team (especially at the older levels), which makes learning all their names a little challenging. Giving each player a name tag to wear during the first practice or two speeds up the process. Slap a name tag on yourself and on any of your assistant coaches, too, so that your kids feel like you're all in this together. Never too early to start team bonding!

Choosing the skills to focus on first

Before the first practice arrives, you should have a plan in place for which drills you want to begin with and how those drills will lead into the more intensive practices to come (see the earlier section "The Big Picture: Creating Your Practice Plan"). For the scoop on some basic drills for beginners, flip to Chapter 12; if you're looking to upgrade your drills, Chapter 13 offers some advanced ones to incorporate into your practices.

If you're coaching a beginning-level team, chances are many of your kids have never played baseball before — or any other type of organized sport for that matter. Because of the somewhat complex nature of the game — from the fundamentals of batting to the art of playing the infield and outfield — your best bet is to ease your players into the first practice by picking out some basic drills to focus on first.

Using the first couple practices of the season to cover some of the most fundamental skills — such as batting stances and proper glove positions for grounders and pop ups — establishes a solid foundation that you can build on without overwhelming your players in the process.

If you're coaching players with a little more experience, you can utilize the first week of practices to refresh your players on some of the basics. Use the first couple practices to really evaluate your players and your team's strengths and weaknesses (see Chapter 5). For example, you can cover the most basic elements quickly, but you should move on to more advanced techniques, such as executing bunts to move runners into scoring position, hitting the cutoff man, and turning double plays, among others, almost immediately.

Functional, not Filler: Making Each Practice Beneficial

Every practice plays an important role in your players' and your team's development, which is why planning them is so important (see the previous sections of this chapter). However, planning a practice isn't enough. After you carefully design your practices, you have to follow through and successfully execute them. You have to make sure that your players have fun and learn about the game of baseball, which means all your practices need to be beneficial in the short time you have with your team.

Because you may have at least a dozen kids on your team, it can be quite a challenge to make sure that every player benefits from your practices. In this section, we map out a plan that you can use to turn all your practices into fun-filled, dynamic learning sessions.

Building your players' skills

A good way to approach your practices is to look at them as building blocks in your players' development. You need to establish a solid foundation for each particular skill before you can jump ahead to another skill or a more-advanced form of the same skill. Building a foundation takes a really focused effort on your part, because you'll be eager to teach your players as much as you can in the relatively short amount of time you have with them.

For example, when working with your infielders, your initial focus should be on teaching a player the basics of fielding a ground ball that's coming directly at him. After he gets pretty comfortable bending his knees to field the ball, you can teach him where to position his glove hand and his bare hand, and you can show him how to watch the ball into his mitt to cut down on errors. After he improves on these tasks, you can begin working with him on fielding balls while on the move to his left and right. Likewise, when working with a hitter, you want to help him hone his swing, hitting pitches down the middle of the plate. Eventually, as he gets comfortable swinging the bat and gains some confidence, you can incorporate other aspects of hitting, such as squaring up to bunt or hitting the ball to the opposite field.

Helping players who need it

Even though you're a great coach (or preparing to become one) — which we know because you're taking the time to read this book — you're bound to have some kids who struggle with different aspects of the game. After all, baseball is a hard game to play, from the bottom to the top levels. If a child is having difficulty learning a skill, you need to acknowledge his efforts. If you stick by him — encouraging and motivating him during each drill — he'll pick up the skill eventually, or at least get better at it.

If a child is really struggling with a particular skill, don't be afraid to take a closer look at how you're teaching the skill. Just because the other players picked up on it doesn't mean that a better teaching method doesn't exist. Try one of the following techniques with the player:

✔ **Alter your instructions.** For example, your instructions to your infielder to keep her eye on the ball while she's fielding grounders may not be having much impact. So, change the focus and zero in on her footwork and how she moves toward the ball instead. If she's able to get in front of the ball more quickly, she'll have more time to adjust to it coming her way and will probably be more efficient at handling it.

✔ **Break down the skill into smaller parts and work on them individually.** For example, teaching a child the art of bunting requires mastering several steps. Work with the child on sliding his right hand up the bat to get it in the proper position. Don't worry about anything else until he's got the hand positioning down. Once he's comfortable with that, focus on his feet and where they must be when he squares around. By teaching a skill one piece at a time, you give the player a better chance of putting it all together.

✔ **Find a different drill that teaches the same skill.** For example, if you're working on helping the youngster hit to the opposite field, you can kneel down near the batter and toss balls underhanded to him to drive to the opposite field; or you can utilize a batting tee and have the youngster swing at balls from there.

Anytime you're devoting a little extra time to a particular player, make sure that your practice doesn't come to a standstill for the remainder of the team. If you have assistant coaches helping you out, make sure they keep drills going so players aren't standing around. If you don't have any help, start up a drill that the other kids know well then spend a few moments with the child who is having some difficulty.

Stay positive while give your instructions. You'll get much further with the child, and the child will enjoy playing for you more, if you say something like, "That was excellent how you bent your knees to field that ground ball. Just remember to follow through with your arm toward the target." This approach is much more effective than saying something like, "You didn't follow through — again."

Youngsters who don't pick up skills as quickly as their teammates will get frustrated. You can help minimize their disappointment by making sure you acknowledge even the slightest hints of improvement. For example, if a youngster is really struggling to hit the ball, but he's beginning to foul some pitches off, build on that momentum by applauding the contact he makes.

Resist the temptation to tell a struggling player to watch how one of his teammates performs a skill. By doing so, you may send the message that one player is better than another.

Accentuating the positive

Everyone loves receiving congratulations for jobs well done or praise for their efforts. It makes people feel good when they receive ego boosts every now and then. Kids who play youth baseball are no different. Hearing praise for performing a skill well — especially in front of teammates — is like being handed a bag of candy or a new toy. Praise is that powerful and uplifting.

Make it one of your goals to praise every child on the team during every practice. You can praise anything — from the way a player hustled down to first base to the way a player demonstrated great teamwork by congratulating a teammate for a nice play. You can ensure that you distribute your praise equally by carrying a roster in your practice planner and making a mark next to a player's name every time you make a positive remark to him.

Don't surrender discipline for the sake of being a pal to the kids. You're still their coach and their leader, and you don't want them to lose respect for you. You can be demanding while maintaining a positive tone and disposition; and, along with your encouragement, you can provide constructive criticism that helps them improve.

Good coaches can find the proper balance between praise and discipline in order to help their players reach their potential. The following list presents a few more ideas on giving positive feedback to your players:

- **Start praising early.** A great time to offer some positive feedback is during warm-ups at the start of practice. For example, as you oversee the stretching, you can mention to a youngster that you're really impressed with how quickly he picked up a certain skill in your last practice and that you're anxious to watch him put the skill to use today.

- **Be innovative with your acknowledgment.** If you're creative, the kids will get a real kick out of your praise. For example, you can do something other than the routine high-five. You can use low-fives, where you and the player slap hands while you're both reaching low to the ground.

- **Be specific with your praise.** General comments like "Thatta boy" and "Way to go" are okay, but you can pack a powerful punch by zeroing in on exactly why you're applauding the player. Something like "Great job bending your knee on that hook slide" hits home and is more likely to stick in the child's head when he attempts that slide in the future.

- **Use the sandwich method.** Surround your corrective comments with positive remarks. For example, when talking to your second baseman, you can say, "Billy, your ready (fielding) stance was perfect before the pitch, but when you bent down to field the ball, you took your eye off the ball to see how quickly the runner was getting to first base."

- **Bring practice to a halt.** Don't be afraid to interrupt practice momentarily when a player does something the right way. Think about the pride you'll give those youngsters who turned a double play if you stop practice and praise them right in front of everyone.

✔ **Don't use excessive praise.** Yes, you want to praise your players to make them feel good about what they've done or tried to do to the best of their ability. But you shouldn't throw out praise just for the sake of doing so. Praising without merit takes away some of your credibility and believability with the team.

Putting smiles on their faces with fun practices

Every practice drill you run should fulfill three requirements:

✔ It must be safe.

✔ It must help the players improve specific areas of their game.

✔ It must be fun.

If you consistently meet all three criteria with your practice drills, you'll treat your kids to a wonderful season of baseball. The following sections give you some safe ideas for teaching the game in a fun manner.

Enhance practice with some fun drills

With just a little imagination, you can turn routine practice activities into really fun exercises that have all sorts of benefits for the players. For example, instead of having the kids lightly jog around the field as part of their warm-up, you can pair them up and give each twosome a ball. As the players jog parallel to one another, they can toss the ball back and forth, using their gloves to make the catches. This drill serves many purposes: It gets the players loosened up for practice; it helps build their hand-eye coordination, which pays big dividends in the field and at the plate; and it makes running much more enjoyable for the kids.

If you're coaching an older or more advanced team, you can take the same creative approach and tweak it to fit your players' needs. Because the competitive level of these kids is much higher than with younger kids, you can turn drills into fun competitions. For the same throwing drill, challenge the kids to see which pair can toss the ball back and forth the most times without dropping it. The winners get a couple of extra swings of the bat during a hitting drill, or they get to choose the next drill to be used during practice. These types of fun activities not only enhance your players' skill development, but also will have them begging to play for you again next season.

Get some help from mom and dad

Moms and dads can be much more than chauffeurs for their kids' games and practices. They can become part of your practices. All it takes is a little creativity on your part to include them in your sessions. Your kids, especially at the younger age levels, will get a kick out of having their parents on the field with them. Getting involved in practice will also be fun for the parents — much more so than balancing their checkbooks and chatting with other parents, we're sure.

You can involve as many interested parents as you want in your practices. Here are some ways you can pull it off:

- ✔ **Notify the parents.** Let the parents know, well in advance, that you'd like to involve them in one your practices. Give them options for dates and times. If you give busy parents time to plan ahead, they'll likely be happy to join in.

- ✔ **Make it a big deal.** Set a fun tone for the practice involving the parents by talking about it in the preceding practice. Be enthusiastic about the drills you have planned, and show your excitement for the adventure.

- ✔ **Set up a parent-child scrimmage.** The kids will really love seeing their moms at bat, their dads running the bases, and their friends' parents chasing down balls in the outfield. You can play an inning or two at the end of practice to conclude the day on a fun note, or you can devote a mid-season practice to the scrimmage as a nice break from the routine.

- ✔ **Pair kids and parents in drills.** You can liven up a routine drill with the help of the parents. For example, you can put a parent on the base paths, and you can have the players run through a rundown situation (where the base runner is caught between bases with no safe place to turn). The kids will love the challenge of trying to tag a mom or dad out.

Not every parent is going to want to participate; you'll have some parents whose schedule doesn't allow them to hang around for your practices; and some kids, for whatever reason, may not want their parents involved. That's okay, because even having just a handful of parents involved gives your practice a different look and the kids another type of drill to participate in.

Fun for the Road: Ending Your Practices on a Positive Note

How you start a practice is essential for setting the tone for the day, but how you end a practice is equally important. You want your players to head home with smiles on their faces instead of feeling relief that the practice is finally over. Here are a couple tips to keep in mind when the sun is fading and your practice time is about up:

✔ **Conclude your practice with a bang.** Save one of the team's favorite drills for the final few minutes of practice. You'll ensure that everyone has a good time, and your players will eagerly anticipate the next practice.

✔ **Give a quick closing chat.** Before turning the players loose to their parents, gather them for a quick chat — and the emphasis is on *quick*. Talk about how much you appreciate the hard work and effort they put in, and zero in on specific areas of the game where they're improving.

Wrap up your practice with a quick review of the upcoming schedule — particularly if the league has altered any practice or game dates because of cancellations due to weather. If the next time you'll see your players is at a game, find out if any players will be unavailable that day. Thank the team for working hard and paying attention, conclude with a team cheer if you have one, and call it a day.

A good way to get the most out of your practices is to take a few minutes afterward to evaluate what happened. Ask yourself which drills the kids really enjoyed and which ones didn't seem to generate much enthusiasm. Writing in a practice notebook while the practice is still fresh in your mind is a great way to organize your thoughts. If you have assistant coaches, consult with them to get their feedback, too.

Chapter 7

Game Day

Game day provides players — and coaches — with all sorts of exciting new challenges. Players have to adjust to unfamiliar pitchers, translate practice skills to game skills, and get used to the speed of an actual game. As a coach, you have to meet with opposing coaches and umpires, conduct warm-ups, and deliver a motivational talk — and that's all before the opening pitch. During the game, you have to pump up your kids after they strike out or bobble ground balls; orchestrate substitutions to ensure equal playing time for all your troops; communicate plays; and direct your kids on the base paths, among other duties. Toss in the post-game talk, and you can imagine the busy day that's on tap for you.

How you handle the avalanche of coaching responsibilities impacts how much fun your kids have on game day. In this chapter, we share all the secrets for handling your various game-day coaching tasks so that your kids — and you — can look back on your games and smile.

Mowing Down Your Pre-Game Checklist

Your coaching duties begin prior to the umpire calling out, "Play ball!" Before you hit the field, you need to tend to various pre-game responsibilities. The tasks, which can be completed in succession, help you ensure the safety of your players, nail down the rules specific to your league, and acknowledge any special circumstances that may exist. Here's a checklist to help you navigate your way through the pre-game chores.

Do your best to arrive at least 20 minutes before your game, which gives you plenty of time to deal with your pre-game responsibilities. If you're running late, make sure you contact an assistant coach so he can get there and assume some of your duties.

Inspecting the field

Because all it takes is one small piece of debris to injure a baseball player, you need to inspect the playing field before your game starts. This responsibility is too important to leave to the opposing coach or the grounds crew. All the players are your responsibility, and you need to take every step you can to ensure their safety. Be sure to take a look around for any item or piece of debris that poses a safety hazard, including the following:

- Rocks and broken glass
- Raised sprinkler heads
- Loose pieces of sod

Meeting with the opposing coach and umpires

Before the game gets underway, you have to play a baseball businessman and hold a couple of important meetings with colleagues and supervisors. Take the initiative to walk over to the opposing coach and shake hands. This display of good sportsmanship sets a great example for the players on both teams, the parents, and any other spectators.

While you're shaking hands with the opposing coach, check to see if any of his players have any special needs that you and your players should be aware of. For example, if an opposing player has a visual impairment, his team may have a brightly colored baseball that they use when he's up to bat. Let your kids know that the ball will be in play when the child steps to the plate.

In addition to meeting the opposing coaches, be sure to meet with the umpiring crew prior to the game. Offering a friendly welcome to the umpires is another way you can set the tone for a positive game. During your conversation, ask the umpires to inform you if any of your players say or do anything unsportsmanlike. Also, be sure to alert the umpires if any players on your team (or any opposing players) have any special needs.

At the younger age levels, leagues usually hire only one umpire, who works behind the plate and makes the calls on the bases. At the more advanced levels, leagues usually place an umpire behind home plate and one or two in the field.

Checking your equipment

Game days are exciting and hectic moments for most kids and parents, so it isn't uncommon for a player to forget a cap, bat, or even a glove. As the kids arrive at the field, do a quick inventory to make sure the players have everything they need. Of course, with all the other responsibilities you have, checking each child may not always be possible. So, when you gather your team for warm-ups, do a quick check to make sure that everyone has the necessities.

Of course, you may be responsible for transporting equipment (such as helmets, balls, and bats) to the games, too, so before you leave the house, make sure you have all the necessary bags packed and loose ends tied (see Chapter 2 for advice on finding out who needs to bring what equipment).

Penciling in players

The time to fill out your lineup is prior to arriving at the game, maybe the night before or at the office (just don't let the boss catch you). At the beginning levels of play your batting order has no significance, but in the older age divisions how you arrange players impacts the strategies you're employing.

In your last practice leading up to the game double-check whether all the players will be at the game. This lessens the chance of you filling out a lineup and then scrambling to rearrange players to account for a youngster who doesn't show up.

Warming Up

After you handle your pre-game responsibilities and all your players arrive at the field, you can begin your pre-game warm-ups. The goal of a pre-game warm-up is to prepare your players for competition and reduce the chances of them suffering injuries. The older the kids get, the more susceptible they are to pulling or straining muscles. And for kids of all ages, warming up their arms and going through some hitting and fielding practice improves game-time performance. As such, a well-designed pre-game warm-up stretches the kids' muscles and loosens up their bodies so they can swing their bats, run the bases, field the balls, and make the throws. The following sections take you through such a warm-up.

Know how much time your league allots for pre-game warm-ups so you can adjust yours accordingly. Because games are often played one after the other, you'll likely have a limited amount of time to get your players ready. Also, make sure that you give your opponent equal access to the field.

Running and stretching

Before you get into any game-skill specific warm-up drills, you should put your kids through some running and stretching drills to get them limbered up and ready to play. Specifically, do the following warm-up activities:

- ✔ **Do some light running.** Before you ask them to stretch out, have the kids perform some light running to get their bodies warmed up. You can line them up on a foul line and have them jog to center field and back a couple of times.

- ✔ **Loosen up the major muscles.** The pre-game warm-up needs to cover stretching all the major muscle groups — arms, legs, neck, and back — that the kids will put to use. See Chapter 16 for details on some specific stretches you can use with your team.

Depending on the size of your team, you should conduct this warm-up activity on the field (if it's available for you to use) or off to the side of the field far enough away so that the kids are protected from wild throws and batted balls if a game or warm-up is taking place on the field. Also, try to create a fun and upbeat atmosphere for the running and stretching part of warm-ups. You want your players to look forward to loosening up before the game so they don't just "go through the motions." You can choose different players to lead the warm-ups before each game to help keep the kids interested.

Throwing

Here is a glimpse at how your players can run through some pre-game throwing:

- ✔ **Infielders:** When your players are throwing the ball back and forth to warm up, you want them to begin close to their partners and lightly toss the ball back and forth. Once they begin to loosen up, they can gradually move farther away from each other and make longer throws.

- ✔ **Outfielders:** Outfielders also begin by lightly tossing. After they've made short throws back and forth with their partners for several minutes, they can gradually make longer throws to simulate the types of throws they'll make in the game. They should be throwing at half speed and then three-quarter speed for the bulk of the warm-up period. After they are fully loosened up, they can make a couple of full-strength throws.

- ✔ **Pitcher and catcher:** Your battery should begin by standing and playing a simple game of catch, throwing the ball back and forth at less than half speed. Gradually, the players work their way up to the distance between the pitching mound and home plate. After they are warmed up the pitcher can begin throwing pitches to the catcher, who can assume his normal squatting position.

If your team has access to the field prior to the game, use the outfield on your dugout side for warm-up throwing sessions; otherwise, find a spot away from the field and spectators that provides a safe spot for the kids to get loose.

Hitting

Giving kids a quality hitting warm-up can be pretty challenging, especially if the league doesn't allow batting practice on the field before games, which is pretty common. If you can't get the kids on the field to take a couple of swings, consider some of these alternatives to get them ready for their appearances at the plate:

- ✔ **Toss some imaginary pitches.** Have all the players grab a bat and spread out. You stand in front of them and deliver an imaginary pitch and have them take their normal swing. This helps them visualize the ball coming toward them, focuses them on making a good swing, and loosens those muscles that they'll rely on when hitting live pitching in a few minutes.

- ✔ **Hit the batting cage.** If your league has a batting cage at the facility, gather the team there before the game to get some swings in. Of course, make sure to follow proper safety at all times, including having only one child in the batting cage at a time wearing a properly fitting helmet.

- ✔ **Use the soft toss drill.** Check out Chapter 12 for details on this drill, which you can use with wiffle balls on your side of the field to help your kids get in some swings. Be sure to conduct drills like this far enough away from the field so you don't cause disruptions for another team.

Fielding

Some leagues allow time for each team to get in some practice in the field, though it's often pretty brief. In order to make the most of this time, have your players, armed with their gloves, ready as soon as it is your team's turn.

Infield/outfield practice (covered in Chapter 13) is a great way to give all the kids some action in a short period of time. You can also take a look at other drills covered in Chapters 12 and 13 and tweak them however you'd like to fit your pre-game warm-up needs. If your time is really limited, focus on giving each infielder a ground ball that he throws over to first base, and each out-fielder a pop fly that he catches and throws in to the infield.

Holding a Pre-Game Team Meeting

A quick pre-game team meeting (under five minutes) for the older kids and even shorter for the younger ones helps your kids focus and prepare for a fun-filled day of baseball. You can conduct these in your dugout, or find an area that has the fewest distractions. During the pre-game meeting, pass along any game-specific instructions you have, and give your players a rousing pep talk to fire them up for the big game.

Keeping your instructions simple

You can follow a basic rule when giving pre-game instructions: The simpler you can keep everything, the better off you and your players will be. When delivering pre-game instructions, zero in on a couple of main points. With a younger team, you can keep the conversation basic by reminding them to step toward the intended target when throwing, for example. With an older team, you may discuss something more strategy-oriented, such as reminding the players to look for opportunities to challenge the opposing team's out-fielders and take extra bases on hits.

Here are some other tips to keep in mind for your pre-game instructions:

✔ **Focus on fun and good sportsmanship.** Make sure your kids understand that you want them to enjoy themselves — whether your team is up by several runs or trailing by a bunch. You also want your team to model good sportsmanship at all times. Stress respect toward umpires — regardless whether calls go in your favor or against you — and opposing players and coaches.

✔ **Avoid strategy sessions.** Minutes before the opening pitch isn't the time to introduce a new strategy or discuss implementing a different style of play (using more hit-and-runs, for example). The kids won't be able to grasp a new concept in such a short period of time. Stick to what you worked on in practice.

✔ **Use specific comments.** Your players are more likely to respond when you give them specific feedback or instructions. General comments like "Let's get some hits today" won't be as productive as more specific remarks, like "Let's see the smooth swings, with your eyes on the ball, that you had working in practice yesterday."

✔ **Tone down the constant instructions.** Do your best to stay away from saying the same things every game. Otherwise, your players may begin tuning you out. Just like a good pitcher mixes up the types of his pitches to keep batters off balance, good baseball coaches vary their comments to keep everything fresh and the players more attentive.

✔ **Run down your field observations.** Relay any important information you gathered during your pre-game check of the field (see the earlier section "Inspecting the field"). For example, maybe a certain spot in the outfield is a bit muddy.

Executing the inspirational talk

Pulling the best efforts out of your players every time they take the field can be pretty challenging, which is why you may want to reach into your coaching bag of tricks and pull out the pre-game inspirational talk. This talk, when drenched with motivation and oozing enthusiasm, is a great way to get your players excited about the game and inspire them to give their best effort every inning. The following list presents some more tips that help ensure that your pre-game words pack a punch and convey the proper messages:

✔ **Be upbeat.** You should exude positive energy at all times, but be particularly upbeat before the opening pitch of a game. Focus your talk on areas of the game that the team has excelled in, and let your players know how eager you are to see them put those skills into action.

✔ **Steer clear of pressure phrases.** Setting performance goals — like scoring eight runs or stealing five bases — may seem motivational on the surface, but you usually just set the kids up for disappointment. Keep in mind that the children can only give you their best effort; they can't control the outcome of games.

✔ **Recall your youth baseball experiences.** In the hours before your game, when you're deciding what to tell your team, reflect on your playing days. Think about your old coaches and the pre-game talks that really hit home with you. Have a chuckle at those that left you bored and baffled. Steal from the good ones, and steer clear of the ineffective ones.

✔ **Shun clichés.** Baseball clichés — like "Don't get caught napping!" or "We're going to have to manufacture some runs against this team today!" — will likely produce blank stares from your players. You don't need to turn to off-the-wall phrases to prepare your kids for a game. Speaking from the heart, with genuine passion, serves you and your team far better. (To discover more effective baseball lingo, check out Chapter 3.)

✔ **Conclude with a cheer.** Finish your talk with a team cheer, such as "One . . . two . . . three . . . Team!" The cheer is a symbolic gesture that reminds all your players that they need to work together and support one another.

Play Ball!

After you handle your pre-game responsibilities (see the previous sections in this chapter), you and your kids should be all set for the game to begin. No rest for the weary, though; after the opening pitch leaves the mound, a whole new list of responsibilities and challenges awaits you. You have to motivate the kids, keep up constant communication, orchestrate substitutions to ensure equal playing time, and make adjustments based on your observations — inning after inning. You'll also be relying on your assistant coaches to help out with many of these chores. Of course, you'll get together with them during your practices, as well as before the game, to go over everyone's responsibilities so everything runs smoothly. The following sections give you a closer look at some of these game-related coaching tasks.

Motivating your players

Even though you gave a pre-game speech that put goose bumps on the kids' arms and raised their excitement level (see the previous section), your players may quickly forget everything you said after the ball goes into play in the first inning — especially if you coach younger players. Follow up your pre-game talk with plenty of encouragement and motivation during the game. Keep the following motivational tips in mind:

✔ **Don't make a big deal out of mistakes.** Give kids a little time and space when they make mistakes so they can figure out how to respond to them and learn from them. Barraging a player with instructions the second he makes a miscue reduces the chances of him learning, adapting, and improving.

✔ **Stay positive — and put a muzzle on the yelling.** Avoid yelling in a negative fashion or with a frustrated tone. Keep your emotions in check, and remind yourself that the kids (and their parents) are at the field to have fun — not to listen to you shout and scream all game long.

- ✔ **Don't be a dugout distraction.** Being enthusiastic is great, because your attitude can be highly contagious and rub off on the kids. But you don't want to cross over into overbearing territory and become a distraction during the game. Be liberal with the high-fives, just don't be so animated all game long that you become a distraction to your players.

- ✔ **Constantly applaud kids who hustle.** Hustle is one area of the game that your players can control, regardless of talent or athleticism. A modestly talented player can make himself an above-average player simply by hustling every second he's in the game.

Using hand signals to communicate

When you watch baseball on television or attend a game, you see coaches and players on the field who look like they're playing charades. Using signs to communicate is one of the more unique aspects of coaching and playing this great game — an aspect unchanged by technology. *Signs* are simply series of hand motions used by coaches to relay information to their players without the other team knowing their intentions. For example, the coach may take his left hand and touch his ear first, his nose second, and his chin last and then have his right hand touch his stomach followed by the bill of his cap. When the player sees this signal, he knows he's supposed to *take* the next pitch (not swing).

Work on your signals with your players during practice, and go over them during your pre-game preparations. If you coach very young players — T-ball or coach's pitch age — don't bother teaching your players signs. Signs can be confusing, and you don't really need to run specific plays at these levels.

You use several sets of signals while coaching — some before the pitch, and some while the ball is in play. The following sections outline both types.

Before the pitch

When your team is up to bat, you can use signs between pitches to let your batter know what you want him to do, such as swing at the next pitch or let it go. Here's how it works:

1. **The hitter steps out of the batter's box and looks to his coach — who's usually positioned in the coaching box by third base (see Chapter 3) — for the sign.**

2. **The coach gives the hitter his sign.**

   Keep your signs as simple as possible; the more complicated they are, the more likely your players are to mix them up during the game. Try to give the kids an easy device for remembering the signs. For example, belt = bunt, skin (of arm) = steal, and top (of hat) = take. You can mix in meaningless signals to keep the other team from stealing your signs.

3. **The hitter accepts the sign.**

   To make sure the player understands the signal you want him to let you know he's got it. This can be something as simple as nodding his head to you or touching the top of his batting helmet.

4. **The hitter steps back into the box and prepares to execute your order.**

Make sure you frequently let your players know how many outs you have — when you're at bat *and* in the field. Simply hold up the number of fingers for the number of outs (or a fist for no outs), and yell out the total as well.

When the ball is in play

Coaches also rely on hand signals to tell the base runners what to do when the ball is in play. Players headed to first base on a ball hit in the infield need to listen to their first base coach while keeping their eyes focused on the bag. Any base runner who's approaching second or third base needs to locate the third base coach, who uses signals to let the runner know what to do: Stop at the base, keep running, or slide into the base. Here are the commonly used signals for third base coaches:

- ✔ **Slide:** The best way to signal for a runner to slide into second or third in anticipation of a close play is to drop down to a knee and wave your hands, palms down, toward the ground. Yelling "slide" or "get down" works, too, but crowd noise may drown out your efforts; a coach's visual signals are much more effective most of the time.

- ✔ **Keep running:** To signal for a runner to continue running — from second to third or from third to home — swing one arm in a windmill motion and point toward the base.

- ✔ **Stop:** To signal for the runner to stop at a base without sliding, hold both hands above your head, with your palms facing the runner.

At the advanced levels of play the on-deck hitters can also help a teammate coming home by getting behind home plate (far enough away so that he doesn't disrupt play) and signaling to the runner whether he needs to slide or cross home plate standing up.

Substituting players

Many youth baseball programs, especially at the beginning levels, allow coaches to make unlimited substitutions and lineup changes during the course of games. Your main objective is to make sure your kids receive an equal amount of playing time; you don't want to leave someone stranded on the bench for an uncomfortable amount of time. If you're juggling a large group of kids and moving them in and out of the game, be sure to keep them updated on who will be playing specific positions each inning. While the team is batting, you can run down who will play each position in the next inning.

At the more advanced levels of play, your league may limit how often you can substitute. Many leagues don't allow players to reenter a game after they've been taken out. You need to know all your league's rules so you can plan accordingly (we discuss this topic in Chapter 2).

In many leagues — except at the youngest levels — you need to notify the opposing team (and the umpire) when you make a lineup change.

Try to substitute for players after they do something *well* rather than after they make a mistake, if possible. If you take a youngster out of the game after he makes a throwing error, he'll most likely relate making mistakes to losing playing time. (If you go over who will be playing certain innings before the game, though, this situation won't pose any problems for you.) When you remove a player from the game, give him a pat on the back or a high-five to recognize all the effort he put forth. Kids love that kind of recognition.

Making mid-game adjustments

Plotting your game strategy ahead of time is a great idea, but as a game rolls along, you shouldn't be afraid to fine-tune your plan based on what's happening on the field. Use the following pointers to help you make those mid-game moves:

- **Observe and adjust.** Don't be afraid to be flexible during a game. For example, maybe early on in the game you told your team to take a few pitches each time up because the opposing pitcher didn't have great control. Midway through the game, the opposing coach brings in a new pitcher who throws plenty of strikes. You now tell your kids to be more aggressive at the plate, because they'll see many more good pitches to hit.

- **Take advantage of your players' insights.** Your kids are great resources because they're on the field in the middle of the action. Because of all your responsibilities during the game, you may not be able to catch everything that goes on. Plus, when kids know that you value their feedback, they'll stay focused on the action, hoping to pick up a tidbit or two that they can share with you.

  For example, maybe your catcher has noticed that several of the opposing team's hitters swing at the first pitch. If that's the case, have your pitchers throw their first pitches outside of the strike zone so the hitters swing at bad balls.

- **Adapt to the home-plate umpire's calls.** Each umpire has a unique interpretation of the strike zone, so your players need to adjust to increase their effectiveness at the plate. If you and your hitters recognize that a particular umpire is calling high strikes, instruct your hitters to be more aggressive in swinging at higher pitches.

Winning and Losing Gracefully

Teaching your kids the art of winning and losing with dignity and class is a tall order. However, it is an order of the highest importance. You have to spend time talking to your team about the need to play fairly, abide by the rules, and behave with class in both victory and defeat. Ask your players how they feel when they win and lose, how they want to be treated when they lose, and how they should treat opponents after a win. Consider their responses, and base your teaching on them.

During games, if your team abides by the guidelines in the following list, you'll be the coach of a classy bunch:

- **Get excited, but don't embarrass the other team.** You want your players to be enthusiastic when they make great plays, score a run, and win games, but make sure they don't direct their celebration at the opposition. For example, if one of your players hits a home run, he should reserve his celebration until he crosses home plate and can high-five his teammates. Posing at home plate and watching the ball sail over the fence, like many pros do, is poor sportsmanship.

- **Don't taunt.** Whether in the dugout or on the field, don't let your players direct negative comments toward the other team (or umpires). For example, if the opposing pitcher walks several batters in a row, your players shouldn't tease or laugh at the struggling pitcher. All comments should be positive and directed at your team.

- **Do the little things.** Encourage small gestures of respect and kindness toward teammates and opponents. For example, when the other team's catcher hustles after a foul pop up, your batter can show good sportsmanship by picking up his mask and handing it to him.

- **Compliment good play.** Teach your kids to praise the efforts and good play of opponents. A simple "nice hit" or "good play" will suffice and show the class of your players and your team.

No matter the situation, never let your players throw equipment, swear, or blame the score of the game on the umpires (or, even worse, on their teammates). These behaviors are *really* unacceptable — at every level of play. (Jump to Chapter 17 to find out more about dealing with bad behavior.)

After the game ends, make the following a part of your team's routine — win or lose:

Play to win, not to embarrass

Many leagues feature a pretty big range of skills between the players and teams, which means your season may feature many mismatches. If your team begins to dominate an opponent, do your best to not run up the score and embarrass the other players and coaches.

If your team finds itself in a lopsided game, consider some of the following approaches that work to keep your team's interest level high, focus on a broad range of skills, and avoid humiliating your opponent:

✔ **Tone down the aggressiveness on the base paths.** If you build a comfortable lead, continuing to steal bases is a slap in the face of the other team. Even if you coach an aggressive team that swipes bases as often as possible, one-sided games aren't the venue to continue playing that style.

✔ **Move kids around.** Lopsided games provide you with the perfect opportunity to play your kids at different positions. Moving your kids to unfamiliar positions gives them new challenges and keeps the game fresh and exciting. And, who knows, maybe you'll discover a new power pitcher or a slick-fielding third baseman in the process.

✔ **Play your reserves.** Giving your reserves more game-day action than they're used to is possible after you build a comfortable lead (assuming, of course, that you aren't giving all your players equal playing time).

✔ **Work on weaknesses.** Encourage your players to work on weak spots in their games. For example, if one of your players is a natural pull hitter, perhaps you can have him work on hitting the ball to the opposite field in his future at-bats.

✔ **Always shake hands.** No matter what happens on the field during the game, your players should line up and shake hands with the opposing team afterward. Make sure you stand in that line, too, to congratulate the other kids and their coaches.

✔ **Be sincere and congratulatory.** Encourage your players to acknowledge a well-played game and solid effort from the opposition and to congratulate individuals that had a good game.

✔ **Thank the umpires.** You don't see many baseball players or coaches thanking umpires anymore, but it's the classy thing to do. Players who get in the habit of thanking the umpires for their work during the game gain the respect of everyone involved in the league and set a shining example of model behavior.

Delivering the Post-Game Talk

The message you deliver to your team following a game has a big impact on the kids. Regardless of how the game turned out, one of your most important tasks as a coach is to send your kids home feeling good about themselves and the effort they delivered. A good start is to be generous with the pats on the back and to dole out plenty of encouraging words following the game. When kids feel that a coach appreciates their efforts, they'll look forward to taking the field again.

The following list presents some additional tips for giving your troops a good send-off:

- ✔ **Keep the focus on fun.** Stay consistent with the pre-game talk you gave by stressing the fun element. Tell them about the fun you had during the game, and inquire if they had fun.

- ✔ **Accentuate the positive.** Wins and losses don't define your players' effort, the strides they've made in many areas of the game, or how much fun they're having playing baseball. Whether your team played its best game of the season or got clobbered, your job as a coach is to point out the good things your kids can build on.

- ✔ **Recognize good sportsmanship.** Don't overlook the displays of good sportsmanship that occurred during the game. Making your players aware of classy behavior sends the message that conduct is as important as the skills that go into playing the game.

- ✔ **Remind players about your next practice or game.** Let the kids and parents know when you'll meet again, and encourage them to practice on their own in between sessions (without burning out the kids, of course; see Chapter 4 for more on interacting with the parents).

Chapter 8

Refining Your Coaching Strategies throughout the Season

*Y*ou can be very proud of yourself as a coach if the season has started successfully — which means that the kids are having fun, learning new skills and fundamentals, and improving on others. However, just because the season has started well doesn't mean you can go into cruise control. You can count your season as a success only if your players keep having fun, keep learning, and keep improving. And keeping the learning rolling along and the smiles going strong requires the ability to adjust to the ever-changing dynamics of your team throughout the season.

In this chapter, we take a look at how you can adjust your coaching strategies to meet the demands of the season as it rolls along. We give you tips on handling any shifts in team dynamics. We outline your key mid-season responsibilities, including revising coaching strategies, adjusting practice plans, setting goals, and reviewing the progress of your players. And we give you tips on gleaning information from parents so you can keep tabs on your players' feelings. How you handle these areas and adapt determines whether the kids' fun and skill development continues or comes to an abrupt halt.

Dealing with Shifting Team Dynamics

By around the midway point of the season, you should have a pretty good idea of what your team's strengths and weaknesses are. Perhaps the majority of your players have really improved their fielding skills — to the point where your team is sound defensively. Now you can focus on getting the players some additional work on certain offensive skills. Regardless of what part of the game they come from, improvements (and areas of weakness) impact the makeup of your team. As the coach, you must shuffle players into different positions, tweak your practice drills to account for the team's changing skills and needs, and — if you're coaching an advanced-level team — probably even fiddle with some of your game-day strategies to account for newfound strengths (and to compensate for any weaknesses that come to light).

In the following sections, we help you take a closer look at where your team is overall in its development, and we assist you in revising your coaching plans to focus on areas you want to strengthen during the remainder of the season.

The scoreboard isn't the best indicator of your team's progress. One of the benchmarks of good coaching is being able to push the final score out of your mind — win or lose — and to put the magnifying glass squarely over the kids' performances. Was a player able to execute the sacrifice bunt you spent a bulk of the last practice working on? Did your players use proper form when sliding into bases? Even if your team lost by a substantial margin, your players may have played one of their most fundamentally sound games of the season. Recognize and applaud their efforts so you can build on the improvement.

Recognizing improvements

As your kids begin to improve their skills and gain knowledge, they'll become more proficient at executing during practice and games. Nothing will make you prouder than seeing the kids improve and succeed, but this situation does present some new challenges for you. The following list gives you a peek at some of the common challenges you face when coaching a team with improving players:

- ✓ **Moving players around in the field:** After a few games and many practices, you may realize that kids you penciled in at certain positions are better suited to handle entirely different positions. As the season unfolds, you need to be a constant evaluator of talent. During practices, pay close attention to the smallest details. Watch how your outfielders deal with hard-hit balls rolling on the ground. If they handle them with no trouble, they may be pretty good scooping up grounders in the infield. Watch how your shortstop reacts to shallow fly balls, since he may be pretty good at reading how the ball comes off the bat and better suited to help your team in the outfield. Watch how your catcher makes throws to different bases. If he has a strong and accurate arm, he can be a perfect fit for third base. You may discover that a youngster would be able and eager to play a new position that can really help the team. At the very least, you can identify valuable backups for spots on the field if any players have to leave a game or get injured.

Make sure you keep parents informed about any position changes you make to reduce the chances of disputes unfolding. Share with the parents why you think their child is better suited for a different position and how his skills at that position will be an asset to the team.

✔ **Moving hitters around in the batting order:** At the advanced levels of play, as certain players become more proficient with the bat, you'll want to take advantage of these improvements and shuffle your batting order around. Maybe you've noticed a player in the middle of the lineup has emerged as an excellent bunter and is better suited to hit in the number 2 spot where he can bunt the leadoff hitter over if the opportunity presents itself. Or, maybe a player at the bottom of the order is getting on base so frequently that he can be more of an asset hitting from the number 1 spot.

✔ **Reducing tension caused by your decisions:** If you coach an advanced-level squad and determine playing time by your players' skill levels, you may discover that players who lose their starting jobs may have great difficulty adjusting to their backup status or their new positions if you simply move them. After all, feelings get hurt when a player's skills are indirectly criticized in front of teammates.

Make sure you take the time to explain to the player that he's a valued and important member of the team. Encourage him to keep working hard in practice and to support his teammates.

A lot of times this type of news doesn't go over well with parents who won't agree that their child is less talented than someone else's. This situation can lead to hurt feelings, tension, and disagreements. Chapter 17 offers some tips on dealing with upset parents.

✔ **Diffusing teammate tension:** Youngsters who lose their spot to a teammate will naturally be disappointed, much like you would be losing out on a job promotion to a co-worker. Keep in mind that kids often get attached to certain positions and that moving them elsewhere can be upsetting. In these cases, pay some extra attention to the child who is unhappy that he got shifted. You want to ensure that he remains passionate about the game and supportive of his teammates. Let the child know that you think with the type of skills he has that he is better suited to help the team in his new position. Also, you can let him know that no move is permanent. Any number of things can unfold during the season — injuries or a change in strategy, for example — that can return him to his original position or perhaps even somewhere else on the field.

✔ **Revising your game-day approach:** As the season moves along, your team may become significantly different than the one you began the first practice with — and you have to adjust accordingly. If your infielders or outfielders show big improvements as a unit, you can begin shifting them around to take advantage of their new strengths. For example, if your outfielders have shown they're good at reading how the ball comes off the bat and react quickly, have them scoot several steps closer to the infield, which enables them to catch balls that might otherwise fall in for hits.

Keeping close tabs on each player's progress makes it easy for you to be there to deliver a high-five whenever the kid learns a new skill or makes an improvement. Maybe the action is subtle, such as the youngster positioning his feet properly to execute a bunt, or maybe he is becoming pretty consistent at fielding ground balls backhanded. Either way, be sure to show plenty of enthusiasm. The ultimate goal of improvement may be winning the games, but you should focus on improvements as vehicles to have more fun and to appreciate the game more.

Dealing with weaknesses

One of the many unique aspects about baseball is that it requires pretty diverse skills, and youngsters on your team aren't going to pick them all up as easily as you would like. Sometimes kids may struggle with different aspects of the game for the bulk of the season, which puts a premium on you being able to change players around to fit the best interests of the team. If you're coaching a beginning-level team, wins and losses take a back seat to learning and skill development and giving kids the chance to play several different positions. At the advanced levels of play, however, you'll likely encounter situations where sliding players into new positions will benefit the team. Let players know before the season gets started that as you get a good sense of their skills and abilities you'll be moving players around in order to make the team the strongest it can be. Stress to the kids that if you're moving them to a new position, you're doing so because you think that their skills are better suited in this new position.

Revising your current plan

One prospect that all coaches should hope they get to face is having to revise practices and game plans to accommodate the ever-improving skills of their players and the ever-changing needs of their teams. You don't want to suffocate your kids' learning by turning to the same set of drills at *every* practice. Your kids will gain the most out of their participation with you, and improve the fastest, if you constantly challenge them with new drills (for advice on practice drills you can run, turn to Chapters 12 and 13).

To mix up your practices and to keep your players motivated for games, grab some of the drills you've used in previous practices — try to pick ones that have been popular with your players — and look for ways to tweak them. For instance, you can increase the difficulty level to provide new challenges if your players have shown improvement in the skill. (You can jump to Chapter 13 for a rundown on some advanced drills.) By using a little creativity, you can alter virtually any drill to fit the needs of your team while maintaining the fun factor.

For example, if you often throw pitches to kids during basic hitting drills, try this: Instead of just throwing each player ten pitches to swing at, turn the drill into a fun challenge. Challenge your players to hit the first five pitches to right field, and see if they can hit the next five pitches to left field. Award a point for each successful swing. You can conclude the challenge with a bonus pitch that the player has to hit while choking up on the bat to simulate hitting with two strikes (these and other types of strategies are covered in greater detail in Chapters 14 and 15). The kids will love the challenge, and you get bonus points because it helps the players focus more on doing well instead of just swinging away.

Even if a specific drill has been wonderfully effective in helping the kids grow as players, don't be afraid to make alterations to it midway through the season. These types of tweaks keep drills fresh and exciting. If your team is struggling in a specific area of the game, pay special attention to the drills you are using. If the majority of the kids just can't seem to get a handle on hitting, for example, chances are you may need a complete overhaul of your hitting drills. Although you don't want to spend all of your practice time on one area of the game, you do want to devote some extra time to areas where the kids are struggling.

Rounding Second on Your Season with the Mid-Season Review

By the time you reach the season's halfway point, you'll notice all sorts of changes and improvements among your players, and — hopefully — you'll see that your team has really bonded under your leadership.

However, you can't stand pat on your successes. You should take the time to review how the team is progressing at the midpoint of the season. This practice benefits both you and the players. It helps keep a season that's been headache-free to this point headed in the right direction, and it can rescue a season that's drifting a little off course.

We all enjoy getting progress reports — in school, at work, or in other endeavors — especially when we receive glowing feedback about how well we've been doing. Pointing out progress and improvement with your players really drives home the point that you have their best interests in mind and that you're committed to helping them get the most out of their experience this season.

After you reach the midpoint of the season, you've seen enough practices and games to know your players really well and understand what their strengths and weaknesses are both individually and as a team. In the following sections, we explain how you can set goals for your players and the team for the remainder of the season, and how to go about giving feedback to the kids based on their progress toward these goals.

Setting goals

Setting goals for your players pushes them to reach their full potential by presenting challenges that they can have fun meeting. When done the right way, setting goals is one of the most effective coaching tools available. When you reach the season's halfway point, put the knowledge you've gained from watching your players in practices and games to good use by setting goals for them for the rest of the season. By setting goals at this point in the year, you refocus your players and present them with something new to strive for. You can meet with each player briefly either before or after practices to outline your goals for him.

To make goal-setting successful at the midpoint of the season, keep the following points in mind:

✔ **Use multiple goals.** Have several goals in place for your players to shoot for, based on what you've seen from them so far in the season and on their age level and experience. Create some that are fairly easy to reach and others that will require plenty of work to attain. By giving a player multiple goals, you ensure that the youngster — no matter how much his skills develop — gains some satisfaction, even if he doesn't reach the top goals.

For example, for hitting you can set several different batting averages — such as .275, .325, and .350 — so the kids have different levels to strive for. Team goals can include errorless games or a designated number of hits per game.

✔ **Encourage extra practice.** At the advanced levels, you get to see the kids a few times a week; however, if they really want to upgrade their skills, they have to take some initiative themselves. Encourage (rather than demand) your kids to spend a few minutes working on their games on non-practice days with their moms, dads, or friends. Doing so will keep their skills sharp.

For example, talk to the kids about having their mom or dad throw them ground balls in the backyard for a few minutes a couple times a week to help work on their fielding skills. You can suggest a fun approach to the parents that works this way: Have them set up a goal that can be marked by two towels, empty plastic containers, or some other safe household item. The parent, who stands about 20 to 30 feet away from the child, throws the grounders. For every ball that gets by the child in the designated area, that's a "goal" worth one point for the parent, and for every ball that the child fields and prevents from scoring he receives a point. The two can even switch roles to make it a fun game and see who fares better at making more stops.

✔ **Avoid performance goals tied to games.** When setting mid-season goals, don't encourage per-game quotas — such as getting two hits each game for the rest of the season. In any given game, a youngster may have some great at-bats that don't result in base hits, which would leave him short of his goal and disappointed, even though he doesn't deserve the disappointment.

Instead, keep the focus on those areas that he does have complete control over. For example, if he has a tendency to be overanxious at the plate and swing at bad pitches, set a goal for him of not swinging at pitches way out of the strike zone. Or if he tends to pick his head up and take his eyes off ground balls coming toward him, set goals for him related to how many times he can keep his head down and use proper form watching the ball into his glove. Remember, just make sure these goals fit with the player's skill level.

✔ **Hold your players' interest.** The younger the players, the shorter the attention spans they bring to the field. At the midpoint of the season, the players may start to lose interest and turn their focus elsewhere. Also, a child's focus often is on what's happening today, not weeks from now. You can issue short-term challenges so that your kids can see progress and improvement immediately, which holds their interest for the remainder of the season. Including only goals that take weeks to meet serves no useful purpose.

For example, if you're working on sacrifice bunting skills, a long-term goal to strive for achieving later in the season would be the child laying down a bunt that moves a teammate over a base. But, to keep the child's interest, you can start out with a short-term goal, such as having him be able to square around with the bat and make contact with the ball. Regardless whether the player pops the ball up, lines it to the catcher, or drops it down into fair territory, he's hit the goal.

✔ **Talk about the goals with the kids.** Your players will have a lot more fun with the goal-setting process — and get a lot more out of it — if you involve them from start to finish. Find out what areas they want to improve in, and then map out plans to help them reach their goals.

For example, if your shortstop tells you that he wants to improve his ability to catch pop ups hit to shallow left field, you can set up a drill each practice where his goal is to catch a certain number in a row.

✔ **Don't overlook the fear factor.** Anytime a youngster has gone through a traumatic experience, such as being hit by a pitch or getting hurt while sliding, take that experience into account when setting goals. Adjust the goals based on the nature of the situation and how much time the child missed. When the child is healthy again and back on track, you can adjust the goals to match his level of play.

For example, if the youngster has missed several games due to being hit by a pitch and injuring his hand, tone down the goals you set for him until he's healthy again. So, if your goals for him when he is healthy are to make solid contact with the ball each time he steps to the plate, a reasonable goal for him coming back from an injury and being out of action would be making solid contact one time during the game. If he's one of those players who bounces back from injuries quickly, you can bump up the goals accordingly.

✔ **Get the parents involved:** You may want to include parents in the goal-setting process, because it can be a fun activity for everyone, particularly at the younger age levels. You'll also be doing your part to promote parent-child bonding. A quick chat with the parents as they arrive with their child at practice, or meeting with them following a practice, is all it takes to get them involved.

Let the parents know that they can make colorful charts that can hang on their refrigerators at home or on the kids' bedroom walls. The kids will get a kick out of seeing their progress being tracked in full color. Plus, parental motivation provides great incentive to continue the learning process. (See the upcoming section, "Getting Feedback from the Parents," to find out more about getting parental feedback.)

If you're coaching a beginning-level team, keep the mid-season emphasis on having fun and downplaying winning and losing. By keeping the goals realistic, your share of wins will come, but more importantly, you'll create an environment that allows your players to reap the rewards of playing and achieving together.

Making a plan for your players

Anytime you're mapping out the mid-season review for your players, you start by establishing goals that they can realistically reach through hard work and following your lead (see the previous section). You always want to set your players up for plenty of successes — not failures — and create the proper environment in which they can flourish. From there, you act on the goals by creating plans for your players to achieve them.

Mapping out a plan that helps your kids build their skills requires gradually working up to the goals one step at a time. If you're building confidence with each step in the progression, your players will reap the benefits. To help your youngsters gauge their progress, make sure you compare their current performances with those from earlier in the season. Many times kids tie their progress to how the team is performing, which isn't a good indication, because wins and losses don't play a role in how a player has grown and developed in different areas of the game.

For example, say your shortstop has become pretty good at fielding ground balls that batters hit directly at him or that require him to move to his left by the midpoint of the season. You work with him on his goals going forward and decide that you want to upgrade his skills and help him become a more complete player by increasing his range to his right and improving his ability to backhand grounders. When putting together your plan to help the player succeed, you should start off easy and work your way up as he learns and improves.

A sample plan can look something like the following, conducted on the field over time:

1. **Position yourself several yards away from the player and roll tennis balls to his right so that he gets used to making backhanded stabs at slow-moving balls that aren't bouncing all over the place.**

2. **To increase the difficulty level a bit at the next practice, you can toss the tennis balls so that they have just a little hop to them.**

3. **Later on in the season, when he starts to field more than he misses, you can increase pace and the bounces in the tennis-ball grounders to raise the challenge.**

4. **When the player masters the rolling tennis balls, you can start using a bat to hit the tennis balls to the player.**

5. **After the player gets a pretty good handle on the fundamentals of resorting to his backhand — and has become pretty proficient fielding the tennis balls — you can move up to baseballs.**

   At first, just roll the player grounders with the baseballs, and then you can progress to hitting him grounders that he fields with his backhand.

Sharing progress

Once you go to the effort of setting goals for your players and orchestrating drills to help achieve them, you need to let kids know how they're doing. Weekly updates are a great way to keep the kids informed and enthusiastic about their progress. While the kids are warming up or stretching before a practice you can pay them a quick visit and let them know how they're doing. You may also want to mention a quick tidbit on something you want them to focus on in the upcoming practice to continue their progression toward the long-range goal.

Always end update chats by praising the kids' development and encouraging them to continue working hard so the positive results keep coming. This type of approach energizes the kids and keeps their confidence running high.

Getting Feedback from the Parents

On a list of smart coaching moves, keeping parents in the loop all season long deserves a spot near the top. Setting aside time to talk to parents one-on-one to find out how their child is enjoying the season so far not only shows how much you care, but also is a great way to get the scoop on what type of impact you're having. These one-on-one chats can be especially comforting to parents who are new to the world of organized baseball.

When you're about to reach the halfway point of the season, give the parents some advance notice that you want to set aside a few moments in the upcoming week to speak to them about their kids and how the season has gone so far. Making this announcement after a game usually works well because most youngsters have parents on hand to watch. The discussion with the parents should be brief and conducted out of the earshot of the youngster; this provides the best environment for receiving honest feedback about how their child feels. (In Chapter 4, we cover the importance of conducting a preseason parents meeting to open up the communication lines.)

During your conversation, which you can hold over the phone or in person before or after a practice, asking the following questions can help produce the information that will be most helpful to you — and most beneficial to the child. In order to make the meeting as convenient as possible for you and the parents, don't make house calls or expect the parents to take time out of their schedules to drive to your home to meet with you.

Is your child having fun?

Because you see your players for only a few hours a week, you can't gauge their true feelings and determine if they're enjoying the season as well as their parents can. Asking parents if their child is having fun usually results in an honest answer. They can tell you whether their son can't sleep the night before a game because he's too excited, or they can warn you that he dreads putting on his uniform on game day.

Be prepared for the honest answer. Even though you may be doing a wonderful coaching job, the child may be having a miserable experience. What some parents divulge to you may sting, but you'd rather have honest feedback and an open conversation than hear that everything is great when it really isn't. If a child isn't enjoying the season, you owe it to him to explore every possible way to reignite his interest and restore the fun.

What else can my coaching staff do?

When you find out from the parents that their child is having a blast, be proud, but don't be complacent. In order to keep those smiles on the kids' faces, take a close look at what you're doing to instill fun and learning, and explore ways to improve upon your approach. Challenge yourself to make the second half of the season even better than the first. For example, take the team's favorite drill and figure out ways to make it more challenging and more fun. Even the slightest alterations to several of your drills can make a big difference.

On the other hand, if you find out that any problems exist, act quickly to correct them. Don't allow problems to linger for another couple practices or games after you become aware of the situation. Maybe his parents can provide a solution for you, or perhaps a chat with the youngster can tell you everything you need to know to make his situation better. It's never too late to rescue a child's season.

The following list presents some solutions to a couple of the more common problems that make a child's season an unpleasant one:

✓ **Finding a different position for the player to play:** Sometimes, all it takes is giving the youngster a shot at playing a new position. At the younger age levels, you can change positions pretty easily because you should be rotating the kids around anyway in order to give them a feel for as many different positions as possible. (See the first section in this chapter for tips on handling hurt feelings due to position changes.)

✓ **Helping the player conquer his fears:** There's a good reason why many kids are afraid of getting hit by the ball — because it hurts! Whether a player gets hit by a pitched ball or by one that ricochets off a bat, he'll have lasting memories of the pain and may be afraid to give it his all for the rest of the year. You're bound to have some kids on your team who are preoccupied with these thoughts.

If a child is afraid of being hit by a pitch, make sure you tackle this problem as soon as you become aware of it. Have the player take his stance in the batter's box, and then toss tennis balls at him so he can practice moving out of the way of pitches. You can even turn this into a fun game and see which of your players is the best at avoiding pitches. After the child gains the confidence that he can step out of the way of wild pitches, he'll be much more comfortable at the plate — and probably more successful, too.

Part III
Working on the Fundamentals of the Game

The 5th Wave   By Rich Tennant

"That's right, Kevin, it's a fair ball...coming right your way. Hang up Kevin! Kevin — hang up and put your glove on!!"

In this part . . .

This part is the meat and potatoes of coaching baseball. Here, you find out how to teach the basics of hitting, fielding, pitching, catching, and base running, among others.

We also offer up a variety of practice drills you can use to teach the basic fundamentals of the game. You also find a collection of advanced drills that will propel your players' skills to higher levels.

Chapter 9

Teaching Offensive Fundamentals

*I*f you've had a chance to meet your players, or if you've had a little experience with youth baseball before, you know what's on their minds and what has them excited to get to the field: hitting and running the bases. And we're sure scoring runs has you excited, too. But know this: Coaching a youth baseball team that hits well and scores runs due to efficient base running requires a sound understanding of the offensive fundamentals of the game — and the ability to teach these fundamentals to your kids. By helping your youngsters learn many all-important offensive skills and improve on others, you open the door to a fun-filled season at the plate and on the base paths.

In this chapter, we dive into the ways your team can generate offensive production: batting (including bunting) and running the bases (including sliding). We also outline the fundamentals of hitting and base running, and we present the best ways to teach these fundamentals to your players.

Becoming a Master of the Box: Batting Fundamentals

No question about it, hitting is what youngsters love most about baseball. The problem is, hitting can be as difficult as learning a foreign language. And when you do get the hang of it, you have to practice regularly to maintain your progress and improve further. Even the best hitters in the Major Leagues fail to get a hit roughly seven out of ten trips to the plate. But those three hits are what keeps them coming back for more!

Many details go into being a successful hitter: from the grip and stance to the swing itself. And like with a golf swing, if one part of the setup or swing breaks down, the result can be affected. In the following sections, we outline the techniques your players need to practice to be productive with the bats in their hands.

Teaching the grip

Although the players on your team don't have the same-sized hands or even fingers, they need to hold the bat in much the same way. The standard batting grip generates the proper wrist action during the swing. Use the following list to teach your players how to grip the bat the right way:

1. **A right-handed batter should place his left hand near the bottom of the bat, with his pinky finger resting against the inside of the bat handle.**

2. **He then places his right hand above the left so the two are lightly touching each other (see Figure 9-1).**

3. **He aligns the middle knuckles of his right hand between the middle and lower knuckles of his left hand.**

   A left-handed batter simply reverses his hands (left on top of right) and alignment position.

4. **He grips the bat with his fingers, not with his palms.**

Figure 9-1: Grip the bat with the knuckles aligned.

5. **He holds the bat firmly, but he shouldn't squeeze it too tightly.**

   A tight grip cuts down on how quickly the batter can swing.

   Instruct your hitters to keep a firmer grip on the bat with the bottom hand than with the top, because the bottom hand is responsible for driving the bat through the ball on the swing.

Choking up on the bat refers to a player sliding his hands up the bat handle a few inches (see Figure 9-2). In the normal grip, the pinky finger of the player's bottom hand rests against the bottom of the bat. The choked grip is good for younger players to use because it gives them more control over the bat (which is why players of all ages tend to use the grip with two strikes against them). The disadvantage of the choked grip is that the players sacrifice some power to gain that control. However, at the beginning levels, you want kids to learn to gain control over the bat before you start worrying about how hard they're hitting the ball.

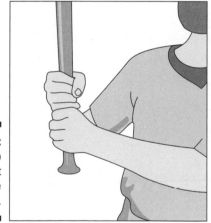

Figure 9-2: Choking up on the bat to improve control.

Taking the proper stance

Assuming the proper hitting position in the batter's box is vital for a hitter's success. The proper stance allows a player to make contact with inside pitches, outside plate-painters, high risers, and low divers. The following list explains what it takes for a hitter to achieve the right batting stance:

1. **The player positions herself in the center of the batter's box so she can swing at pitches all over the strike zone (and those that come close).**

   The *strike zone* is the area over home plate between the batter's armpits and the top of her knees. The home-plate umpire determines the strike zone; only he has a say about which pitches are strikes (even if the parents in the stands seem to disagree).

2. **The batter keeps her feet parallel to the direction home plate is pointing and digs them in approximately shoulder-width apart (see Figure 9-3).**

3. **She bends her knees slightly and keeps her weight evenly distributed on the balls of her feet.**

4. **She moves her hands (and, of course, the bat) about 5 to 7 inches away from her body and approximately even with (or just below) her shoulders.**

5. **She points the bat upward and angles it slightly toward her body.**

6. **The player turns her head toward the pitcher and focuses her eyes on the upcoming action.**

Figure 9-3:
A proper
batting
stance is a
balanced
batting
stance.

Depending on the age and experience level of the players you coach, you may want to introduce more advanced feet positions that can improve a player's situational hitting, or you may want to stick with the standard stance.

Even (or square) stance

For youngsters who are new to the sport and the basics of hitting, teach them the *square stance* (see Figure 9-4). In this stance, a player simply positions both her feet an equal distance from home plate (see the previous list in this section for the complete description). The square stance is the most commonly used hitting position, and it's the easiest one to teach younger players.

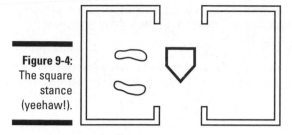

Figure 9-4:
The square
stance
(yeehaw!).

Open stance

In an *open stance,* the player angles her feet slightly toward the pitcher, and she moves her back foot closer to home plate than her front foot (see Figure 9-5). This stance opens the batter's body and allows her to face the pitcher, giving her a better look at pitches. It also makes pulling the ball easier. However, it puts a premium on the batter not moving away from the plate or further opening her hips too soon, because her front foot is already angled away from the plate. Because players who choose this stance are farther off the plate, they need to focus on not moving away from the plate too soon while swinging; otherwise, their power will be crippled.

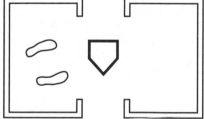

Figure 9-5:
The open
stance.

Closed stance

In a *closed stance,* the hitter moves her front foot closer to home plate and moves her back foot slightly farther away (see Figure 9-6). She also angles her feet more toward the catcher than the plate. This stance allows a player to generate extra power on her swings because they're on top of the plate and their body is less likely to pull away from pitches, like in the open stance. A drawback is that it is a little more difficult to get out of the way of errant pitches.

Swinging at a pitch

After a batter takes his grip on the bat and positions himself in the batter's box (see the previous sections), he awaits the pitch. When the pitcher lets loose, the batter makes a split-second decision: Swing or take. No matter the situation, when the young batter decides to swing, you want his swing to be consistent and technically sound. The following list looks at how you can teach your kids to produce an effective swing:

1. **As the pitcher goes through his windup, the batter's head should remain still, and he should focus on the pitcher's hand with both eyes.**

   The bat should remain steady during this time as well.

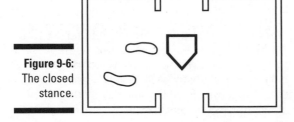

Figure 9-6:
The closed
stance.

2. **As the pitcher releases the ball, the hitter steps forward with his front foot — about 6 inches is standard — and begins his swing a fraction of a second later (see Figure 9-7).**

   As the player's body moves forward, his head should remain centered over his body. This is the point where the hitter must decide to continue his swing or stop it right there. Throughout the entire process the player's eyes should always be focused on the ball.

Figure 9-7:
The player
strides and
begins to
swing when
the pitch is
released.

3. **With his front foot now planted, the batter uncoils his entire body to drive the ball (see Figure 9-8), letting his hips lead the bat through the strike zone.**

   The bat travels through the zone at a slightly downward path, though it will level out when it makes contact with the ball. As his swing flattens out, the youngster straightens his elbows, rotates his hips so his belly button faces the pitcher, and rotates on the ball of his back foot. He keeps his hands back.

   Give your kids a nice visual by instructing them to "squash the bug" with their back feet as their hips rotate forward during a swing. They rotate on the balls of their back feet like they're squashing bugs beneath their shoes.

Figure 9-8:
Before impact, the hitter straightens his elbows and rotates his hips.

4. **At the point of contact, the player keeps his front leg stiff while pushing off his back foot (see Figure 9-9).**

5. **Following impact, the hitter begins his follow-through by rolling the wrist of his top hand over to send the ball sailing and to continue the bat on its trajectory.**

6. **Upon completion of the swing, the toe of the player's back foot should be pointing downward; more of his weight should end up on his front foot; and the bat should end up in the middle of his back (see Figure 9-10).**

Figure 9-9:
The
footwork of
a good
swing at
impact.

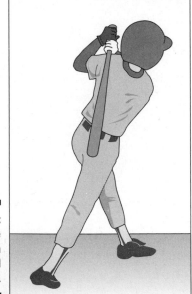

Figure 9-10:
The
conclusion
of a good
swing.

Sacrifice bunting

The sacrifice bunt is a great skill for your hitters to have in their offensive toolboxes. Sure, collecting base hits is what puts a smile on a young batter's face, but laying down a sacrifice bunt — particularly in a closely contested game — can be just as exciting. The play can help the team score runs, and the other players and coaches will all congratulate and celebrate the youngster — if that won't make the kid smile, nothing will.

The *sacrifice bunt,* the most common type of bunt, is a strategic move to advance a base runner by bunting the ball in play while sacrificing an out (in the form of the batter). See Chapter 14 for more on bunting strategy specifics.

Use the following list to teach your players how to execute a sacrifice bunt:

1. **As the pitcher begins his delivery, the batter takes a quick step to the side with her front foot and then steps forward with her back foot so that she faces the pitcher.**

   Her feet are now perpendicular to the direction home plate is pointing, and they are shoulder-width apart.

2. **The hitter slides her top hand approximately halfway up the bat and lets the bat rest between her thumb and first finger (see Figure 9-11).**

   Make sure your hitter keeps her thumbs and first finger off the face of the bat so the ball doesn't hit them. As your kids get more comfortable with bunting, they can start to move their fingers toward the front of the bat for better bat control.

Figure 9-11:
The proper
sacrifice
bunting grip.

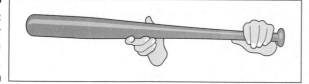

3. **While moving her top hand up the bat, the hitter firmly grips the bat at the handle with her bottom hand.**

   Her knuckles should be on top of the bat, and her thumb should be stretched out along the length of the bat.

4. **While adjusting her hands, the batter drops into a slight crouch and shifts her weight onto the balls of her feet.**

   As your players gain experience, Steps 1 through 4 will begin to happen simultaneously, because the windup of the pitcher lasts only a second or two with runners on base.

5. **As the pitcher releases the ball, the hitter extends the bat out in front of home plate — between her waist and shoulders — holding the top of the bat a bit higher than the handle (see Figure 9-12).**

This angle helps her make contact with the top half of the ball. Instruct your players to always try to bunt the top half of the ball so that it goes directly to the ground. Bunting the middle of the ball sends it flying to a fielder, and bunting the bottom half of the ball often results in a pop up, which is an easy out. To execute a bunt down the first- or third-base lines, the batter needs to make some minor adjustments. To direct the ball toward first base, the batter extends the handle out a little farther from her body and angles the barrel of the bat in the direction she wants the ball to go; bunts toward third base require the player pulling the handle in toward her body while angling the barrel so it's facing third base.

Figure 9-12:
Keeping the barrel of the bat above the handle.

6. **The batter decides if the pitch is a strike or a ball. If the pitch is a strike, she proceeds to Step 7; if the pitch is a ball, she quickly pulls back the bat to take the pitch, because if she leaves the bat out and misses the pitch, it counts as a strike against her.**

Advise your hitters not to bunt pitches higher than the starting position of the bat, lower than their knees, too far inside where they can't extend their hands to comfortably get the bat on the ball, or too far outside where they can't keep their hands in proper position on the bat because they're reaching too far with it. In a nutshell, they should only try to bunt strikes.

7. **The player attempts to deaden the ball, or reduce the force of the impact, at contact by pulling the bat back a bit (just a few inches).**

This technique should send the ball to the ground and send the runners on base to their next destinations.

A bunt toward third base usually has the most upside, because it forces a longer throw to first base, which may turn the sacrifice into a hit by giving the batter extra time to reach base safely. Ideally, you want the ball to come to rest midway between the catcher, pitcher, and third baseman. Another effective area is down the first-base line, midway between the catcher, pitcher, and first baseman.

Players are more vulnerable to being hit by errant pitches in the bunting position, because they expose their entire bodies. Facing the pitcher also makes it more difficult to dodge wild pitches. When you're teaching kids this aspect of the game in practice, begin by using tennis balls, which cuts down on the pain factor of having hard balls pinch fingers, as well as protecting other body parts from foul balls.

Bunting for a hit

Most bunts are the sacrifice variety, but they don't have to be. In the Major Leagues, for example, many fleet-footed players work diligently on their bunting skills because they can frequently parlay their speed and bunting ability into base hits. A deftly placed bunt forces the opposing defense to react quickly to try to throw out the hitter at first base.

If any of your players display bunting ability, encourage them to try to bunt for a hit occasionally. During games, monitor the opposing team's third baseman and first baseman. A good bunting opportunity arises if either of them is playing *deep* (well behind their respective bases), and a bunt placed right down the line, about halfway to the base, may result in a hit.

The drag bunt is a weapon your left-handed hitters can use to get on base. Drag bunts catch a defense off guard and can lead to rushed throws and errors, which lead to more bases for your runners. However, they require that the hitters begin moving before they make contact with the ball, which makes solid contact more difficult to achieve. The following steps outline how the drag bunt works:

1. **When the pitcher releases the ball, the hitter quickly shifts his weight to his front foot while pivoting and stepping toward first base.**

2. **He slides his top hand up the barrel of the bat while keeping his bottom hand on the handle.**

3. **Holding the bat firmly, he lowers the barrel until the end of it points toward third base (see Figure 9-13).** His knees are slightly bent and his body is leaning forward.

4. **He makes contact with the ball, trying to send it toward first base, with the bat nearly parallel to the ground (see Figure 9-14.)**

Figure 9-13:
The drag bunt catches defenses off guard due to its late revealing.

During contact, the hitter already should be striding toward first base; his back foot should be pushing out of the batter's box or already be in the air.

A perfectly placed drag bunt goes past the pitcher, about halfway between first base and the mound. With this placement, the second baseman has to charge in to try to make the play, and the runner can usually get to first base safely.

Figure 9-14:
The drag bunt requires movements before the pitch arrives.

Hitting troubleshooting

One of the most important responsibilities that comes with coaching a youth baseball team is recognizing when your kids are performing a skill incorrectly and making the necessary adjustments to get them back on track. The harder you work to recognize and solve your kids' problems — especially hitting-related problems, which tend to frustrate kids the most — the more fun they'll have learning from you. The following sections work to troubleshoot hitting and bunting issues.

One case where you can't blame poor technique or a failure to follow instructions for a child's struggles is when she has problems with her eyesight. If you notice that a youngster is really struggling, and none of your suggestions are working, ask the child to read something in the distance to gauge her eyesight. If she can't read what you pointed out, alert her parents of your discovery. A pair of glasses or contacts may bring the pitches coming her way into focus.

Swinging away

Even the best hitter experiences some difficulty with her grip, stance, or swing at some point during her playing days. Consistency is very important and, unfortunately, hard to maintain. The following list runs down some common problems children encounter at the plate and what you can do to help:

- **Stiff wrists:** A player has trouble rolling her wrist over following contact when she grips the bat too far back in her palms. Until she gets back on track, have her, during practice time, place the barrel of the bat on the ground and rest the bat handle across the middle knuckles of her left hand (if she's right-handed). She then puts her right hand in a similar position above the left (see Figure 9-15) and raises the bat up. This way, the bat barely touches the player's palms.

- **Fear at the plate:** Players who are afraid of being hit by pitches usually step backward before or during their swings to get farther away from the plate, which makes hitting the ball much harder. A great drill to help kids overcome their fear is to pitch tennis balls rather than baseballs during practice. Facing tennis balls helps the kids gain confidence and develop the reflexes necessary to avoid wild pitches. When you see the kids getting more comfortable in the batter's box, you can gradually work up to pitching baseballs.

- **A handcuffed swing:** A player who has trouble reaching pitches may be standing too erect, which handcuffs her ability to maneuver the bat. For instance, in an erect position, a hitter may not be able to handle low or inside pitches. Have her bend her knees slightly and adopt a more relaxed posture at the plate.

Figure 9-15:
Ensuring a
proper grip
on the bat.

✓ **Weak contact:** Check the following potential causes:

- **Bat position:** Too far away from the body produces a swing with a longer arc, which means the swing won't be level. Too close to the body limits the player's ability to move, which cuts down on the amount of power she can generate. See the earlier section, "Taking the proper stance," for the right distance.

- **Head movement:** If a player's head is moving during her swing, chances are she won't make solid contact. Hitters need to keep their heads still during their swings, with their eyes locked on the ball.

✓ **A lack of power:** Kids lose bat speed, and consequently power, when they move their hands forward right away with their strides, or if they're opening their hips up too quickly. A hitter needs to keep her hands back for a split second after she takes the initial step. When her hands are back, she generates the power needed to drive through the ball.

✓ **A slow bat:** A hitter can have trouble getting around on pitches for a few reasons:

- A player that puts her weight on her heels often has a slower swing. If you notice this problem, have her shift her weight to the balls of her feet.

- Also, check her bat position while she awaits the pitch. If she rests the bat on her shoulder or points the barrel at the pitcher (see Figure 9-16), her bat has to travel much farther, resulting in a late swing.

- Finally, make sure the bat she's using isn't too heavy for her!

Figure 9-16: Pointing the barrel of the bat at the pitcher is poor form.

Bunting

Executing bunts can be tricky to master because of the fear factor and because youngsters are so accustomed to swinging away. The following list presents a couple common problems kids have while learning the art of bunting:

- **Pop ups:** One reason youngsters pop up bunts is because they allow the barrel of the bat to drop too low in their stances. When the bat drops below chest level, a player is forced to hit up on the incoming ball, which pops it up. For advice on the proper position, see the section "Sacrifice bunting."

- **Line drives:** This often results from the player making contact with the ball while the bat is level. To get the ball on the ground quicker, and with less speed, she needs to raise the barrel higher in her stance and hit down on the ball rather than pushing the bat straight out.

- **Poor timing:** When kids are continually fouling balls off, you can usually trace the problem to their timing. Make sure the kids are getting into the proper bunting position right away, rather than hurrying to get the bat in position while the pitcher is delivering the ball. Have them hold the bat in the proper bunting position while the pitcher is standing on the mound until they become comfortable making the transition to that position after the pitcher begins his windup.

Running to Safety: Base-Running Fundamentals

Fast kids who have the ability to get on base are great assets for generating offensive production; however, you can still produce runs without great speed if you have a roster full of kids who know how to run the bases properly. Base running may receive less focus than other aspects of the game, but you shouldn't lose sight of its importance. Players who run the bases well can turn routine singles into doubles and routine doubles into triples. Their mere presence on the bases can cause havoc with a pitcher's timing and force the infielders' attention away from the batter.

Speed is a gift kids are born with; you can't turn a slow-footed runner into a speed burner who tears up the base paths. However, you can make a difference in a child's effectiveness on the bases by teaching proper technique, sound base-running judgment, and game situations, which we explore in the following sections.

Proper running technique

You shouldn't assume that your players know how to run properly and efficiently. The following list outlines the basics of good running form; teach these basics to your players before you advance to base-running technique:

- **Run with the eyes looking straight ahead and the face muscles relaxed.** Looking this way and that throws off a runner's rhythm, and clenching the jaw or the teeth leads to tighter muscles and slower movements.

- **Run on the balls of the feet while pumping the arms.** The elbows should stay close to the body; don't allow them to move from side to side. Make sure the runner cups his hands loosely.

- **Run with the shoulders level and body leaning slightly forward.** This posture keeps a runner's momentum going forward.

Leaving the batter's box

A quick start out of the batter's box after hitting the ball increases a player's chances of reaching base safely. Even on weakly hit balls right to the infielders, opponents can make fielding or throwing errors, so hustling to first is good practice. The following list explains how a player should move out of the batter's box:

1. **After making contact with the ball, the hitter drops the bat behind him with his bottom hand, leans forward, and takes a step with his back foot.**

2. **The player keeps his first few steps out of the batter's box short and compact, gradually working up to a full sprint.**

3. **When he has an idea of the outcome, such as a ground ball hit directly at the shortstop, the player should run straight ahead to his target and only avert his eyes to get instruction from his coaches.** If he sees the ball is going to fall in for a hit, he runs hard out of the batter's box and takes the proper angle to round the base, while also keeping an eye on the action. If he continues to second base, he looks to his third base coach for further instructions.

Legging out a ground ball

The difference between an infield grounder turning into a hit or an out often depends on the batter's ability to *leg out* the grounder — or beat the throw to first base — by running hard all the way through the base.

1. **If the batted ball stays on the ground in the infield, the runner should keep his eyes focused on first base and aim for the front edge of the bag, never breaking stride until his foot hits the base.**

2. **As he crosses the base safely, the runner continues in a straight line for a few steps before veering off to the right into foul territory.**

   If the runner is out, he continues veering until he reaches the dugout. If he's safe, he returns to the base. See the following section, "Rounding the bases," for techniques to use on sure hits.

A runner must stay within the base line. If he runs outside the base line in an attempt to avoid a tag, or if he simply isn't paying attention to where he's running, the umpire will call him out (this applies to all base lines).

Remind your kids that they won't get to first base any quicker by sliding. The only time a runner should slide into first base is when an errant throw pulls the first baseman off the bag, and the runner needs to slide to avoid being tagged (for more on sliding, see the later section "Getting Dirty: Sliding Fundamentals"). If the first base coach sees that the throw is off target and sliding into the bag will increase the player's chances of being safe, he can instruct him to slide. Also, lunging at first base actually slows down runners. Remind your players to run *through* the base.

Rounding the bases

When a player collects a base hit, his run down the first-base line is much different than when he has to beat out an infielder's throw. On a base hit, a runner needs to *round* first base — taking an angle outside the first base line so he can step on the bag at full speed without breaking stride — to put himself in a better, more efficient position to advance. For instance, a runner may advance to second base if he hits the ball well enough to achieve a double or triple, or if an opposing player misplays the ball.

Here's how rounding the bases works:

1. **After a youngster takes his first five or six steps out of the batter's box and determines that he has a base hit, he begins moving to his right about 3 feet outside the first-base line (see Figure 9-17).**

   The runner continues to steadily move away from the line on his subsequent few steps.

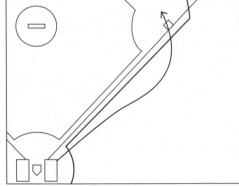

2. **About three-quarters of the way down the line, when the runner is roughly 10 to 15 feet away from the bag, he turns in toward first base and hits the bottom-left corner of the bag at full speed while also glancing to see where the ball is.** The runner can use either foot to touch the bag, though making contact with the left foot makes the turn a little shorter (see Figure 9-18).

3. **As the runner crosses the bag, he dips his left shoulder and leans toward the inside of the infield to keep his momentum going toward second base.**

4. **When he leaves first base, the runner continues on his path and listens for a command from the first base coach.**

   The coach should let the runner know whether to continue to second base or stop and retreat to first.

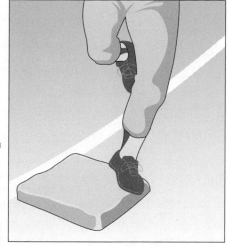

Figure 9-18:
Targeting
the bottom-
left corner
of the base.

Leading off

A *leadoff* refers to the distance a base runner stands from the base he's on. Most youth programs don't allow base runners to step off a base until the pitch crosses home plate or reaches the catcher's glove. If your league enforces this policy, use this list to teach your players the leadoff:

1. **The runner starts by facing the next base on his path.**

   He keeps his head angled slightly toward the batter so he can see the ball.

2. **He puts the ball of his right foot on the edge of the base (see Figure 9-19).**

3. **He keeps his hands at waist level and forms light fists with his fingers.**

4. **When he can run, the child uses his right foot to push off the base, he turns his eyes toward his destination, and he takes a short step.**

Tagging up

When a runner is on base with fewer than two outs and the batter hits a ball in the air — either on a line or way up high — the runner must make a quick judgment (with the help of his coach, of course): Should he get back to the base and tag up, assuming the ball will be caught, or should he advance? *Tagging up* refers to a base runner remaining on a base until the ball is caught, at which point he's allowed to advance to the next base. If he advances without tagging up, the fielders can force him out. (Refer to Chapter 3 for a rundown on the terms and rules of the game.)

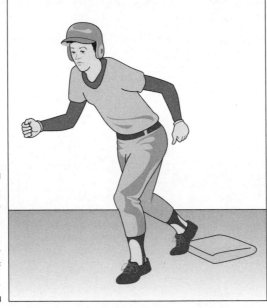

Figure 9-19:
The ready base-running stance for no-leadoff leagues.

The following list explains the technique your runners should use when tagging up:

1. **While the ball is in the air, the runner retreats to his base.**

2. **He faces the next base on his path and puts the ball of his right foot on his current base.**

Thievery on the base paths

Base stealing can be an effective part of your offensive arsenal. However, the practice usually is limited, or not allowed at all, at the younger age levels (normally 12 and under).

As kids get older (usually 9 to 12 years old), leagues begin to allow steals, but only after the pitch crosses the plate. Given this limitation, only the speediest runners can successfully swipe bases. You need to keep this in mind when instructing your kids on the base paths.

Check your league rules for its policy on pilfering bases (see Chapter 2). If you coach in a league that allows leadoffs and (unregulated) stolen bases, check out *Baseball For Dummies.* This book is written by Hall of Famer Joe Morgan, one of the most successful base stealers in major league history. He offers plenty of great insight on taking leadoffs, reading pitchers, choosing counts to run on, and much more.

3. **He stays low to the ground, in a semi-crouch, keeping his knees bent and his arms at waist level.**

4. **He locates the ball; the moment he sees the ball touch a player's glove, he pushes hard off his right foot and takes a couple short strides, building up to a full sprint.**

Some players, especially younger ones, prefer to get a signal (both verbal and visual) from a base coach that lets them know when to run. For example, a coach can hold his arm in the air, and as soon as a fielder touches the ball, the coach drops his arm and shouts "Go!" (see Figure 9-20). Signaling is helpful for all players if the fly ball sails behind the runner (for instance, a fly ball to left field when the runner is on third base).

Figure 9-20:
Tagging up on a fly ball with a coach's assistance.

A player isn't *required* to advance after tagging up. He can start to run, change his mind, and retreat to the base.

Here are some other important situations to keep in mind regarding tagging up:

✓ **Foul fly balls:** On a foul fly ball, the runner should always tag up, because he can't advance if the ball lands in foul territory. Therefore, he needs to be on the base in case a player makes the catch, at which point he *can* advance.

✔ **Outfield fly balls:** Fly balls to the outfield present the most difficult tagging decisions for youngsters, because so many factors are involved. A player has only a second or two to assess how deep the ball has been hit, decide which outfielder will make the play, and recall how strong his throwing arm is.

Base coaches can instruct players on what to do. A coach can give a verbal cue, such as "halfway" (the runner should come halfway toward the next base) or "tag" (the runner should tag up and prepare to advance).

Base-running troubleshooting

Runners face many challenges on the base paths; likewise, youngsters face many challenges when learning how to run the bases. We detail some of the more common mistakes you'll encounter when teaching this skill in the list that follows:

✔ **Poor jumps out of the batter's box:** If you notice this trend, watch to see if the child is guilty of standing in the box for a split second to watch his hits. Younger kids especially are so proud of making contact with the ball that they waste valuable time admiring their work. Advise them to get out of the box as quickly as possible, and make up for the lost admiration time by praising them to the nines.

Also, some kids take too much time setting down their bats before they begin running. Instruct your players to quickly drop their bats rather than squander important seconds by bending over to set them down. Just make sure they don't go to the other extreme and throw them!

✔ **Often getting doubled off:** At the youngest levels, base runners get excited to run whenever a ball is hit, even if it sails in the air. Unfortunately, their excitement can translate into plenty of double plays for the other teams. Advise your base coaches to instruct the kids to stay close to the base when balls are hit in the air. And always make sure your base runners know the number of outs — especially when you have two outs so they can run on any ball that's hit.

Getting Dirty: Sliding Fundamentals

Kids love mixing grass stains and dirt stains on their uniforms, which is why they enjoy learning how to slide during base-running drills. Sliding is an important part of base running for a couple reasons:

✔ It helps players avoid being tagged out.

✔ It allows players to stop at a base instead of overshooting it.

Proper sliding technique is critical, though, to avoid the risk of injury. This section takes a look at the most common types of slides your players will use on the base paths and how to execute them safely.

When you first introduce the art of sliding, find a soft patch of grass for the kids to practice on (wet grass works great, too). Your best bet is to head to the outfield, because that part of the field receives the least amount of wear and tear, leaving it smoother and softer. Don't allow your kids to practice on a base when you first start out. Plop down a towel in the outfield to serve as the base. Now, when some of your players begin their slides too late — and they will — they'll slide right over the towel instead of having their feet jam into a base.

Don't allow your kids to wear plastic cleats or spikes when they first practice sliding. (Metal spikes are generally only allowed in the advanced leagues, where most kids probably have a basic handle on how to slide already.) Spikes can get stuck in the grass, potentially causing a child to twist his ankles or knees. If a child has spikes only, have him remove his shoes and run in his socks during practice. Adopt this policy until your kids are comfortable executing the proper sliding techniques.

In a game, when a player slides or dives into a base, he'll likely emerge covered in dirt. He can ask the umpire for a quick timeout to step off the base and dust himself off without being tagged out by the opposition. Just make sure to remind your players never to leave the bag until they have been granted the timeout.

Bent-leg slide

You should always teach the bent-leg slide to your players first because it's easy to learn — good news for both the kids and you — one of the safest to use, and one of the most common. The following list breaks down how it works:

1. **Running at top speed toward the base, the player waits until she's within about 8 to 10 feet of the base before she starts the sliding motion.**

   A good rule of thumb for gauging the distance is to mark two body lengths of the player as the starting point.

2. **The player starts to slide by pushing off her back foot and lifting both her legs up (see Figure 9-21).**

   In this position, the player's body glides forward feet-first.

3. **She bends her left leg and tucks it under her right leg as she hits the ground, and slides on her bottom with her torso leaned back and her right leg stretched in front of her.**

Figure 9-21:
The bent-leg slide.

4. **As she hits the ground, she raises her hands partway above her head and makes partial fists with her fingers.**

5. **She tucks her chin into her chest and focuses her eyes on the base.**

6. **She slides into the base with her right foot and lowers her left arm. Her bottom leg remains bent underneath her.**

Head-first slide

When executed properly, the head-first slide gets a player to the base the quickest, because the momentum of his upper body is already going forward as he begins the slide. A player may want to slide head-first into a base in the following situations:

✔ If he anticipates a very close play

✔ If he's prone to injuring his ankles or legs

Many youth programs, especially at the younger age levels, don't allow head-first slides because of the risk of injury. The slide is more dangerous because the base runner can jam his fingers, hands, or wrists into the base; he can injure his neck or shoulder in a collision with the opposing fielder; and the fielder can step or land on the runner's hands or arms with his spikes. Make sure you know your league's policy regarding head-first slides. You don't want to waste practice time and put your players at unnecessary risk by going over a banned technique (see Chapter 2 for more on league-specific rules).

The following list outlines how a head-first slide works:

1. **As with the previous slides, the player begins his motions about 8 to 10 feet from the base.**

2. **Staying low to the ground, the player dives ahead, extending his arms and landing first on the palms of his hands (see Figure 9-22).**

Figure 9-22: The head-first slide.

The heels of the player's hands and his upper chest absorb most of the impact.

3. **As he nears the base, the runner keeps his fingers pointed slightly upward so that he doesn't risk jamming them into the bag.**

He also looks directly at the base, arching his back slightly.

4. **As he touches the base, the runner plants his hands on the bag and digs his toes into the ground so he doesn't slide past the bag.**

Of course, if he's sliding into home, it doesn't matter if he comes off the plate — as long as he touches it.

Pop-up slide

The pop-up slide is a variation of the bent-leg slide (see the "Bent-leg slide" section earlier in this chapter). This slide quickly puts the runner back into running position, allowing her to advance if a fielder has made an error. The following list explains how it works:

1. **For this slide, the player begins the sliding motion only about 5 feet from the base.**

   Sliding closer to the base gives the runner more force with which to pop up.

2. **The child executes the same sliding motion that she uses for a bent-leg slide.**

3. **The player stops abruptly by planting the cleats of her right foot into the base and pops up by pushing up on the calf of her folded leg.**

   The player's momentum will help her pop up easily, taking most of the pressure off the calf of her folded leg.

   During the pop-up slide, the player's hands shouldn't touch the ground.

 Because the pop-up slide requires the player's foot making solid contact with the bag and using that force to spring up into a standing position, the injury risk to the foot or ankle is higher. Stress using the proper form when executing this type of slide to minimize the chances of a player twisting his ankle or wrenching his knee.

Hook slide

Players can use a hook slide when they need to avoid a tag on a close play. You often see the pros do this at home plate, because it doesn't matter if you slide over and past the base, but you can teach your kids the technique at any base. Here's how:

1. **The player begins the hook slide about 8 to 10 feet from the base.** This slide is done on the opposite side of wherever the tag will occur.

2. **To hook slide to the right, the child, at the proper distance, pushes off on his left foot and drops to his right side.** He extends his right leg outside of the base while angling his left leg toward the base (see Figure 9-23).

3. **As he slides past the base, he uses the toes of his left foot to hook the base at its nearest corner.** As his momentum carries him over the bag he can reach to grab it with his hand.

 At the major league level, you see players going out of their way to slide out of the base path in order to break up double plays at second base. Never allow your players to use a hook slide to take out an infielder. Whenever a double play situation arises, instruct your players to use a bent-leg slide and head directly for the bag.

Figure 9-23:
The hook
slide.

Sliding troubleshooting

Sliding can be a difficult concept for kids to grasp right away, because it seems a little awkward and scary to drop to the ground while running full speed. Here are some common problems kids face while learning how to slide:

- ✔ **Isn't reaching the base:** When a player comes up short of reaching the base, he may be dropping into his sliding motion too early. If you think this is the case, simply instruct him to take another step or two before going to the ground. Another culprit is leaning too far backward in the sliding motion. Check to make sure the player's lower back isn't contacting the ground, which will bring a slide to a premature stop. Finally, check the youngster's hand position; he may be dragging his hands on the ground, which also slows down a slide.

- ✔ **Is sore or bruised:** Kids performing the bent-leg slide often jump to the ground instead of dropping into the proper motion with their legs bent, which is a surefire route to soreness and bruising. They may be landing on their tail or hip bones, which leads to aches and pains. Work with them so they can practice putting the weight of the fall on their bent legs and sliding on their butts.

Chapter 10

Teaching Infield and Outfield Fundamentals

In This Chapter

▶ Breaking down the responsibilities of the infielders

▶ Teaching infielding techniques

▶ Perusing an outfielder's job description

▶ Focusing on proper outfield fundamentals

Baseball is one of the most unique sports around — and one of the most challenging to coach — because you have to teach two totally different skill sets: offense and defense. Playing defense is a major element of baseball, although a solid defensive effort may not get as much attention as a run-producing offense. But even if your team is a run-scoring machine, your kids won't have much success on the field if they don't have a handle on the basics of playing defense.

As a coach, you have to cover many different positions on the field, and each position requires different skills to achieve success. For example, on just one play, your outfielder may have to field a base hit and throw to an infielder; the infielder catches the ball and relays it to third base; and the third base-man catches the ball and tags out a runner. Three different positions, three different skill sets all working together. How comfortable your players become with the defensive fundamentals of the game impacts how much fun they have manning their positions.

This chapter focuses on the fundamentals of good defense and runs down the basics of how to makes plays at all the infield and outfield positions (minus the pitcher and catcher; see Chapter 11). And because some of these skills can be pretty difficult to learn, we provide handy troubleshooting tips you can use to help youngsters who are having problems. (For drills you can implement in practice to further the skills we present in this chapter, check out Chapters 12 and 13.)

When coaching defensive techniques, you want to employ the same approach you use to teach a kid how to ride a bike: Start with the fundamentals and build from there. Chances are, you'll be with your team for only a handful of hours each week, so you need to keep your expectations realistic. You don't have a whole lot of time to teach, so you should introduce the kids to as many different skills and positions as possible to make their experiences fun-filled and well-rounded.

Protecting the Infield

Every time a batter puts a ball in play, the infielders are on the move — whether the ball lands 2 or 200 feet away from home plate — in order to prevent base runners from advancing. Because infielders are so active, they have to work on a variety of fielding skills. Grasping the fundamentals of these skills and working to master them are key elements for a winning team.

In this section, we first cover the skills and techniques that all infielders need to succeed, and then we present advice for teaching some specific skills for each position in the infield.

Grasping general fielding skills

Some fundamental skills and techniques apply to every position in the infield. In order to thrive at their positions, the infielders need to have sound stances; make the routine plays on ground balls, pop flies, and line drives; and make accurate throws to all the bases. The following sections outline these basics.

Getting into proper fielding position

Every time the pitcher goes into his windup (see Chapter 11), youngsters in the infield need to be ready for a ball hit in their direction. Preparing to handle ground balls by moving into the proper stance is one of the most important components of playing the infield. If an infielder just stands around and waits for a pitch, he won't be as mobile or as quick to field batted balls. The following steps present a basic stance that you can teach to your infielders, whether they're just learning the nuances of the game or have strayed from teachings of the past:

1. **Position the child's feet slightly wider than shoulder-width apart. Her knees should be bent, and her weight should be on the balls of her feet (see Figure 10-1).**

2. **She should allow her hands to hang between her legs, keeping her glove open and the palm of her bare hand facing the hitter.**

Figure 10-1:
An infielder's basic pre-pitch stance.

3. **Instruct her to keep her head up and her eyes zeroed in on the hitter.**
   As the pitch is released, she raises her hands to about waist level in preparation to field the ball.

Fielding ground balls

When a batter hits a ground ball, an infielder must react as quickly as possible to get in position and make a play to get the hitter out. The following list teaches your infielders how to be playmakers:

1. **The infielder moves to position himself in front of the ground ball.**

   When the ball is hit a few feet to the infielder's left or right, he shuffles his feet while keeping his body facing the ball.

2. **When in position, the player bends his knees, stays low to the ground, and keeps his glove open (see Figure 10-2).**

3. **As the ball approaches, the fielder bends down and extends his arms in front of his body to reach for the ball.**

   The player should keep his head down to watch the ball into his glove, and he should use his bare hand to trap the ball in his glove (see Figure 10-3) while moving his glove into his body.

4. **With the ball secure in his glove, he brings the glove up to his waist and points his non-throwing shoulder at the target.** The weight comes back on his right leg (if he's a right-hander). His right leg braces his body and pushes it forward. He steps toward the target with his left foot and releases the ball.

   In this position, the infielder is prepared to make a throw.

Figure 10-2:
Getting low
to field
ground
balls.

Figure 10-3:
Using the
bare hand to
secure the
ball.

TIP

When teaching the steps in the previous list to your infielders, keep in mind the following tips regarding fielding ground balls and recite them to your players:

✔ **Greet the ball.** Encourage your players to move toward the ball instead of waiting for it to get to them, when possible. Short, quick steps get a player to a ball quicker, which gives the hitter less time to reach base.

Another reason to greet the ball is to try to field it on the best (or highest) hop possible. A common baseball cliché is, "Play the ball; don't let the ball play you." What that means is that players should control a situation by moving forward to field a grounder on a nice, easy hop rather than stepping backward and increasing the chances of having to field a weird, difficult hop.

✔ **Use two hands.** Bad hops and unexpected bounces are a part of an infielder's job description. Instill in kids the habit of keeping their arms out in front of them and using two hands to field every grounder — even the most routine ones. Knocking down a ball often is enough to give a player a chance to retrieve it, make a throw, and still record an out.

✔ **Keep your head down.** If you can't see the top of a child's cap as he's fielding a grounder, you should instruct him to keep his head down and watch the ball into his glove. Don't allow the kids to take peeks at base runners, because doing so leads to errors.

✔ **Use your glove.** On hard-hit balls, kids have no choice but to use their gloves. Kids need to use the same approach for slow rollers, too. Young players tend to want to pick up balls with their bare hands — especially if they've seen their favorite pros do it on television. Instruct your infielders to bare-hand balls only when the balls aren't moving or are barely moving.

✔ **Get dirty.** You want your infielders to do everything possible to get in front of ground balls — especially with runners in scoring position. Knocking down a ball often prevents a runner from scoring from second base. Encourage your kids to get their uniforms dirty by diving for balls — they'll love it!

Making infield throws

When the infielder secures possession of the ball, she can turn her attention to executing a throw to the appropriate base to record an out. The following list presents the steps for making an accurate throw around the infield:

1. **With her bare hand, the player grips the ball across the seams, with her middle and index finger about an inch apart. She places her thumb underneath the ball, directly below her middle finger (see Figure 10-4).**

Figure 10-4:
The finger placement for an infield throw.

2. **Ball in hand, the youngster points her glove-side shoulder toward the intended base (see Figure 10-5) while keeping her eyes on the target.**

After a youngster looks the ball into her glove, she needs to focus on her target, not the ball. Staring at the ball in order to grip it wastes precious seconds and throws off the timing and accuracy of her throw. Therefore, your kids should practice this grip all through the week before games and stick with it during pre-game warm-ups, too.

Figure 10-5:
Aiming the left shoulder at the target.

3. **While aligning her shoulder, the youngster prepares to carry out the throw by taking a small skip forward, planting her right foot (for a right-hander), and swinging her throwing arm back in an arc.**

When bringing her arm back, the player should cock her wrist.

4. **The player steps toward the target with her left foot and pushes off with her right foot while bringing her glove-side elbow toward the target (see Figure 10-6).**

After a youngster has a good grasp of these fundamentals, you can work with her on bringing the ball directly to her ear (on her throwing side), because this technique cuts down on the amount of time the infielder has the ball in her hands before delivering a throw.

Figure 10-6:
Stepping
forward on
infield
throws.

5. **With the torque created by her lower body and left arm, the player swings her throwing arm forward and snaps her wrist downward to release the ball.**

   The player's momentum carries her forward toward the target on the follow-through.

Catching line drives

For an infielder, snagging a line drive is all about having quick reflexes — and being in the right spot at the right time. Because the ball is coming so quickly, a player has little time to think and simply must rely on his reflexes. Instruct your infielders to raise their gloves from their fielding positions and squeeze the line drives as they impact their gloves. On line drives that force the fielders to move to their left or right, or to jump in the air, advise them to rely on more of a stabbing motion to snag the balls. They'll also have to use a quick crossover step to make plays on balls hit to their left or right. During your practices be sure to mix in some line drives for them to field along with the grounders and pop ups. Using tennis balls works well to help players get accustomed to fielding line drives, because these hard-hit balls can be pretty intimidating to some kids.

Camping under pop ups

Fly balls that don't make it out of the infield (often called *pop ups*) seem like sure outs, but they can drop in for hits if the infielders don't get into position as soon as the ball goes into the air and communicate with each other. (Also, check out the "Catching fly balls" section later in this chapter; the techniques for catching pop ups and fly balls are very similar.) The following list outlines how infielders should handle pop ups:

1. **As soon as the ball is airborne, the infielder runs to where he expects the ball to land, keeping his glove by his side and letting his teammates know that he's in position to make the grab.** Yelling out "I've got it" reduces the chances of teammates colliding while going for the ball.

   If possible, the player should run sideways — like a football receiver running a pass pattern over the middle — instead of backpedaling to move under the ball. The sideways motion reduces the chances of the player's feet getting tangled.

2. **The player should position himself behind the ball at its probable landing spot and stand still, with his eyes on the ball.** Being behind the ball makes it an easier catch for the player because he can clearly see the ball rather than having to reach for it over his head. He's also in a better position to make a throw to a base if one is required.

3. **When the player's feet are in position, he raises his glove slightly above his head, with his throwing hand lightly touching the outer edge of the glove.**

   The player should position his glove slightly toward his throwing-arm side to prepare for any future action.

4. **As the ball hits the glove, the player squeezes the glove shut, using his other hand to help trap the ball.**

5. **He lowers the glove to his chest and grabs the ball (see the section "Making infield throws") in case he needs to make a throw.**

Applying tags to base runners

Often, infielders receive throws from teammates and need to tag out base runners who are trying to advance around the base paths. Keep these tips in mind when teaching infielders how to apply tags:

✔ **Get your feet positioned:** At first and third base, the infielder straddles the base, facing the thrower. At second base, the throws can come from a variety of different positions; he keeps his feet about shoulder's width apart, facing the thrower, while keeping his feet clear of the base runner's path.

✔ **Provide a nice target:** The infielder needs to position his glove about waist-high, giving the thrower a nice target to throw toward.

✔ **Tag what's closest.** A player should tag whatever part of the runner's body comes closest to the bag. Many body parts come into play (see Chapter 9 for more info on the different types of slides):

- **Foot:** When the runner slides feet first

- **Hand:** When the runner dives headfirst

- **Chest:** When the runner comes in standing up

✔ **Hang onto the ball.** The fielder should squeeze the ball tightly in the web of his glove and apply the tag with the back of the glove. The runner has a better chance to knock the ball loose — a legal play — and reach base safely if the player tags with the front of his glove. If the fielder doesn't have to reach to make the tag he should use two hands to secure the ball so that there is little chance of it being knocked loose. Of course, there are many times when the fielder will have to stretch to make tags and he won't be able to rely on his free hand for that extra support.

Also, make sure the infielder secures the ball before applying the tag. If they too hastily try to apply a tag, fielders often drop the throw.

Covering bases on stolen base attempts

When the opposing team tries to steal a base, your infielders cover the base — that is, they run to the base and straddle it — and receive the throw from the catcher. After receiving the throw, they apply the tag (see the preceding section).

Typically, on swipes of second base, your shortstop covers when a left-handed batter is at the plate, and your second baseman covers when a right-handed hitter is at the plate. On steals of third base, you guessed it, the third baseman covers.

Whenever an opposing base runner tries to steal a base, communication among your players is vital. If, for example, the runner at first takes off for second, have your first baseman let everyone know by yelling "Going!", or something similar. This warning gives your fielders time to scramble to the bag to receive the throw, and it allows the catcher to prepare to make the throw.

Getting players out in rundowns

Whenever a runner is caught between bases (known as a *rundown* or a *pickle*), he's in a whole lot of trouble —as long as your infielders understand the following techniques:

✔ **Limit the throws.** The fewer throws your players make back and forth, the better. Fewer throws means fewer chances of a bobbled, dropped, or misplayed ball, which rescues the runner from his base-running blunder.

- ✔ **Force him back.** Make your infielders run hard toward the runner, forcing him back to the base he left. Then, even if your fielder makes an errant throw, the runner hasn't gained any advantage because he's right where he started. When the runner is forced to retreat quickly, he'll have a hard time switching directions after your fielder makes the throw.

- ✔ **Hold the ball high.** Whenever a player has the ball he holds it up high so his teammates can see it clearly. He also keeps his arm still so that he can make a quick and accurate toss. Discourage a player from faking a toss, because he may just end up faking out his fielder instead of the runner!

- ✔ **Offer good targets.** The player waiting to receive the throw positions himself a couple of steps in front of the base. If the player with the ball is right-handed, the fielder receiving the throw stands on the left side of the runner to give his teammate an unobstructed throwing lane.

- ✔ **Stay out of the baselines.** Infielders must stay out of the baselines for a couple of reasons. One, they risk colliding with the runner, which can result in an obstruction call and the runner being awarded the bag; and secondly, in the baseline the runner blocks the view of teammates.

Infield troubleshooting

The following list helps you address some common problems infielders have:

- ✔ **Off-target throws:** If a child places his fingers so they go with the seams on the baseball, rather than across them, the ball has a tendency to sink or sail on throws. Refer to the section "Making infield throws" for the proper technique.

- ✔ **Weak throws:** A player can lose velocity on his throws when he places the ball back in his palm instead of grabbing it with his fingers. In the back position, kids have a tendency to squeeze the ball, which drains a lot of power from their throws.

- ✔ **Grounders going under the player's glove:** A lot of players have a tendency to lift up their gloves, which opens the way for balls to scoot underneath for hits. Try this tactic: When kids get in their ready position, have them open their glove and have the top of the glove firmly touching the ground. Hit a series of grounders to them, with the emphasis on having that glove contacting the ground before each one. This will help them develop the habit of keeping the glove low to the ground.

- ✔ **Taking their eyes off the ball out of fear:** Whenever kids take their eyes off the ball, they're actually increasing their odds of being hurt because they can't see where the ball is headed. During practice, use tennis balls for the kids to field, which helps take away the fear factor of being hurt by an incoming ball. Gradually, hit them harder and harder and eventually the players will gain the confidence that they can stop those hard baseballs, too.

The blooper-scooper: Playing first base

Youngsters who play first base have an important role: Coaches and teammates count on them to field a variety of throws from the other infielders. No matter how good the other infielders are at knocking down balls and making throws, if the first baseman can't catch the good ones and scoop the bad ones, your defense won't be very effective. Of course, first basemen also have to perform their normal chores: fielding ground balls, pop ups, and line drives. The following sections outline how a first baseman should position himself and how he should receive throws from around the infield.

Moving into the ready position

With no runner on first base, the first baseman typically positions himself about 6 feet to the right of the bag and approximately 6 feet behind it. The deeper a first baseman can play, the better, because a deep position allows him to cover more infield territory. However, he needs to be able to get to first base in time to receive throws. (For more on the general fielding position for an infielder, see the earlier section "Grasping general fielding skills.")

The first baseman has an advantage over the other infielders most of the time because he can drop to one knee, field a ground ball, and still record the out. He should take advantage of this whenever necessary. Being closer to the bag buys him a little extra time to get the out himself or to toss the ball to the pitcher covering first base (see Chapter 11).

Receiving infield throws

When a batter hits a ground ball to an infielder, the first baseman must get to first base as quickly as possible, set up on the bag, and give his teammate a good target at which to throw. Here's how a first baseman prepares for and receives throws:

1. **The first baseman sprints to the bag and places the ball of his right foot (for a right-hander) or his left foot (for a left-hander) on the edge of the base (see Figure 10-7).**

   Make sure the youngster doesn't plant his foot on top of first base. The runner can step on his foot and cause an injury, particularly if he's wearing cleats.

2. **He bends his knees slightly and faces the infielder who's about to make the throw.**

3. **He holds his glove about chest-high and extends it toward the fielder to provide a good target while also stretching his left leg (if he's catching the ball with his left hand) toward him.**

Figure 10-7:
Keeping
your foot out
of harm's
way at first
base.

Every throw from an infielder won't be right on target, so the first baseman has to be ready to handle a variety of throws. Two of the more challenging throws are low liners that skid in the dirt and high risers that force the first baseman to jump off the bag.

Remind your first basemen that their top priority is catching the ball. Sometimes, players at this position worry too much about keeping their feet on the bag, so balls may get past them, allowing runners to advance.

Handling low throws

Balls that bounce in the dirt before they reach the first baseman are some of the toughest for him to handle. In order to field these throws cleanly (or at least to stop them), he has to do the following:

1. **He gets his body low and keeps his eyes on the ball when he sees that it will bounce.**

2. **When the ball nears the bag, he stretches out, places his glove low to the ground (see Figure 10-8), and holds his bare hand near his glove to scoop the ball.**

   If he can't field the ball cleanly, his body position allows him to block it so the runner can't advance to second base.

Figure 10-8:
Stretching
out to field
(or block)
throws in
the dirt.

Snaring high throws

On a high throw, the first baseman should try to reach for the ball by raising his glove and left knee into the air while keeping his right toes on the bag. If he can tell that he has to jump to snag the ball, and his jump pulls him off the bag into fair or foul territory, he should try to tag out the runner when he hits the ground while avoiding a nasty collision.

First base troubleshooting

The following list helps you address some common problems that youngsters playing first base are likely to encounter:

- **Takes his foot off the bag while making catches.** This often happens when a youngster puts his foot on top of the bag. It's difficult to maintain contact with the top of the bag on throws to the left or right. See the section "Receiving infield throws" for the proper technique.

- **Has trouble with routine throws.** Make sure the player keeps his eyes on his teammate making the throw and not on the base runner(s). Also, when he gets into position to field a throw, make sure he has his glove up around chest level. If he holds his glove too low, he'll waste time bringing it up into proper position to catch the ball, which makes the catch more difficult.

✔ **Struggles to scoop low throws out of the dirt.** Most kids tend to flinch and turn their heads when attempting to field low throws in the dirt, which makes the task next to impossible. One solution is to use tennis balls to throw them balls in the dirt during practice. When they get more comfortable scooping up low throws, you can gradually mix in baseballs.

The double-play don: Playing second base

Playing second base presents a variety of challenges. Along with the normal ground-ball fielding duties, a player at this position must work with the short-stop to make outs at second base, turn double plays, and cover unmanned bases. The following sections provide a glimpse of what it takes to succeed when fielding grounders and receiving throws as a second baseman. (For drills focused on turning double plays and for other second-base skills, check out Chapters 12 and 13.)

Moving into the ready position

The second baseman's stance is just like that of the other infielders. Her feet are shoulder-width apart and her weight is distributed evenly on the balls of her feet. Her knees are slightly flexed. When the pitcher goes into his windup, she keeps her eyes focused on the batter. As the pitch is released, she raises her hands to about waist level in preparation to field the ball.

A second baseman plays at different ready positions. In the standard position, the second baseman plays fairly deep — four to five steps behind the base path — because a deep position gives her a better chance of getting to more balls. However, if a speedy player is at the plate, she should scoot in several steps because it gives her more time to throw out the quick batter. However, the second baseman adjusts her position in a couple of different situations:

✔ **Runner on first base:** The second baseman should move two to three steps closer to second base and the same number of steps closer to home plate — a position referred to as *double-play depth*. At double-play depth, the second baseman is in better position to cover second base on a stolen base attempt, and she has a better chance of forcing out the runner at second base on an infield ground ball.

✔ **Runner on third:** The game situation dictates the position she takes. In most instances, she'll assume her normal position. If your team is trailing with less than two outs in the late innings of a close game, however, you may elect to have your infielders move in several steps. Scooting in gives her a better chance to throw out the runner at the plate on an infield grounder. For more on defensive strategies, check out Chapter 15.

Flipping (and receiving) the underhand toss

One of the basics of good defensive baseball is making sure you get at least one out on a ground ball put into play with a runner on base — and many times, this out occurs at second base in the form of a force out. A *force out* occurs when a fielder steps on base with the ball in her possession to make an out on a base runner who has to move forward due to the hitter becoming a base runner. (For more information on terms and rules of the game, refer to Chapter 3.)

With a runner on first base, the second baseman plays at double-play depth (see the previous section). And when a ball is hit in the vicinity of second base, she can make an underhand toss to the shortstop covering second base for a force out. If you have fewer than two outs, the underhand toss can start a double play. The following list explains how to execute the underhand toss:

1. **The second baseman fields the ball in her glove and raises it to chest level.**

2. **She turns her body toward second base, grabs the ball with her bare hand, and steps toward second base.**

3. **She tosses the ball underhanded to the shortstop, releasing it as her hand moves slightly above waist level (see Figure 10-9).**

   The second baseman should finish the toss with her hand facing the shortstop. The underhand toss works especially well when the two fielders are close to each other.

Figure 10-9: The underhand toss is accurate and quick.

Besides making underhanded tosses, your second baseman also will be on the receiving end of the shortstop's tosses. She catches the tosses to secure force outs and to start double play attempts (we cover drills that practice double plays in Chapters 12 and 13). When receiving a toss, the youngster

- Straddles the base. If she needs to relay the ball to first base for a double play, as she catches the ball she steps on the bag with her left foot while turning to make the throw; kids with stronger arms may prefer catching the ball behind the base and stepping on it with their back foot and then using the bag to push off to deliver the throw to first.

- Holds her glove up between her waist and her chest, facing the shortstop, to provide a target for the toss.

- Squeezes the ball as it hits the webbing of her glove.

Delivering a backhand toss

Many times, the second baseman doesn't have enough time to set up for her normal throw, or to even get off an underhand toss. When there's a runner closing in on second base, the best option — and the only one for getting the runner out — is resorting to the backhand toss. It's also an effective technique when the second baseman is on the ground and doesn't have time to stand and set up, or when she's forced to dive away from the bag to stop the ball. She executes the toss by picking the ball out of her glove and tossing the ball. When she's facing home plate her hand rotates so that the palm faces the outfield as the ball is released. She extends the arm all the way and locks her elbow.

Second base troubleshooting

If one of your youngsters has some difficulty learning the art of playing second base, be patient with her. The following list presents a couple areas where a second baseman may struggle and how you can make the necessary corrections:

- **Makes wild throws:** First, find out if the player is following proper throwing mechanics (see the earlier section "Making infield throws"). If she is, look to other sources. For instance, if a youngster doesn't field the ball cleanly, she'll naturally start to panic and rush her throw, which can lead to throwing errors. Remind your second baseman of the slight advantage afforded to her by playing close to first and second base. If she doesn't field the ball cleanly, she has a little extra time to recover and focus on making a good throw.

- **Makes poor underhand tosses:** You want your second baseman to use an underhand toss when she's close to second base and she doesn't need to throw overhand. When you first teach this skill, your youngster may develop a habit of putting too much pace on the toss, which handcuffs the shortstop. Teach the child to make the toss as if she's lobbing an egg to her teammate.

The diamond diva: Playing shortstop

The shortstop is the anchor of the infield because of all the responsibilities she has, which range from covering a large amount of territory, to making long throws across the infield (both after fielding grounders and after receiving relays from the outfield), to turning double plays (for which we include drills in Chapters 12 and 13). In this section, we help you teach your shortstops how to field balls hit to their left and right.

Moving into the ready position

The shortstop positions herself between second and third base, typically shaded a bit closer to second. She usually stands 10 to 15 feet behind the base line (from second to third, which isn't marked).

Where you position *your* shortstop depends on many factors, such as her arm strength, the hitter at the plate, and the situation on the base paths. For example, in the section "The double-play don: Playing second base," we discuss how the second baseman plays at double-play depth with a runner on first base with fewer than two outs. The shortstop does the same in most situations.

Moving on grounders to her left and right

The most effective shortstops can range to their left *and* right to gobble up ground balls, turn double plays, and make throws all over the field. The following list explains the proper technique for moving to the left:

1. **As the pitch is delivered, the player takes two small steps forward, keeping her body in fielding position.**

   The steps put her body in motion and her weight on the balls of her feet. Reacting to a ball is easier when the body is moving rather than standing stationary.

2. **When the batter hits the ball to the shortstop's left, the fielder makes a crossover step (assuming she's a righty).**

   She pivots on her left foot and takes a big step across her body with her right foot.

3. **When she reaches the path of the ball, she bends down, keeping her eyes on the ball, and puts her opened glove low to the ground to field it (see Figure 10-10).**

4. **With the ball in glove, the shortstop rises up, pulls her glove in toward her waist, turns her body toward her intended base, and delivers a throw.**

Figure 10-10:
Using the
crossover
step.

Ground balls hit to a shortstop's right are some of the most difficult plays for her to make. If the play is at first, she has to field the ball backhanded and then make a long throw while her body is moving in the opposite direction. This is how this type of play is executed:

1. **The player turns her back to second base by using the crossover step to her right — right foot pivot and left foot across the body.**

2. **She rotates her glove hand while bending down with her left knee to field the ball, and she places the glove on the ground in the backhand position (see Figure 10-11).**

   The player really needs to keep her eyes on the ball when making this movement to ensure a clean scoop.

Figure 10-11:
Making the
backhanded
play.

3. **As soon as she secures the ball, the shortstop plants her right foot and makes the throw.**

   Younger kids may not have the arm strength to make these types of throws. Instead, after they've secured the ball, encourage them to stop and take a mini-hop forward to generate some momentum toward first base to help them get the ball there.

Shortstop troubleshooting

The following list presents some of the more common problems kids encounter when learning how to play shortstop:

- ✔ **Slow reaction time:** Keep a close eye on where the player puts her hands when your pitcher delivers the ball. If she tries to rest them on her knees, correct this behavior. By going to her knees, she puts herself at a disadvantage because she has to waste time getting her hands in the ready position. Refer to the section "Grasping general fielding skills."

- ✔ **Makes off-target throws when ranging to her left:** Check the positioning of the player's left foot (for a right-hander). After she scoops up a grounder, she should step directly toward first base with her left foot before she releases the throw.

The hot corner: Playing third base

To play third base regularly, a youngster should have good reflexes and an arm that can hurl the ball across the infield. Having no fear is another advantage at the *hot corner*, so named because hard-hit balls often come the third baseman's way. However, another common (though not as glamorous) occurrence during a game is a softly hit roller down the third-base line that's just out of the reach of the pitcher. If a third baseman can make this play, he sets himself apart from the pack. We cover this topic and more in this section.

Moving into the ready position

Ground balls and line drives reach the third baseman quickly, so being in the proper position to react to them is key for playing well here. Here's an effective stance to teach your third baseman:

1. **His feet are shoulder-width apart, with his left foot slightly in front of his right foot. His knees are slightly bent.**

2. **His glove is down and faces the batter, along with the palm of his bare hand.**

3. **The youngster's back is low so that it's almost parallel to the ground.**

4. **As the pitcher delivers the ball he brings his right foot forward and puts his weight on the balls of his feet.**

The third baseman usually plays about four or five steps to the left of the foul line and three or four steps behind third base in a normal defense. Of course, game situations often influence his positioning. For example, in the late innings of a close game, you may want to position your third baseman closer to the foul line to try to prevent doubles hit down the line. If you suspect a bunt is coming, you may have your third baseman play even with the bag and begin creeping toward the batter. (For more on defensive strategy, check out Chapter 15.)

Handling slow-moving balls

A third baseman often faces the challenge of handling a slow-moving ball that results from a bunt or poor contact on a full swing. And if the ball is rolling very slowly, he may not have time to scoop it up with his glove and get set to make a regular throw, making the play even more challenging. In this case, the player's best chance to record the out is by picking up the ball barehanded and delivering a throw, all in one motion.

This play is tricky — even Major Leaguers can struggle with it — but your players will have fun giving it a try. Here's how you teach it:

1. **The third baseman charges toward the ball when it dinks off the hitter's bat.**

2. **As he nears the ball, he shortens his steps (or chops them) to prepare to field the ball.**

3. **He plants his left foot to the left of the ball (for a right-handed player) and starts to bend down with his right arm.**

4. **He picks up the ball by coming across the side of it.**

5. **With his momentum going forward, he plants his right foot and pulls his arm back at waist level, turning his focus toward first base.**

6. **He throws the ball sidearm across his body while swinging his left foot across his body (see Figure 10-12, which illustrates the entire technique).**

Third base troubleshooting

A third baseman must have a broad mixture of skills, which makes the position challenging to learn and practice. A young third baseman may struggle with the following areas while discovering what it takes to play the position:

✔ **Has trouble handling slow rollers:** Scooping up a slow roller isn't easy (and making an accurate throw is even harder). Many youngsters have problems because they pick up the ball incorrectly. A player shouldn't pick it up like a toy, with his fingers pointing down — this method is inefficient. You want the player to scoop it from the side, which helps him transition into his throwing motion much more quickly and easily.

✔ **Timid going after grounders:** Encourage your third baseman to go after every ball hit to his left. A child may have a tendency to let balls go by, thinking the plays belong to the shortstop. Encourage him to try to make a play on every ball he can reach. If a ball ends up being out of his reach, no problem. Just instruct him to continue on so the shortstop can attempt a play without being obstructed.

✔ **Backs up on grounders:** Players are more likely to field the ball cleanly — and make accurate throws — when their bodies are moving forward and they take control of the situation. Watch your third baseman and help him practice moving forward the moment the ball contacts the bat. Remember, he should be taking a step forward with his right foot as the pitcher goes into his windup.

✔ **Makes wild throws on slow rollers:** Fielding a slow roller is difficult; making an accurate throw after corralling the ball is even more challenging. When a youngster's throws are veering off to the right, the likely cause is side spin generated from his sidearm throwing motion. Have him aim just slightly left of the first baseman to account for the spin on the ball.

✔ **Has difficulty handling balls hit hard directly at him:** This is a tough play for the third baseman. The key is staying low in front of the ball. Even if he can't field it cleanly, by knocking it down and keeping it in front of him, he still usually has enough time to track down the ball and throw out the batter.

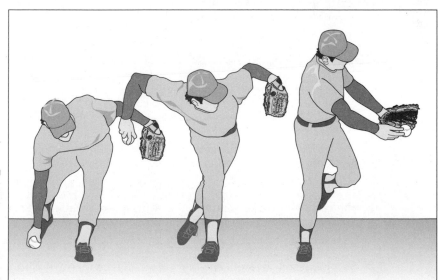

Figure 10-12:
Making a
sidearm
throw on
a slow-
moving ball.

Patrolling the Outfield

Outfielders may be a long way from most of the action on a baseball field, and they may not field as many balls as the infielders, but they're very important to a defense. It takes plenty of skill and an understanding of the game to excel in the grass. An outfielder must

- ✔ Make catches while running in a variety of directions
- ✔ Field hits that scream into the gaps
- ✔ Back up infielders and the other outfielders (see Chapter 15)
- ✔ Toss accurate throws to all the bases (or their cutoff men — see Chapter 15)

Adding to the difficulty of an outfield position are the sun and wind, which can create havoc with fly balls, and a player's mind, which can wreak havoc with his confidence. An outfielder is the last line of defense (not counting the wall, of course), so if he misplays a ball, the error results in extra bases and more runs.

If you coach an advanced-level team, you should try to put your most gifted and best all-around outfielder in center field. A center fielder has the most territory to cover, so having speed and quickness, as well as sound fundamentals, is a big advantage for the team (see Chapter 5 for more information on evaluating your team and players).

Moving into the ready position

The most efficient (and successful) outfielders can move quickly in any direction as soon as a batter makes contact with the ball. An outfielder's ready fielding stance should look like what we describe in the following list:

1. **She keeps her feet shoulder-width apart, her knees slightly bent, and her feet pointed toward home plate (see Figure 10-13).**

   This is her base position for most of the action.

2. **She rests her hands on her knees during downtime, but she drops them into ready position when a pitch is delivered.**

   When in the ready position, her bare palm should face her opened glove.

3. **As a pitch is delivered, she takes a small step forward with her left foot.**

   This keeps her on the balls of her feet so she can react quickly to a batted ball.

Figure 10-13:
The ready
fielding
stance
for an
outfielder.

Remind your players about the following tips that concern positioning in the outfield:

✔ **Play the count.** Not only does paying attention to the count keep an outfielder focused on the game, but also gives her an edge. For example, if the pitcher falls behind in the count — like two balls and no strikes — he'll probably throw a pitch down the middle of the plate. The outfielder should take a couple steps back before the pitch, because the batter may take a pretty good rip at the ball.

✔ **Know base-running situations.** If a speedy runner is on second base, for example, the outfielders may want to take a step or two forward so they have a better chance of throwing out the runner on a hit or sacrifice fly.

✔ **Understand game conditions.** Late in games, the score helps dictate the positioning of outfielders. If your team is clinging to a one- or two-run lead in the last couple innings, you may position your outfielders a little farther back to prevent balls from going over their heads, which can erase your lead quickly.

✔ **Know your teammates.** If certain infielders possess good speed and are adept at handling short fly balls, your outfielders may position themselves differently. For example, if your third baseman and shortstop are great at tracking down short fly balls, your left fielder can move back several steps.

Catching fly balls

Although younger outfielders have been known to watch butterflies and chase grasshoppers, the most high-profile job that accompanies an outfield position is catching fly balls (and line drives). The following list presents the basic steps a player takes to secure a fly ball:

1. **When the ball flies into the air, the outfielder with the best chance to make the play runs to where he thinks the ball will land.**

   He should keep his eyes on the ball and his hands in the proper running position the entire time.

2. **When he gets to the proper spot, he raises his glove hand above his head, angling the fingers of the glove slightly to the right (see Figure 10-14).**

Figure 10-14:
Angling the glove to catch a fly ball.

The glove should be on the throwing-arm side of the player's body.

3. **After squaring his body and raising his glove, the player positions his left foot (if he's a righty) in front of his right foot.**

   This footing ensures that after making the catch, the player will be ready to deliver a throw, if necessary.

4. **As the ball descends on the player, he moves his bare hand next to his glove, with his fingers pointing straight in the air (see Figure 10-15).**

5. **The player squeezes his glove shut around the ball and places his bare hand over the top of his glove to keep it from popping out.**

Not every fly ball will be routine, however. Outfielders often need to charge in on short pop flies and go back on deep drives. The following sections explain how.

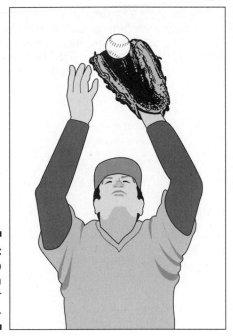

Figure 10-15:
Using two
hands on a
fly ball for
security.

Making a running catch: Charging in

Here's how your outfielders should handle fly balls that force them to charge in:

1. **The player sprints forward on the balls of his feet.**

2. **When he's ready to make the catch, he assesses the position of the ball:**

   - If the ball is chest-high or higher, the player holds his glove in front of him, palm facing away from his body, with his fingers pointing straight up and his bare hand next to his glove.

   - If the ball dips below his waist level, he turns his glove over so his fingers are pointing down and the palm is facing away from him.

3. **With either position, the player watches the ball into his glove and squeezes it, using his bare hand to cover it up.**

If a player decides that he can't make the catch, he should slow down so he can keep his body and glove in front of the ball and field it on a bounce.

Making a running catch: Going back

One of the toughest catches for an outfielder to make is a ball hit directly over her head. The following list explains how your youngsters can track down these balls:

1. **The outfielder takes her first step back in the direction the ball is hit (see Figure 10-16).** If the ball is hit over her right shoulder she steps back first with her right foot; if it's over her left shoulder, she steps first with her left foot. If she's stepping back with her right foot, she rotates it clockwise; if she's using her left foot she moves it counterclockwise. This move is called a *drop step.*

Figure 10-16:
Getting a good jump on a deep fly ball.

2. **She follows her drop step with a big step across her body with her other foot (see Figure 10-17).**

   The player is now turned around and in a position to sprint back.

Figure 10-17:
Tracking a fly ball by making a big crossover step.

3. **She sprints back, keeping her eyes on the ball at all times and her glove at waist level until the time comes to raise it up to make the catch.**

Catching line drives

Handling line drives hit directly at them poses a lot of problems for young outfielders. The biggest challenge is that the youngster doesn't have an angle to pursue the ball, like he does on those hit to his left or right. Instead, he has to move forward and make a quick determination whether he can make the grab or field it after it bounces in front of him. As he's running forward, he keeps the glove at his side, which allows him to cover more ground in a short amount of time. If he can make a play on the ball, he extends his glove hand out so he can catch it around chest level. If he realizes that he can't get to the ball, he slows down and puts his glove in front of his chest to snag the ball on the bounce.

Fielding hits

When the bases are empty, an outfielder should focus on keeping hits in front of him, because he doesn't have to make a quick throw to a base (although he shouldn't take too much time). As the ball approaches on the ground, the player drops to one knee (see Figure 10-18) to eliminate any room for the ball to squeak by him. He keeps both eyes on the ball so that he's prepared for any bad hops.

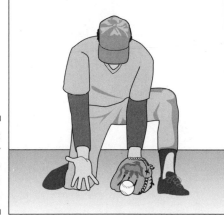

Figure 10-18:
A player should keep all hits in front of him.

With runners on base, an outfielder can't be so lax. He must charge the hit much more aggressively, gain possession, and get it back to the infield quickly to keep the runners from advancing extra bases. When an outfielder is sprinting toward a bouncing or rolling ball, he follows this technique:

1. **He approaches the ball from his glove side.**

2. **When he gets within a few feet of the ball, he slows down so he can keep his body under control.** The player bends his left knee slightly as he bends over to collect the ball.

3. **The top of his glove contacts the ground, and he scoops up the ball with his glove to the side of his left leg (if he's a right-handed thrower).** He takes a short hop forward to continue his momentum, strides with his left foot, and delivers an overhand throw.

Making throws

Outfielders who possess accurate (and strong) throwing arms make it difficult for opposing teams to enjoy success on the bases. Use the following list to teach your outfielders how to deliver on-target throws:

1. **After fielding the ball, the player grips it across the seams (much like an infielder) and squares up to the target.** She uses a small hop, which involves stepping forward with her left foot and then taking a short hop forward with both feet to gather momentum for her throw.

2. **She takes her arm back, with her elbow leading the way, and rotates her shoulders and hips to her right (for a right-hander).**

   Her weight should be on the ball of her back (right) foot when cocking back (see Figure 10-19).

Figure 10-19: Rotate the hips and shoulders before throwing.

After the rotation, her non-throwing shoulder is pointing at the target and the wrist of her throwing arm is cocked.

3. **She brings her throwing arm up to her head, her elbow still leading the way; as she continues her arm motion, she steps forward with her left foot and shifts her weight accordingly.**

4. **She releases the ball when her arm passes her ear, with her non-throwing elbow driving toward the ground and carrying the player to her follow-through.** Remind outfielders to use a full arm motion, which is much different than how their teammates in the infield deliver the ball.

For a young player especially, the best throw to a base is one that bounces once before reaching the infielder. A throw that lands at the infielder's feet is tough to handle, and a throw that sails in the air for a long time requires quite an arc, which gives the base runner exactly what he wants — more time to reach base safely.

Outfield troubleshooting

Playing the outfield tests kids' coordination, arm strength, and ability to make split-second decisions. Here are some of the common problems that young kids (and even grizzled vets) encounter while learning to play in the outfield:

- **Misses the mark with throws:** When kids throw the ball from the outfield with a sidearm motion or don't come over the top, they put side spin on the ball, which causes it to tail off to the left or right and miss the target. Instruct your players to come over the top to produce balls with backspin that go straighter. Also, if an outfielder doesn't grip the ball across the seams, his throws may be wild (see the earlier section "Making throws").

- **Bobbles ball when charging in:** When a player gets a hit with runners on base, a charging outfielder may rush and panic and bobble the ball. Work with your outfielders to run under control and to not take their eyes off the ball to peek at base runners.

- **Gets poor jumps:** On balls hit over their heads, young outfielders tend to react by backpedaling, which is a big no-no. Practice using the drop step so they can get to balls more quickly and get better looks at the ball in the air.

- **Has trouble building up speed to pursue balls:** Outfielders who run after fly balls with their gloves already in the catching position hurt their chances of making plays, because this type of running slows them down. Teach your outfielders to keep their gloves at waist level during their pursuits, only raising them when they're ready to make the catch.

✔ **Gets a case of the drops:** If a child regularly botches fly balls, the youngster may be holding his glove at an improper angle. Many young players stick their gloves straight up in the air, which results in the ball bouncing off their palms. Adjust their glove angles slightly to the right (if they're right-handed), which puts their hand in a more natural position to catch the ball by exposing more of the webbing of the glove.

✔ **Takes bad angles on balls hit in the gap:** During your practice sessions, encourage your outfielders to experiment with less-aggressive angles to balls hit in the gap. Gradually, they'll begin to get a sense of choosing the right angles during the heat of the action of game day.

Chapter 11

Teaching Pitching and Catching Fundamentals

- -

In This Chapter

▶ Instructing pitchers

▶ Coaching up your catchers

- -

Your pitcher and catcher share a special bond during games. All the action starts and ends with them. How effectively they handle their responsibilities influences how well your team plays. If these two players — often referred to as the *battery* — aren't in sync, they can throw your entire defense out of whack, because how they perform affects what the other players must do. However, when they're working well together, they can make playing defense much easier for the rest of the players in the field by putting them in a position to succeed.

In this chapter, we head to the mound to introduce everything from the stance and windup to the delivery and follow-through. We also take you behind the plate to give you the scoop on teaching kids how to crouch properly, block wild pitches, and throw out base runners. If that's not enough, we include some handy troubleshooting tips for dealing with some of the more common problems youngsters encounter learning these positions.

Sending Youngsters to the Mound

Every part of a car, from the tires to the interior to the brakes, serves a valuable purpose, though the engine is arguably the most important. The same holds true in baseball, too, where every player in the field has an important job to do, though pitchers carry just a little more weight simply because of the impact they can have on the game. Even if your team is struggling at the plate in a game, a strong outing by your pitcher can save the day. This section touches on the fundamentals of sound pitching. (Chapter 5 offers some tips on choosing the right players to hand the ball to on game day.)

Focusing on the fundamentals of baseball pitching

Although baseball is a team game, the pitcher is usually recognized as the most important player on the field — and the position is regarded as one of the most challenging to master, too. A young pitcher has to figure out the proper stance, grip on the ball, and delivery, for starters. In the following sections, we cover the basics of baseball pitching, from the stance on the mound all the way to the follow-through.

Taking a stance on the mound

Delivering a quality pitch starts with the stance (much like hitting at the plate). The setup is important in most every sport, from football to golf to baseball. A pitcher can use a number of different stances to deliver a pitch, but we suggest the following basic stances. As pitchers gain experience, they can make adjustments based on what works best for them.

1. **The pitcher stands on the *rubber* (the rectangular slab on the pitching mound), facing home plate, with his body straight (see Figure 11-1) and his weight evenly distributed.**

2. **A right-handed pitcher should make sure his right foot contacts the rubber in the middle of his shoe. His left foot should either touch the rubber, too, or be slightly behind it. (A lefty should follow the same advice with the opposite feet.)**

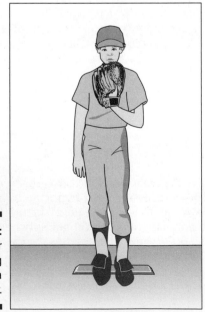

Figure 11-1: The proper starting stance for a pitcher.

3. **With his feet in place, the pitcher can hold his glove, with the ball in it, in front of his chest. His pitching arm can hang relaxed at his side, or it can hold the ball inside the glove.**

Forming fastball and changeup grips

Kids in youth baseball leagues need to keep their focus on throwing fastballs. Fastballs are easy to grip, throw, and control, and they're easier than curveballs on the muscles and ligaments of the arm.

A pitcher can throw a fastball with a couple of different grips. The *four-seam fastball* is the most basic of pitches. The following steps detail how the youngster should grip the ball:

1. **The pitcher puts his middle and index fingers across the seams at their widest point (see Figure 11-2), about a half-inch apart.**

2. **He should let his thumb rest under the ball, across the bottom seam.**

3. **His ring and pinky fingers should be off to the side of the ball (see Figure 11-3).**

   When the grip is complete, the ball should rest in the pitcher's fingers rather than on his palm.

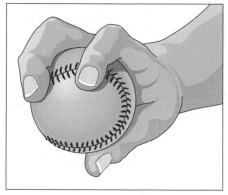

Figure 11-2:
The four-seam fastball grip.

At the more advanced levels of youth play (from ages 11 and above), you can introduce your pitchers to the *changeup,* a pitch that calls for the same arm speed and motion as the fastball (see the following section), but which comes to the plate slower in an attempt to fool the hitter. The reduced speed is due to the grip. The changeup doesn't put any extra strain on the pitcher's arm, but it will put extra strain on the batters' minds.

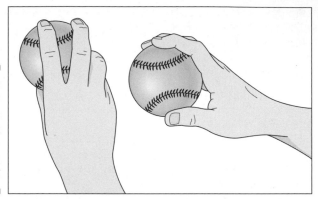

Figure 11-3:
A fastball grip uses the index and middle fingers and thumb.

The following list explains how to grip a changeup:

1. **Take a grip similar to the fastball grip, with the middle, index, and ring fingers across the seams and the thumb and pinkie under the ball.**

2. **Keep the wrist stiff and the finger tips slightly above the ball.**

3. **Keep the grip hidden in the glove so that the batter can't tell that a changeup is coming.**

   With the change-up, the pitcher keeps the ball a little farther back in his hand (see Figure 11-4) and holds it a little bit looser. The grip should provide the loss in speed, not the arm motion or speed of the pitcher.

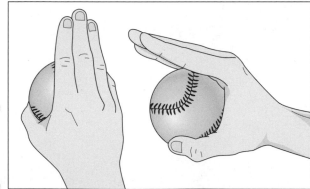

Figure 11-4:
The changeup grip.

Young pitchers may want to imitate the big leaguers by experimenting with *breaking balls,* or pitches that curve and sink across the plate. Breaking balls include curveballs, sliders, and variations on the two. However, don't teach this type of pitch at the younger levels, because it puts additional stress on the arm that isn't healthy for the child. We recommend that you don't teach breaking balls until the age of at least 14.

Winding up and delivering a pitch

After the pitcher takes his stance and prepares his grip, he's ready to wind up and deliver his pitch. (He also may take a sign from the catcher; see the section "Crouching in stance behind the plate," later in this chapter, for more info on pitcher/catcher signs.) If you've watched baseball at the upper levels, you know that windups and deliveries are personal things. Each pitcher has a unique style, from crazy leg whips to twisting and turning. However, each pitcher started in a youth league with a basic delivery, and each unique delivery they've developed is rooted in the fundamentals.

The following list details a fundamental windup and delivery:

1. **The pitcher begins by focusing his eyes on the catcher's target while gripping the ball in his glove.**

2. **When he's ready to pitch, the pitcher takes a short step backward behind the rubber — about 6 inches — with his left foot (if he's right-handed; see Figure 11-5).**

   Reverse right and left for left-handed pitchers throughout these steps.

3. **While stepping backward, the pitcher should bring his hands above his head, still gripping the baseball.**

4. **While behind the rubber, he pivots on his right foot, bringing it parallel to the front of the rubber (see Figure 11-6).**

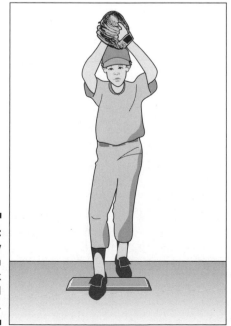

Figure 11-5:
The delivery begins with a step back and raised arms.

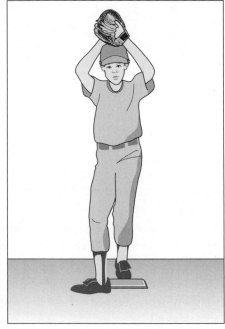

Figure 11-6:
Bringing the
right foot in
front of the
rubber.

5. **Turning his body so that it's perpendicular to home plate, the pitcher lifts his left leg so that his knee is at waist level (see Figure 11-7) while lowering his glove to waist level, too.**

   At this point, the pitcher is ready to bring his momentum forward from a stable yet powerful position. He can begin to bring the ball out of the glove. Note how the pitcher's eyes haven't strayed from the target.

6. **The pitcher begins shifting his weight forward to gain momentum toward the plate.**

7. **He steps forward with his left foot, driving his leg toward home plate and pointing his toes in the same direction, while pushing off the rubber slightly with his right foot (see Figure 11-8).**

8. **While driving toward home plate with his lower body, the pitcher should use his left shoulder and elbow as guides, keeping them pointed toward the target and close to the body, and then bring his right arm forward toward the target (see Figure 11-8).**

   When the pitcher releases the ball, he should snap his wrist and keep it stiff, following through with the heel of his hand.

   On a changeup, the pitcher should bring the ball straight down, using the same type of motion as if he's scratching his fingernails on a chalkboard.

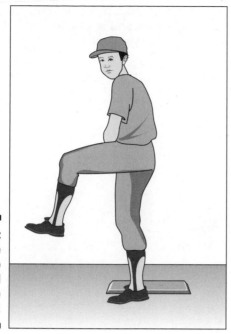

Figure 11-7:
Raising the left leg to waist level continues to build power.

Figure 11-8:
Toes of the left foot pointing toward home plate.

9. **After release, the pitcher follows through by completing his arm motion and swinging his right foot around so that his body faces the hitter, keeping his eyes on the pitch (see Figure 11-9).**

   Upon completion of the pitch, his weight should be evenly balanced on the balls of his feet. He should bring his glove back chest-high in case he needs to react to a ball hit directly back at him.

Figure 11-9:
Finishing the
delivery.

To be successful pitchers, youngsters need to develop solid, comfortable pitching mechanics, which can come only with plenty of repetition. Work with your pitchers during practices so that they develop fundamental deliveries, and constantly stress to them the importance of repeating those same deliveries.

Troubleshooting for pitchers

As you can see in the previous section, many steps are involved in delivering a pitch, which is why pitcher is one of the most difficult positions for kids to learn. The following list presents some of the common difficulties that young pitchers contend with:

✔ **Throwing pitches too high in the strike zone.** Wildness high in the zone usually happens when kids rush their deliveries. Instruct your player to hold the ball in his glove a split-second longer in his windup.

✓ **Losing his balance easily.** During a pitch, pay close attention to the youngster's head; make sure he's focusing on the batter, not putting his head on a swivel. Another cause of balance problems is when a pitcher takes too big a step backward with his non-dominant foot when beginning his windup. Make sure that your player doesn't step more than 6 inches behind the rubber. (See the section "Winding up and delivering a pitch" for proper instruction.)

✓ **Lacking velocity on pitches.** Following through is critical for getting the most force behind a pitch. Watch your pitchers' arms to make sure they follow through all the way instead of stopping their arm motions as soon as the ball leaves their hands. If a player has a habit of stopping his motion early, have him use an exaggerated follow-through, where he swings his arm well past his left knee. Another cause is when youngsters open up their bodies too soon and lead with their non-throwing arm, which quickly drains their power source.

Working with the Masked (And Armored) Men behind Home Plate

Catching is right up there with pitching in terms of challenging positions to learn, but it can be one of the coolest positions to play, and most coveted, thanks to all the gear the kids get to wear. The catcher is involved in every play, and he gets to direct much of the action that takes place. (For info on the equipment that catchers need, check out Chapter 2.)

In the sections that follow, we explain the basic setup a catcher takes to do his job, and then we outline the many responsibilities of the job and how you can teach them.

Crouching in stance behind the plate

A pitch can't be thrown until the catcher gets into his crouch. A crouched catcher provides a target that spans the strike zone for the pitcher, and the crouched position allows the catcher to move laterally and the umpire to call the action. Here's a look at how you can instruct the catcher to set up:

1. **The catcher picks a spot about 2 feet behind home plate (see Figure 11-10). Make sure his legs are slightly wider than shoulder-width apart and that he evenly distributes his weight on the balls of his feet.**

   The spot he chooses must be far enough behind the plate so when he reaches to catch pitches he doesn't disrupt the batter's swing and get called for interference.

Figure 11-10:
The basic
catching
stance.

2. **He lowers his butt down to below his knees and above his heels (see Figure 11-10).**

   This is the fundamental crouching position a catcher takes.

3. **When in the crouched position, the catcher should move his elbows to the outside of his knees.**

4. **At advanced levels of play, this is the point where the catcher uses his free hand to signal to the pitcher the type of pitch he wants. He presents a signal in between his legs with his fingers to signify the pitch and designates the desired location by angling his fingers in a certain direction.**

   For example, he can point one finger toward the ground if he wants a fastball (see Figure 11-11), two fingers if he wants a changeup, and so on. He can also call for the location: for example, an inside fastball, by wiggling his index finger toward the batter.

5. **When the pitcher is ready, the catcher should begin to move from his setup position to his pitch-receiving stance by raising his butt to just below his knees and keeping his thighs parallel to the ground.**

Figure 11-11:
Giving the
signals.

At the younger age levels, kids may not have the leg strength for this position, so you can instruct them to remain in the squatting setup position. Or, if it makes them more comfortable, they can kneel on both knees, with their bottoms resting against their heels.

6. **He should move his mitt to a position directly behind home plate and hold it still to give the pitcher a good target to throw to.**

7. **With his glove in place, the catcher should protect his throwing hand by putting it behind the webbing of his glove. Or, he can put his hand behind his back to protect it if that is more comfortable for him. He can make a relaxed fist, as you see in Figure 11-12.**

The catcher is now in a functional, safe position to receive the pitch. As the pitch arrives, he keeps his glove steady and waits for the ball to reach the glove.

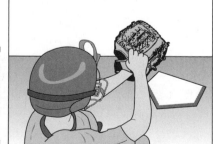

Figure 11-12:
Protecting
the bare
hand from
foul tips.

Never allow a catcher on your team to expose his throwing hand on a pitch, because a foul ball or pitch that bounces in the dirt can cause serious injury. See Figure 11-13 for an example of a bad position.

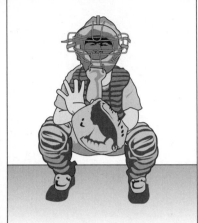

Figure 11-13:
A dangerous position for a catcher's bare hand.

Blocking wild pitches

Being able to prevent errant pitches from rolling to the backstop so that runners can't advance is an all-important skill for a catcher to have. The following list explains how a catcher handles errant tosses that bounce directly in front him. These actions happen almost simultaneously, in one fluid motion, with the catcher concentrating on the incoming pitch:

- The catcher should drop to his knees, with his toes pointing outward.

- He drops his chin against his chest protector to protect his neck and throat, while still trying to look the ball into his chest.

- He drops his glove hand to the ground between his legs, with the top of the glove touching the ground, to prevent the ball from squeaking through. He should keep his bare hand behind the glove to prevent injury.

- He hunches his shoulders and leans forward to provide a wall that will corral the ball.

  If the ball bounces up into the catcher's body, having his shoulders and midsection leaning forward causes the ball to bounce back down in front of him instead of ricocheting away. You can see all these motions together in Figure 11-14.

Wild pitches that bounce in the dirt to the left or right of the catcher really test a young catcher's range and reflexes. The following list explains what it takes to smother these pitches and keep base runners where they are. You can make this more difficult skill easier by breaking down the movements into steps, although each step will happen almost simultaneously when the catcher perfects his craft.

Figure 11-14:
Blocking a pitch in the dirt.

1. **When a pitch bounces to the right of home plate, the catcher takes a step in that direction with his right foot while dropping to his knee with his left leg (see Figure 11-15).**

   The area from the knee to the foot on his left leg should rest flat against the ground. The catcher uses the same technique — in the other direction, of course — for pitches that bounce to the left of home plate.

2. **While moving to his right, the catcher should tuck his chin against his chest and turn his glove so that the top touches the ground.**

Figure 11-15:
Blocking a pitch that bounces to the catcher's right.

3. He moves his bare hand behind the glove while resting his right elbow against the inside of his right knee.

4. He should do his best to angle his right shoulder toward the pitcher to keep the ball in front of him.

Handling high pitches

As we mention in the pitcher's troubleshooting section, a common problem young pitchers have is the tendency to throw high. The good news is that high pitches present fewer problems for catchers than pitches that hit the dirt. Here's how a catcher should deal with a high pitch:

1. **The catcher rises up out of his stance while moving his glove hand above his head, keeping his eye on the pitch.**

2. **Advise him to stop his glove slightly higher than the path of the ball and angle it downward a bit.**

   In this position, if he misses the ball, it's more likely to drop in front of him, preventing the runners from advancing. If he stops his glove below the path of the ball or angles it upward, the ball can glance off the top of the glove and shoot behind him, which means extra bases for the opposition.

Retrieving passed balls

No catcher is perfect, so sometimes a ball will get by your catcher and roll to the backstop. When this happens, instruct him to take the following measures:

1. **Turn and sprint toward the ball, accounting for any possibilities of ricochets off the backstop.**

2. **Scoop up the ball with his glove and bare hand to ensure a clean grab.**

3. **Come up in a throwing position (see the following section) in case he has a chance to throw out a runner attempting to advance.**

Nabbing base stealers

With the proper fundamentals, catchers improve the chances that they'll be able to nab base stealers. The following list presents the steps needed to execute a successful throw to a base in danger — in this case, second base:

1. **When the catcher spots a base runner on the move, he should lean forward slightly before catching the pitch.**

Make sure he knows not to interfere with the batter by reaching out over the plate for the ball.

2. **While catching the ball, he rises from his stance, moving the glove to his throwing hand fluidly.**

   Be aware that the following steps all occur within a very short amount of time and should become a fluid motion for the catcher.

3. **He should grab the ball out of his glove and grip it across the seams with his middle and index finger, placing his thumb below the ball.**

4. **While gripping the ball, the catcher brings his glove hand back toward his right shoulder, turns his left hip and shoulder toward second base, and brings his right hand (with the ball) to a position above his right ear.**

5. **He then brings his right arm forward to throw, following his left shoulder toward second base, while transferring his weight from his back leg to his front leg.**

   The catcher steps forward with his left foot and releases the ball as his right hand passes his head. He should follow through by bringing his throwing hand to his left knee. A quick release is important.

Protecting home plate

Base runners want to get to home plate any way they can, which is why you see the pros knocking each other silly. Although this won't happen in youth leagues, runners will do their best to go around, under, or over your catcher. Catchers who use proper blocking techniques can make getting home safely a little more difficult. Here are the steps a catcher should take to protect home plate when a runner is trying to score:

1. **As the runner approaches, the catcher should stand in front of home plate with his mask on.**

   The mask protects his face from any throws that take an unexpected hop.

   Players on their way to home plate have built up quite a bit of speed, so you should never have your catcher block the entire plate so that the runner has no other option but to run or slide into him. Home-plate collisions put both players at risk of injury.

2. **Have him spread his legs a little wider than shoulder-width apart and leave half the plate available for the runner.**

3. **After catching the ball, he should wrap his bare hand around it while keeping both hand and ball enclosed in the glove.**

   Using both hands reduces the chance of the runner knocking the ball loose during a slide.

4. **When the runner starts his slide, the catcher should kneel on his right knee and apply the tag with the back of his glove.**

5. **If the runner misses the plate, the catcher shouldn't chase him; instruct him to maintain his position at the plate, rotating around it as necessary, and wait for the runner to come to him.**

Tracking foul balls

Catchers who are proficient at catching foul balls behind and above home plate are pitchers' best friends, because they make the pitchers' jobs a whole lot easier. The at-bat stops right there, and no runners will advance. Plus, if the ball drops, the worst that happens is the umpire calling "Strike!". Here's a look at how you can instruct this useful skill:

1. **When the ball flies up in the air, the catcher should rise out of his stance, turn his back to the infield, and look up to locate the ball.**

2. **As soon as he determines the direction and probable landing spot of the ball, he should toss his mask to where he won't trip over it while attempting the catch.**

3. **Instruct him to run near the spot where he thinks the ball will land and stop several feet short of the area.**

   Catchers should try to stay slightly behind the ball so that they don't have to backpedal, which is very difficult with all that gear.

4. **He should then put his glove hand above his head and place his bare hand behind the webbing of the glove for support while he waits.**

   Have him slant the fingers of the glove upward to provide a good cushion.

5. **After the ball hits in the glove, he needs to put his bare hand over the top of the glove to secure the ball.**

Catching foul balls is difficult for a catcher, so anytime an infielder has a legitimate play on the ball (usually when the pop ups are farther up the first- or third-base line), he should call off the catcher and make the play. Remind your team of this whenever you have your catcher practice this skill.

Fielding bunts

When a hitter lays down a bunt, the catcher is the player who should take control of the situation. She either makes a play on the ball — if it stays within her range — or directs her teammates on where they should go with it. For example, if the third basemen is charging hard and scoops the bunt, the catcher may yell "Second base!" if a runner is on first or "Third base!" if a runner is on second, depending on the speed of the runners and how quickly the third basemen made the play.

Here's a step by step breakdown of what the catcher should do when she can reach the ball:

1. **When the bunt hits the turf, the catcher should rise out of her stance quickly and call out to her teammates if she plans to make the play.**

   Being vocal prevents a collision with another player who wants to go for the bunt.

2. **Her body should be facing the base she intends to throw to when she arrives at the ball. She should move her feet slightly wider than shoulder-width apart and place her head directly over the ball.**

3. **Instruct her to scoop the ball by using both her glove hand and her throwing hand (see Figure 11-16).**

4. **She should grip the ball across the seams with her index and middle fingers, step toward the base, and let it rip.**

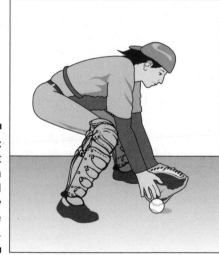

Figure 11-16: Field a bunt with both hands and your body over the ball.

Troubleshooting for the backstops

The list of a catcher's responsibilities is long and challenging. A catcher must digest a lot to learn to play the position, which makes it very tough to break into. The following list presents some of the more common problems young catchers deal with when learning the position:

✔ **Flinching on pitches.** A young player with little experience will naturally close his eyes or turn his head when a ball is coming at him and a bat is entering his field of vision.

When working with young catchers, pitch them tennis balls, and have an assistant coach stand at the plate to swing at them. Instruct the coach to purposely miss the pitches by swinging well above or below them. When the youngster starts to get comfortable, have the assistant swing as close to the balls as possible without hitting them so that the catcher has to focus on the ball coming toward him. When he can confidently make those catches, he should be ready to catch the hard balls.

✔ **Having trouble handling outside pitches.** When your catcher gets into his stance, check the position of his elbows. If he's locking them or putting them inside his knees, he's making it more difficult to reach for outside pitches. (See the section "Crouching in stance behind the plate" for more on proper positioning.)

✔ **Losing balance while blocking balls in front of the plate.** This usually happens when the catcher keeps his toes pointed directly down into the ground when dropping to his knees. He needs to have his insteps touching the ground, which promotes good balance. (See the section "Blocking wild pitches" for blocking instruction.)

✔ **Letting balls bounce away.** Watch to see if the youngster is turning his head away as a ball bounces in front of him. Remind him that his gear provides great protection and that he should pretend he's a hockey goalie when blocking the ball. Let him know that he doesn't have to field the ball cleanly; he just needs to keep it in front of him.

You can practice with tennis balls to help youngsters refine technique without the worry of getting hurt.

✔ **Losing the path of foul balls.** Catchers at all levels tend to overrun foul balls, because they typically come back toward the infield due to their spin. Keep hammering home that the catcher needs to stay a few paces behind the ball, and practice the technique often. (See the section "Tracking foul balls" for more.)

Chapter 12

Fundamental Drills for Beginners

As a coach, you won't have any trouble getting your kids excited about putting on their colorful uniforms and stepping onto the field to play in games. However, one of the keys to being a successful coach is generating that same type of enthusiasm for midweek practices. The drills you use during practice influence how much fun your kids have playing for you and how quickly they develop their skills. The more interesting and challenging the drills are, the more productive they will be in generating excitement and developing all-important skills.

In this chapter, we offer an array of drills that cover many of the offensive and defensive fundamentals of baseball. Whether you're looking for a way to help your outfielders deliver accurate throws to a cutoff man or your catcher to handle tricky foul balls behind home plate, you'll find it all here. These drills give your players a good start on learning and practicing the basics of the game. Best of all, you can easily tweak most of these drills to meet your team's ever-changing needs from week to week. (For more advanced drills to use when your players get beyond the basics, flip to Chapter 13.)

Try to establish good warm-up and cool-down habits with your players. Warming up is especially important in a sport like baseball, where players use so many different muscles to swing the bats, make the throws, and run the bases. Setting aside time for your kids to increase their heart rates and stretch out their muscles before your practices begin helps clear the way for more productive sessions. (For an in-depth rundown of the stretches you can have the kids perform, jump to Chapter 16.)

Preparing to Score: Offensive Drills

Your team's ability to create run-scoring opportunities — and have fun trying — depends on your players knowing and understanding the basics of hitting and base running. You want your kids to be comfortable with performing each of these basic offensive fundamentals, because with comfort and practice come satisfaction and scoring. The drills in this section can help your players establish a solid offensive foundation that they can build on to continue having success in this area of the game.

The age and talent level of your players should dictate what types of drills you use during your practices. If you have a group of talented kids who've been playing the game for years, you may want to jump to Chapter 13, where we provide many advanced drills more suitable for the older kids. Or, if your kids are fairly inexperienced, you can pick and choose from the drills we present in this chapter to address your team's needs throughout the season. A little creativity on your part is all it takes to tweak drills in order to make them appropriate for however large or small your team may be.

When you introduce new drills to your players, keep in mind that simple and fun works best — especially at the younger age levels, where kids' attention spans are really short. Attempting to understand and learn all the basic techniques of the game and trying to put them to use can be overwhelming for beginning players. No matter how creative you make your practices, don't lose sight of the fact that you want your players to develop the solid fundamentals we cover in Chapter 9, and development can take place only if you provide your players with quality instruction. If you find that a drill is too simplistic after running it a few times, you can use your creativity to tweak it to meet the needs of your team.

Hitting

A common complaint from coaches about conducting hitting drills is that you're limited in how many quality swings you can give each player during a practice. Pitching to each child individually isn't a very productive use of practice time, because you leave the rest of the kids to stand around in the field. Allow us to help! The following hitting drills put bats in the hands of your players and give them plenty of swings in a fairly short amount of time. (Chapter 9 provides more information on hitting mechanics.)

If you coach younger kids, the less time you spend talking and instructing and the more time you give your players to swing the bats, the happier they'll be playing for you this season.

Individual toss

The individual toss drill is a great exercise for enhancing hand-eye coordination, and it enables your entire team to work on their swings at the same time.

What you need: Every player, and a bat and five balls for each child.

How it works: Give each player a bat and five balls, and space the players along the third-base line with at least 10 feet between each hitter. Have them face the outfield. Each youngster should start by holding a ball in his left hand and a bat in the other while maintaining the proper hitting position. This allows a right-handed hitter to toss the ball out in front more easily so he can take a full swing.

On your command, the players toss the balls into the air to themselves, get their free hands back on the bats, and swing and hit the balls. When the players hit all their balls, have them sprint to the outfield to gather their shares. When all the players return to the third-base line, you can repeat the drill.

Give each player as many balls as you can so your kids spend less time going back and forth to retrieve them. If you don't have enough bats to go around for everyone, pair up the players and make the partner responsible for chasing down the batted balls to keep the drill moving along.

Coaching pointers: Your young players may struggle early on with this drill, until they begin to improve their hand-eye coordination. Keep providing encouraging words, and make sure the hitters are keeping their eyes on the ball, striding forward with their left feet (for right-handers), swinging the bats on a level plane, and taking full follow-throughs. When the kids begin to make some contact, they'll start to develop a rhythm to their swings and settle into a nice groove that they'll carry with them into your games.

Kneel toss

The kneel toss drill (also known as *soft toss*) helps hitters focus on stepping toward the ball and making solid contact on every swing. It also helps a hitter to make his swing more consistent.

What you need: A player, a coach, and a bucket of balls.

How it works: The player takes his normal batting stance. The coach gets down on one knee several feet away from the hitter, facing him, and about a foot in front of him. The coach begins the drill by tossing a ball out in front of the hitter, simulating as closely as possible a pitch down the middle of the plate. For advanced players, you can increase the difficulty by tossing balls inside or outside to help them work on hitting those types of pitches. The hitter steps toward the ball, swings, and drives it. After hitting the ball, the player returns to his batting stance to await the next toss.

You can also do this drill with multiple players. Pair up players and spread them out along the first-base line, for example, and have them hit into left field. Just make sure you leave plenty of room between each pair.

Coaching pointers: When the youngster takes his batting stance, make sure he sets his feet properly and that he's holding his bat in the right position (see Chapter 9). One of the biggest problems young hitters have is setting up incorrectly. It leads to inconsistency. Hitting a baseball is tough enough without making a mistake before the ball even leaves the pitcher's hands. Make sure each hitter gets set up properly before each swing.

If you're coaching a young team, you can turn the toss drill into a fun challenge by seeing how many balls your players can knock out of the infield. Award a point for each successful swing. If you coach older kids, you can challenge a hitter by announcing which direction you want him to hit the ball right before you toss it up. This wrinkle helps a player develop into a versatile hitter who can spray the ball to all parts of the field.

Here are some other tips to keep in mind:

- ✔ If you're working with your players on pulling the ball, toss the balls out in front of them and to their inside so they can get the bat around the ball easily and gain confidence driving the ball to left field (if they're right-handed hitters, of course).

- ✔ If your focus is teaching the techniques of hitting to the opposite field, deliver balls out in front of the batter and to their outside so they can go with the pitch and knock it into right field.

- ✔ With younger kids, using wiffle balls is a great way to give players a lot of swings in a short amount of time because you won't waste a lot of practice time chasing balls around the field.

T-ball target

The T-ball target drill helps your young hitters learn how to follow through with the bat on each swing — an essential skill for power and consistency.

What you need: One player, two coaches, one tee, and a bucket of tennis balls.

How it works: Place the tee at home plate and have the youngster take his normal batting stance next to the tee. Put a tennis ball on the tee and then stand off to the side. Position a coach or parent volunteer as a target in front of the batter, armed with a glove, about 15 yards away. When everyone is set, the player takes a swing and tries to hit the target in front of him.

Coaching pointers: One area you want to concentrate on during this drill is your players' eyes. Kids have a tendency to look up before making contact with the ball, because they're anxious to see if their hits will nail the targets. One way you can help a player keep his head down and eyes on the ball is to put a small dot on the ball where he can see it. Have him focus on that dot while he swings the bat. One other point: Your volunteer targets need to be ready to defend themselves! An added benefit is that you can do this drill at several different areas around the field — you'll just need to recruit additional parents or volunteers to help out. You can also use this drill with older kids to help them develop consistent swings.

Base running

Many youth coaches push base running to the side in favor of working on more "glamorous" skills, but you shouldn't fall into that trap. You need to make sure your kids understand how to move around the bases efficiently. The more proficient your players are in running the bases and making good slides, the better equipped your team will be to produce those all-important runs. The following drills will show you the way. (See Chapter 9 for more sliding scoop.)

Circle the bases

Circle the bases helps your players become more comfortable rounding the bases at top speed — something you want to see often this season.

What you need: An entire team of base runners and two balls.

How it works: Split your team in half and put one half at home plate and the other half at second base. Give a ball to the first player in line for each team. On your command, the two players begin running around the bases in normal fashion. When they get back to where they started, the players hand off the balls to the next people in line. Continue the drill until all the kids have completed a lap around the bases.

Coaching pointers: Make sure the kids don't just touch each of the bases, but that they make contact with the inside of the bases as they round them, which cuts down on the distance traveled and increases your base runners' speed. As your kids become more comfortable running around the diamond, you also want them to circle the bases with their heads up. This skill is important during games when players have to spot the third base coach quickly and react to his instructions.

You shouldn't have any problems with your kids catching up to one another, but if you do, you can tweak the drill by having one half of the team go first, starting at home plate. You can use a stopwatch to time the players and then challenge the other half to try to beat their time. Just make sure the sides are as fair as possible.

Mystery bases

Mystery bases is a great base running drill for kids at the younger age levels, because it helps them learn how to run the bases while having fun.

What you need: A pitcher, a catcher, a batter, and a third base coach.

How it works: The pitcher and catcher take their normal positions on the mound and behind the plate, respectively, and the hitter takes his stance in the batter's box. The pitcher delivers a pitch at regular speed, and the batter swings to put it in play. As the hitter leaves the batter's box, the third base coach tells him what kind of hit he produced (regardless of what it really was). If the coach calls out "double," the player takes the proper route around first base and heads to second. If he calls out "infield grounder," the batter sprints at top speed straight down the first-base line and runs through first base. If he calls out "possible triple," the player should approach second base with his eyes on the third base coach, waiting for a signal to see if he should continue on to third or stay at second. If you're working with a smaller squad, or are short on players at a particular practice, have the players hit off a tee.

Coaching pointers: Keep an eye on how the kids approach first base after you call out an extra-base hit. If they stay too close to the first-base line or stray too far from it, let them know that they're wasting valuable steps and reducing their chances of reaching second or third base safely. They should make a small banana shape with their path as they approach first base. If your kids are having trouble with this, try marking a spot on the field where they should begin rounding off their runs.

Pillow slide

When base runners don't slide properly, they have a better chance of being tagged out, *and* they risk unnecessary injury. The pillow-slide drill helps you teach your youngsters the proper form for going into a basic slide. See Chapter 9 for more sliding instruction.

What you need: Your entire team and a pillow for each player.

How it works: Ask each child to bring an old pillow to practice — and tell them to leave the pajamas at home. (Bring a few extras, if you have them, for kids who forget.) At practice, have the kids line up with 5 feet between each of them. They should place their pillows directly behind them. On your command, the players drop down into the sliding position, with their right leg extended toward the base and their left leg bent under their right knee. Their chin is tucked to their chest and their hands are raised partway above their head. The pillows cushion their landings so that their bottoms and legs don't get sore.

Coaching pointers: Make sure your players don't lose their concentration during the drill, because a lapse of concentration can mean an injured leg or arm. Remind them to get their legs tucked underneath their bodies in the proper manner.

Get low

One of the biggest hurdles for learning how to slide is figuring out how far away from the base you should begin to slide. Get low helps your players gauge the proper distances for them. Chapter 9 provides pointers on proper sliding technique.

What you need: One base runner, two coaches, and one broom (or any other long item, like a mop or a piece of rope).

How it works: The youngster gets into his ready base-running stance at first base. The two coaches position themselves in front of second base, each holding one end of a broom at about stomach level. On a coach's command, the runner breaks for second base. As he nears the broom, he drops into his slide (see the previous section to practice the proper sliding technique), at which point the two coaches raise the broom so the player's hands don't touch it. Give the youngster feedback on his technique. If he ends up too far away from the bag, move closer to it and tell him to begin his slide a step or two later next time.

Coaching pointers: Always be aware of where the coaches are standing. A good rule of thumb is that kids should begin their slides about two body lengths from a base. The shorter the player, the closer to second base the coaches need to be. Also, make sure the base runner keeps his eyes on the base — not on the coaches — and tucks his chin to his chest during his slide.

Protecting Your Diamond: Defensive Drills

Some kids may think that working on defensive skills isn't as much fun as stepping up to the plate and taking cuts at the ball. Within your first couple practices, you can help change this type of thinking. If you introduce some clever and fun-filled defensive drills, your players will embrace the defensive aspect of the game, and your team will allow fewer runs during games. The drills in this section will help your players become comfortable and confident in executing defensive skills, and they'll leave your players excited for upcoming practices.

Pitchers

All eyes fall on the pitcher every time he steps on the mound, because the action doesn't begin until he delivers a pitch. When he delivers the pitch, his teammates are counting on him to throw strikes and get batters out. Along with getting the ball to the plate, a pitcher is responsible for making plays in the field, just like the other infielders. No wonder the pitchers get all the blame and glory! The following drills address both areas of a pitcher's game.

Strike challenge

Pitchers who can throw strikes, especially when they fall behind in the count, really make their jobs easier (and the jobs of all the defenders) by avoiding walks. Strike challenge helps your pitchers develop the confidence that they can throw strikes in any situation — from their Thanksgiving family games to the deciding games of youth tournaments.

What you need: A pitcher and a catcher.

How it works: With your pitcher and catcher at their normal positions, challenge your pitcher to see how many strikes in a row he can throw. Give him five rounds; if the first ball he throws is a strike, he keeps going until you call a pitch a ball, at which point he begins his second round. Anytime he throws a ball, that round ends and he starts a new round.

Coaching pointers: When a pitcher is trying too hard to get the ball across the plate, he has a tendency to aim the ball rather than throw it. You can pick up on this problem when a pitcher's throws start to lack some of their normal pace. When a pitcher aims, he doesn't follow through, because he doesn't have the confidence to unload a normal throw. Continually stress to the pitcher to concentrate on his mechanics; when he does, he'll discover that he can throw the ball hard and still get it across the plate. (See Chapter 11 for a breakdown of proper pitching mechanics.)

You can create a fun player-coach strike challenge by competing against a pitcher. Let him call the balls and strikes on your pitches. Find out who can throw the most strikes in a row or who can throw the most strikes out of a set number of pitches.

Pitchers' fielding practice

Your young pitchers need to get used to fielding ground balls — which you can practice when hitting grounders to other infielders — but they also have another important role: covering first base when the first baseman has to field a ground ball to his right. This drill covers the covering, so to speak.

When a first baseman has to range to his right, he may not have enough time to beat the base runner to first base. In such a case, the pitcher needs to hustle to cover first base and take the throw from the first baseman.

What you need: A pitcher, a catcher, a first baseman, and a coach.

How it works: The pitcher, catcher, and first baseman take their normal positions. The coach positions himself off to the side of home plate with a baseball. The pitcher goes through his windup, and delivers the ball to home plate. As soon as the ball hits the catcher's glove, the coach throws a ground ball to the first baseman's right. When the pitcher sees the ball going in that direction, he runs toward first base to field a throw from the first baseman. He catches the throw in his glove and steps on the bag for the out.

Coaching pointers: When the pitcher completes his follow-through, make sure he keeps his head and his glove up and stands facing the batter. This fielding stance puts the youngster in position to make a play on the ball and to defend himself against line drives and hard grounders. When covering first, the ideal place to receive the ball from the first baseman is about three steps before the pitcher reaches the bag, which gives him time to locate the bag and step on it for the out. Also, make sure the pitcher looks the ball into his glove before he tries to look down and locate first base.

In order for your pitchers to get the most benefit out of this drill, mix up where you throw the grounders. Toss some in front of the pitcher to simulate bunts. Introducing uncertainty helps your pitchers learn to be ready for anything — like slow-rolling grounders in front of the mound or the need to cover first base — as soon as the pitches leave their hands.

Catchers

Playing behind the plate requires a variety of skills — too many for us to cover in this limited space. But we'd like to highlight two basic skills that often get pushed behind blocking the plate and throwing out base stealers, among others: being able to field balls that stay in the vicinity of home plate and catching foul balls popped up behind the plate. The following drills cover these skills (for more advice on instructing your catchers, refer to Chapter 11).

Slow roller

Slow roller gives catchers a chance to practice getting out of their stances quickly and fielding balls that stay within their range. The drill also is great for helping catchers discover how to handle bunts.

What you need: One catcher, one first baseman, one coach, and five balls.

How it works: The catcher and first baseman assume their normal positions. The coach stands behind the catcher with the five balls ready to go. The coach begins the drill by rolling a ball to the catcher's left — make sure it doesn't go too far. The catcher gets out of his stance, tosses his mask to the side, charges to the ball, scoops it up, and fires to first base. The catcher returns to his position, and the coach continues to roll balls, switching locations to the right and up the middle.

Coaching pointers: All good throws begin with good footwork. When the catcher has the ball in his grasp, make sure he steps toward first base with his left foot (if he's right-handed) and points to the base with his left shoulder and elbow. On balls hit in front of the plate and down the first-base line, remind your catcher to take a couple of steps to his left after scooping up the ball so he has a better angle to make the throw because the base runner obstructs the throw a bit. When kids rush to get off throws, sloppy footwork and errant throws often enter the picture. Tell your players to calm down, concentrate on technique, and fire away.

You can tweak this drill to increase the difficulty and to include more players. For example, you can position an infielder at each base. When you roll a ball, yell out which base you want the catcher throwing to right before he reaches it. You force him to make quick adjustments and focus on tossing an accurate throw, which simulates game conditions.

Find the foul ball

Find the foul ball helps your catchers adjust to making catches on balls that they initially can't see. Foul pop ups can be pretty challenging to grab around the home-plate area — just watch the baseball bloopers on television — so your catchers need all the practice they can get.

What you need: A catcher, a coach, a tennis racket, and a can of tennis balls.

How it works: The catcher takes his stance behind home plate, and the coach stands several feet behind the catcher. Using the tennis racket, the coach hits a tennis ball high into the air behind home plate. When the catcher hears the racket hit the ball — just like when he sees and hears a bat hit a ball — he turns and takes time to locate the ball. When he does, he stands a few feet behind it, waits for it to come down, and makes the catch. (He stands behind it because backpedaling on a foul ball makes the catch much more difficult.) Repeat!

Coaching pointers: Most youngsters are tempted to throw off their masks like the pros before they even know which direction they need to move. Not only can this lead to an error, but also to trouble if player trips over the mask. Instruct your catcher to locate the direction of the foul ball first so he can toss his mask safely in the opposite direction. Also, while he's making the catch, advise your catcher to use both hands to squeeze the ball.

When you first teach this drill, try to keep the balls near the catcher, and don't hit them very high. You want to give him the chance to get comfortable and allow him to gain confidence. When he seems ready for a tougher challenge, you can hit the balls much higher and direct them off to his left and right.

First basemen

The most important job a first baseman has is to catch the throws that come from his infielders. And the most successful first basemen can adjust to a variety of throws — without taking their feet off the bag. Being able to field all throws is important because infielders' throws won't always be perfect, chest-level strikes. Use the following drills to help your first basemen practice scooping up all kinds of throws.

Crazy-angle throws

In this drill, your young first basemen practice getting to the bag quickly and setting up to receive infield throws.

What you need: A first baseman, a second baseman, and a coach.

How it works: The first and second basemen take their normal stances in the infield. The coach positions himself about halfway down the first-base line. He begins the drill by throwing a grounder to the second baseman. As soon as the coach releases the ball, the first baseman must rush to get to first base and set up to receive a throw. For subsequent tries, give the second baseman a variety of grounders so the first baseman gets practice receiving throws from many different angles. A bonus of this drill is that your second baseman gets quality practice fielding grounders.

To keep your first baseman from running over to the bag too soon, mix in some grounders his way. He won't cheat if he has to field some balls himself occasionally. You can also include other infielders so the first baseman gets practice taking throws from different positions on the field.

Coaching pointers: Make sure the first baseman holds his glove at chest-level when he gets to the base to provide a nice target for the second baseman. Also, keep an eye on the positioning of the first baseman's non-stretch foot. You always want it to be on the infield side of the bag and not on top of it.

Short hoppers

First basemen can prevent opposing players from getting on base and infielders from making errors if they can scoop low throws out of the dirt. Short hoppers allows your first basemen to practice the proper scooping techniques.

What you need: One first baseman, one coach, and ten tennis balls.

How it works: The coach positions himself between first and second base, about 20 feet in front of the first baseman, who assumes his stance on first base to receive throws. The coach begins by tossing soft one-hoppers with the tennis balls to the youngster's right and left so that he has to use his backhand, too. Gradually, you can pick up the pace of the throws, and you can vary the height of the bounce you create.

Coaching pointers: Because kids have a tendency to flinch and turn their heads on short hoppers, you utilize tennis balls to speed up the learning process and to instill confidence. Always instruct the first baseman to get his body in front of short hops. Even if he can't field the ball cleanly, he can keep it in front of him so the batter can't advance to second base. You can turn this drill into a fun challenge by throwing your first baseman ten tennis balls to see how many he can dig out of the dirt cleanly.

Second basemen

The ability to move in all directions, make tough plays, and deliver accurate throws in a hurry (and with time) are some of the keys to enjoying success at the second base position. The following drills work to hone these skills.

Double play starter

If you want your second basemen (and your shortstops, if you like) to spend some time working on the techniques for fielding grounders and attempting to turn double plays, start with this drill.

What you need: A shortstop, a second baseman, a first baseman, and a coach.

How it works: Have the three infielders take their normal positions in the field. The coach stands around the home-plate area and begins the drill by hitting a ground ball to the shortstop. At the crack of the bat, the second baseman runs to cover second base, receives the shortstop's throw, pivots around the bag, and fires to first base. You can increase the drill's difficulty and give your second baseman more practice by mixing up the grounders between the shortstop and second baseman. Don't let them know where the ball is going. Also, be sure to hit some balls directly up the middle to give them practice communicating. One player may have to execute the double play by stepping on the bag himself and relaying the ball to first.

Coaching pointers: Make sure the player receiving the throw provides a good target by holding his glove up and facing the thrower. Keep an eye on the throws to second base, too — including underhand and backhand tosses — to ensure that they come in at a comfortable level. You want the receiver to handle the ball and relay it to first base without any wasted motion.

Range reactor

Range reactor provides your second baseman (you can use it with other infielders, too) with the chance to practice moving to their left and right to field balls and making tough throws. It also allows the kids to dive for balls and get dirty — two activities they'll definitely love!

What you need: A second baseman, a first baseman, a coach, and a bucket of baseballs.

How it works: The second and first basemen take their normal positions. The coach positions himself about 20 feet away near the pitcher's mound with a bucket of baseballs. The coach begins the drill by throwing a soft ground ball to the second baseman — a ball that calls for the youngster to move only a step or two. He fields the ball, sets his feet, and throws to first base. As soon as he makes the throw, the second baseman should hustle back into position to receive another grounder. When the player begins to develop some consistency fielding the balls, you can increase the difficulty of the drill by making him use his backhand and placing some balls almost out of range so he has to dive for them.

Although using drills that force your kids to stand in long lines is a big no-no, you can make an exception for this drill. Have two second basemen stand together; as soon as one youngster throws to first base, the other gets into his stance to receive a grounder. By keeping the balls coming, you allow no standing-around time. Remind your first baseman about the benefits of this drill — namely, that he gets a lot of work catching throws in a short amount of time.

Coaching pointers: Remind your kids to keep their hands in the proper ready position while they wait to field grounders. Don't allow them to rest their hands on their knees. A proper ready stance ensures good balance and enhances the players' ability to react to — and field — balls going in any direction. (Chapter 10 covers all the infield fundamentals necessary to make these drills a success.)

Shortstops

If you can count on your shortstops to field balls cleanly, make accurate throws to first and second base (and third base on occasion), get the routine outs, and gobble up double plays along with the second basemen, your defense can be really tough to score against. The drills we offer up here work on the primary skills that all good shortstops need.

Base-throw challenge

Base-throw challenge helps your shortstops develop a comfort level with the throws they have to make to different bases under pressure in game situations.

What you need: A shortstop, a second baseman, a first baseman, a coach, and a bucket of balls.

How it works: The three infielders take their positions, and the coach heads for home plate with a bat and the bucket of balls. He begins the drill by hitting a ground ball to the shortstop. As the player fields the ball, the coach shouts out which base he wants the shortstop to throw to. The uncertainty forces the player to really concentrate. It also makes him a better decision maker during games, when he has to decide if going for the out at second is worth it.

When the second baseman sees the ball heading toward the shortstop, he should run and cover second base and provide a good target to receive a throw in case the ball comes his way. To really keep the shortstop on his toes, you can add a third baseman to the drill so he has three throwing options. You can also mix things up by hitting balls to other infielders so the shortstop doesn't always know where the ball is going.

Coaching pointers: A shortstop needs good hand-eye coordination to enjoy success at his position. Make sure that when he fields the ball, he keeps his head down and watches it go into his glove instead of peeking up to see the base that the coach has called out.

Double-play throws

Executing double plays provides a real boost for a defense — and slashes the workload for the pitcher. The responsibility of starting double plays often falls on the shortstop's lap, which is why he should be your most sure-handed fielder (see Chapter 5 for more on choosing players for certain positions). The double-play throws drill works well for honing those all-important double-play skills.

What you need: One shortstop, one second baseman, one first baseman, two base runners, one coach, and one bucket of baseballs.

How it works: The shortstop and second baseman take their positions at double-play depth, and the first baseman takes his normal position. You place one base runner at first and one next to the coach at home plate. The coach begins by hitting a ground ball to the second baseman, at which point the runners take off. The player fields the ball and, depending on how close he is to second base, delivers an underhand toss or a regular throw to the shortstop, who has run to cover the bag. The shortstop catches the throw, pivots around the bag, and relays the ball to first base. The oncoming runner should simulate game action and make the shortstop's throw to first more challenging. To mix things up, you can also hit some balls up the middle so the shortstop or second baseman — whoever can get their glove on the ball — is forced to make plays on his own.

Coaching pointers: Instill in your players the importance of always getting at least one out; their focus should remain on securing the first out before eyeing the double play. Make sure the youngster who fields the ground ball gets off an accurate, under-control throw to the infielder who covers the bag. Your kids may try to rush the throw and put unnecessary pace behind it because of the excitement of the double play. Also, remind them that their best bet for avoiding sliding runners is taking a small hop step to the outside of the bag before completing the throw.

You can turn double-play throws into a fun challenge by seeing how many times the kids can successfully turn the double play.

Third basemen

When it comes to making accurate throws to first base, the third baseman's position is the most challenging because of the length of the throw and the short amount of time available to make the play. Young third basemen who can deliver strong, accurate throws with high frequency cut down on the scoring opportunities for the opposition — especially if the team is full of right-handers who pull the ball.

Third basemen also have to deal with pop ups that travel in the infield, behind them in the shallow part of the outfield, and in foul territory. Use the following drills to help your third basemen play their position like pros.

Ground-ball mania

Ground-ball mania zeroes in on putting your third basemen in a groove so that making those throws over to first base seems like second nature.

What you need: A third baseman, a first baseman, a coach, and several baseballs.

How it works: The third and first basemen take their normal defensive positions, and the coach stands at home plate with some baseballs. The coach starts the drill by throwing a ground ball to the third baseman's left. He fields the ball, sets his feet, and throws over to first base. After he releases, he should quickly set up again; when he's ready, the coach throws a ground ball to his right, which he fields and delivers to first base. The player sets up again, and the coach throws a grounder with a little less pace, forcing the player to come in a couple of steps. For the final toss, the coach makes him charge forward even farther.

Coaching pointers: Instruct the youngster to step toward first base with his non-dominant foot, and make sure that he throws overhand. If his throws are veering left or right or sailing over the first baseman's head, he may be throwing with a slight sidearm motion. He also may be gripping the ball improperly, so ask him to show you his grip. (See Chapter 10 for more infield throwing tips.) You don't want to wear out the youngster's arm, so limit the number of throws he makes. You can do this a couple of different ways: Have the player take turns with a couple of other infielders so he has a moment to catch his breath, and rest his arm, while another player goes through the drill.

You can make ground-ball mania even more fun for the players by awarding points based on the accuracy of their throws. Give a player two points for every throw that the first baseman catches in the air without having to move his feet; award one point for throws that short-hop the first baseman or that force him to lunge, but still get caught. Deduct a point for an errant throw that would result in a runner reaching base safely.

Find the pop up

The following drill helps your third basemen react to pop ups in the infield, take charge, and make plays on them. (The drill works equally well for the other infield positions, too.)

What you need: A third baseman, a coach, and a bucket of balls.

How it works: The third baseman takes his normal fielding position, and the first baseman does the same. The coach positions himself around the home-plate area with the balls. He begins by throwing a short pop up that the third baseman has to come in on and catch. After he makes the catch, he tosses a throw to the first baseman like he's trying to nab a runner who's late getting back to the base.

Gradually, the coach can make the pop ups more challenging by forcing the third baseman to move back several steps, either into the outfield or foul territory. This also makes his throws more difficult, because he moves farther away. To help him keep track of his progress, the coach can award a point for every catch he makes and deduct one for each drop; he can do the same with the throws based on their accuracy. Another twist to this drill is that you can put youngsters at all the infield positions and send pop ups between two infielders so they get practice learning to call one another off if they have a better play on the ball.

Coaching pointers: Make sure the youngster begins in the proper fielding position — standing on the balls of his feet with his feet shoulder-width apart. He needs to be able to react quickly in whatever direction he needs to run. To keep your third baseman alert so that he doesn't know what's coming all the time, you can mix in some ground balls, too.

Outfielders

Even though the outfielders aren't right on top of the action going on in the infield, they are the last line of defense for a team. Many skills go into playing balls that leave the infield and give the offensive team hope. An outfielder's job description includes making catches, fielding hits, and delivering accurate throws to the cutoff man — the following drills put your outfielders to the test.

Target throws

Outfielders who can hit their cutoff men and make accurate throws to bases really make maneuvering around the bases difficult for opposing players. The target throws drill helps your outfielders practice their throwing skills all over the field. (See Chapter 15 for more on the finer points of cutoff men and relay throws.)

What you need: Three outfielders, four infielders, and a coach.

How it works: The outfielders and the third baseman take their normal fielding positions. The other infielders assume their cutoff positions: The shortstop stands in shallow left field so he can move to either his left or right based on where the ball is hit; the second baseman moves to shallow right field; and the first baseman parks in front of the pitcher's mound.

The coach begins the drill by throwing (or hitting) a ball down the left-field line. The left fielder chases down the hit and throws the ball to his cutoff man, the shortstop, who catches the ball, and turns, and relays to the third baseman. After sending the ball down the left-field line, the coach sends another ball out to the center fielder. The player fields the ball and makes a throw to his cutoff man, the first baseman, in front of the pitcher's mound. If you're coaching a younger squad, you may want to consider having the second baseman serve as another cutoff man to cut down on the distance of the throws between players. As soon as he sends a ball to center field, the coach sends another down the right-field line. The player in right field scoops the ball and throws it to his cutoff man, the second baseman.

Continue doing several repetitions of this drill so your outfielders get plenty of practice hitting their cutoff men. You can even rotate the infielders so both they and the outfielders get lots of practice making and handling cutoff throws with different teammates.

Coaching pointers: Remind your outfielders to use an overhand throwing motion and follow through toward their targets — this improves their accuracy. To help the outfielders really focus on hitting their cutoff men, award points for every throw that a cutoff man doesn't have to take more than a step to catch. By creating a fun competition among the outfielders, you ensure that the players will give their full attention to the drill. Another twist you can add is to include a catcher. You can have your second and first basemen (and your shortstop, if you like) relay balls to home after receiving throws from the outfield.

Fly-ball frenzy

Fly balls rarely sail directly to your outfielders, so they need all the tracking practice they can get. Fly-ball frenzy helps your players practice taking the proper angles to snare balls hit to their left and right.

What you need: Three outfielders, one coach, and one bucket of balls.

How it works: The outfielders take their normal positions in left, center, and right field, and the coach stands in shallow center field with the bucket of balls.

Beginning with the left fielder, the coach points to the player's left, letting him know that the fly ball is coming to that side. The coach then throws or hits a ball up in the air in that direction, and the player makes his break for the ball.

The ball should be high and deep enough to force the outfielder to run several steps before being able to make the grab.

After the left fielder makes the catch, the coach repeats the drill with the other two outfielders. When a player makes a catch, he jogs back into position to await another throw.

You can really keep the kids on the move during this drill by recruiting some parents or assistants to help out so that each outfielder has his own thrower.

Coaching pointers: The purpose of letting the kids know in advance which direction they'll go is that you want to instill in them the importance of using proper footwork when tracking down fly balls. For example, if you hit a ball to your left fielder's left and over his head, instruct him to take a drop step with his left foot, turn and cross with his right foot, and begin running at an angle as he tracks down the ball. After a player develops the habit of using proper footwork, he'll track down balls that normally would've sailed over his head. You can add a communication aspect to this drill by having two outfielders break for the ball at the same time so they get practice talking to one another while the ball is in the air to determine who will catch it.

If you plan on tossing the balls into the outfield, make sure you stretch your arm and loosen up before you start. You don't want to strain any muscles, which will limit much how you can work with the kids the rest of the season.

Combining Your Drills: A Sample Practice Session

Because you have your players for a limited amount of time each week, every minute you spend with them on the field is valuable. As you maneuver through the season, you'll find that the needs of your team will constantly change from game to game, and you'll have to adjust accordingly. Even if you have a month of practice plans carefully laid out, you may have to make slight adjustments — or even major overhauls — based on your team's performance and areas that may require some extra attention. The following list details a sample one-hour practice session — half on offense and half on defense — that uses the drills we cover in this chapter. For more information on planning practices, flip over to Chapter 6. For tips on planning practices that feature more advanced skills, check out Chapter 13.

- ✔ **10 minutes:** Take this time for your warm-up period. (Check out Chapter 16 for a complete rundown on stretching.)

- ✔ **10 minutes:** You can get the kids to work on their swings right away with the Individual Toss drill. If you have enough room and players, you can conduct the Kneel Toss drill deep in the outfield at the same time. As your players go through the Individual Toss drill, you can call one player over at a time to hit five tosses from you.

  If you want to combine these drills, you need to make sure that every child gets a chance to hit with you. Equal playing time is important in games, but having a balance is just as crucial during your practices.

- ✔ **5 minutes:** Conclude the offensive half of your practice by running the Circle the Bases drill. The exercise is good for team bonding, and your kids will enjoy doing a fun relay.

- ✔ **15 minutes:** In foul territory along the first-base line, or in foul territory in the outfield, set up the Strike Challenge for your young hurlers. For your catchers, you can run the Find the Foul Ball drill behind the home-plate area. Use the infield to arrange the Base-Throw Challenge for your first basemen, second basemen, and shortstops. At the same time, your third basemen can work on the Find the Pop Up drill. In the outfield area, your outfielders can have some fun with the Fly-Ball Frenzy drill.

- ✔ **15 minutes:** Have your four infield positions and three outfield positions take their normal places for the Target Throw drill. Meanwhile, away from all the action deep in the outfield, you can run the Slow Roller drill for your catchers and the Pitchers' Fielding Practice drill for your pitchers. For these drills, you need to call out a first baseman to lend his assistance. You can alternate between giving the catcher a ball to field and throw to the first-base area; a ball for the pitcher to field and throw to first base; and a ball for the first baseman to field and toss to the pitcher who runs to cover first base.

✔ **5 minutes:** Conclude the practice with a light cool-down period (see Chapter 16). Gather your kids around and thank them for their hard work. Because you always want to end your practices on a high note, point out the positive things you saw on the field. Send your kids home feeling good about themselves. Remind them about the next practice or game, perform your team cheer (if you have one), and call it a day.

Remain flexible after your practice gets going. In other words, you need to be ready to make any necessary adjustments. For example, if you notice that several kids are struggling with a base-running drill, stick with that drill for a few extra minutes until they get more comfortable. To compensate, simply trim a few minutes off another drill you had planned for later in the practice. Although you want to arrive at the field with a practice plan, consider it written in pencil and not ink. Also, when using drills that require the help of assistants, make sure that they are comfortable in their roles before practice begins. You don't want to spring surprises on them a minute before the drill begins. Go over with them well in advance of your practice how you want the drill to run and what their specific roles and responsibilities are to help ensure that it goes smoothly.

Chapter 13

Taking Your Drills to the Next Level

··

In This Chapter

▶ Conducting challenging hitting drills

▶ Upgrading your defensive drills

▶ Turning your individual drills into effective practices

··

*A*fter you conduct many practices with your team and take the field for some games, you'll begin to notice your players transforming right before your eyes. They'll start to pick up the different aspects of the game that you've been teaching so far this season. Some kids will become more proficient at swinging the bat; some will develop a knack for running the bases efficiently; and others will show more prowess in fielding grounders. Even better, some kids may surprise you with how rapidly they develop in all these areas.

Now, more than ever, is the time to make sure you're sprinkling your practices with newfangled drills and providing fresh challenges for your players to inspire their learning and development. Relying on the same set of drills practice after practice is a big coaching no-no, because repetition brings learning and fun to a grinding halt. In this chapter, we provide a collection of drills — both offensive and defensive — that will not only challenge your players, but also propel them to exciting new levels of performance. We also include two sample practice plans to show you how to design fun-filled sessions that your players will look forward to, as well as give you ideas on how to keep all the kids involved throughout the practice.

From Bats to Bases: Offensive Drills

A lineup full of players who can swing the bat with consistency and run the bases with confidence creates all sorts of problems for opponents. In the following sections, we present a smorgasbord of batting and base-running drills that you can incorporate into your practices to keep them exciting and to help take your team to the next level offensively. The drills are fun, productive, and easy to implement, and they can really make a difference in your players' development.

Keeping the kids safe must always be a top priority anytime you're running a drill. Every player who steps to the plate — as well as any players in the on-deck circle — must wear a properly fitting helmet. Never pitch a ball to a hitter unless you're sure that all the infielders and outfielders are ready and paying attention. Also, remind kids to lay the bat down rather than throw it after making contact with a pitch.

Batting

Hitting a baseball is one of the most challenging tasks in all of sport — and one of the most fulfilling. You can't quite duplicate the feeling a player has when he makes solid contact and the ball rockets off his bat. Constantly stressing the fundamentals of hitting will help your players develop swings that they're comfortable with and confident in. The following drills work toward this goal while also aiming to boost your players' productivity at the plate and keep their interest level in this part of the game high.

Pepper

Pepper is a fun drill that helps players develop hand-eye coordination when swinging a bat. A bonus is that the drill enables players without the bat to hone their fielding skills, making it a versatile and useful drill for any practice.

What you need: Four players, one bat, and one ball.

How it works: One player assumes the role of batter, facing the fielders. The fielders stand facing the batter, positioned about 20 feet away from him and about 8 feet apart from each other. (You can do this drill anywhere on the field.) The drill begins when the middle fielder lobs a pitch overhand to the batter, who takes a half swing, trying to hit the ball back to one of the three fielders on one or two hops. The targeted fielder fields the ball and lobs it back to the batter, who tries to hit it to a different fielder. The object of the drill is for the kids to keep the ball in play as long as possible.

Coaching pointers: You want both the hitter and the pitching fielder to go at about half speed to increase the chance that the ball will be constantly in play and that the kids will have plenty of opportunities to hit and field the ball. Encourage the player with the bat to mix up hitting and bunting so that he gets practice on both skills. Keep a close eye on the fielders to ensure that they use the proper ready position (see Chapter 10) before each pitch.

You can include everybody in the pepper drill simply by breaking the team into groups of four and scattering them around different parts of the field. Rotate the kids every few minutes so that everyone gets a chance to swing the bat and field the balls.

Speed hitting

Speed hitting is a drill that allows hitters to get many swings in during a short period of time. This drill improves a hitter's ability to recognize and react to pitches.

What you need: One coach, one batter, and ten baseballs.

How it works: The hitter takes his batting stance in the batter's box, and the coach stands on the pitcher's mound with ten baseballs. He delivers the first ball for the batter to hit. As soon as the coach releases the first pitch, he grabs the next ball, and when the batter gets set in his stance again, he delivers another pitch. After ten pitches, the batter rotates to a position in the field and the player she replaces heads to the batter's box. You can place several buckets around the field for the kids to deposit the balls in, or have a few assistant coaches stationed at different spots in field that the kids can throw the balls to. You don't want balls scattered around the field where youngsters can trip over them and be injured.

Coaching pointers: Because the pitches will come in rapid succession, you need to make sure that each batter gets her feet set and her bat in proper position after each swing (see Chapter 9 for more on the proper hitting positions). You can incorporate more of your players into the drill by setting up a defensive unit. Because the pitches come quickly, the infielders won't have a chance to make throws to first base, and the outfielders won't be able to throw to infielders, but the players will gain added practice from fielding grounders, line drives, and pop flies. If you have an assistant coach who you can count on to consistently deliver pitches across the plate, have him handle the pitching chores so you can keep a close eye on each hitter and dissect her swing to ensure she's using proper fundamentals.

Progression hitting off the tee

Progression hitting off the tee helps players learn to hit the ball to all different areas of the field. Advanced levels of play often call for hitters to pull the ball, hit it to the opposite field, hit a ground ball or pop fly, and so on, based on different game situations they encounter.

What you need: One batter, one batting tee, ten baseballs, and an entire defensive lineup.

How it works: You put the batting tee on home plate and tell your defense to take the field. You call for a hitter to assume his batting stance at the plate. After he takes his stance, you call out where you want him to hit the ball, and the batter swings to try to put the ball into play at the desired location. The infielders field the grounders and make throws to first base, and the outfielders catch fly balls or field base hits and deliver throws to the proper cutoff men (see Chapter 3 for more on these terms). The hitter then puts another ball on the tee and prepares to hit again.

Coaching pointers: Let the hitter get set in the batter's box before you tell him how and where to hit the ball so he can't cheat and adjust his feet or turn his body — something he won't be able to do in a game. By setting his feet, he has to rely on making a quality swing to get the desired result.

Give each player a variety of situations to hit in. For example, you players to be able to hit the ball into the outfield for sacrifice flies, and you want them to be able to hit the ball to both sides of the field to advance runners. You can turn the progression into a fun competition between the players by seeing which youngster can hit the ball to the right spot the most times.

Mixed speeds

The mixed speeds drill works to help kids improve their reaction time at the plate and quicken their swings.

What you need: One hitter, one catcher, and a coach.

How it works: The hitter and catcher assume their regular positions in the batter's and catcher's boxes, and the infielders and outfielders take their normal spots. The coach stands from about 10 feet in front of the pitching mound and delivers pitches from a bucket of balls. Because the batter has less time to react to pitches at this distance, he really has to concentrate on the release of the ball from the coach's hand and begin his swing quickly.

Coaching pointers: Never allow the kids to handle the pitching responsibilities in the mixed speeds drill. Because the pitcher stands closer to the batter's box, he increases the risk of injury.

When delivering the pitches, the coach should give the kids a variety of different speeds to help them improve their reflexes. Switching speeds is much more beneficial than asking the kids to swing away at the same pitch each time.

Base running

A team's ability to generate runs is linked — in large part — to how efficient its players are on the base paths. Your team can accumulate more runs by knowing when to try for that extra base and when to take a conservative approach. You can use the following drills to help your players understand which situations are best for challenging outfielders' and catchers' arms and when they should be content to advance one base at a time or stay on their current base.

Extra-base challenge

The extra-base challenge is ideal for giving your players opportunities to try for those extra bases (or to put on the brakes and stay put). An added benefit is that your outfielders get the chance to make throws to different bases while under pressure, and your infielders get work on making cutoffs and tagging out runners.

What you need: Your entire defensive team, base runners, and a coach with a bucket of baseballs.

How it works: Your defensive players take their positions in the field. A player for the offensive team stands in the batter's box in his hitting position. The coach stands near the pitching mound, and he either hits or throws a ball into the outfield. As soon as the ball leaves the mound, the offensive player runs down the first-base line and, judging by where the ball goes, which player fields it, and how the fielder handles the play, determines if he should try for an extra base. If he makes it to a base safely, he stays there while the next offensive player steps into the batter's box. You can continue the drill until each offensive player gets a set number of repetitions, or you can stop when the defense records three outs.

Coaching pointers: Run this drill at a quick pace so that you keep all the infielders and outfielders busy and challenged in a variety of ways. Make sure your base runners only attempt to take extra bases when the opportunities are there. If a runner gets thrown out a lot during the drill, remind him of the importance of not being overly aggressive all the time, but picking and choosing spots for aggressiveness. Don't neglect to monitor the throws of your fielders. Make sure that your infielders properly set up to receive cutoff throws. If you have a large squad, you can split the team into offensive and defensive units and turn it into a fun competition between the two. With smaller groups you can simply rotate players from offense to defense.

Swiping bases

Stealing bases gives your offense better opportunities to score, and catching base stealers on defense prevents the opposing team from doing the same. The following drill helps your base runners develop base-stealing skills, and it gives your catchers great practice at getting rid of the ball quickly.

What you need: A pitcher, a catcher, a second baseman, and a base runner.

How it works: The pitcher, catcher, and second baseman assume their normal positions. The base runner heads to first base. When the pitcher begins his delivery (or when the ball crosses the plate, depending on your league's rules), the runner takes off for second base. When the catcher receives the ball, he explodes out of his squatting position and delivers a throw to the second baseman, who started moving to cover the bag when the runner took off for second (for more on catching techniques, see Chapter 11).

You can also incorporate a shortstop into the drill and have him alternate covering second base with the second baseman.

If your league doesn't allow players to take leadoffs, the base runner should begin the drill with his foot on first base and take off for second at the appropriate time. (See Chapter 9 for more base-running basics.)

Coaching pointers: Make sure your second baseman gives the catcher a good throwing target, and that he properly positions his feet — straddling the base so that he won't get injured by the sliding base runner. When the runner takes off from first base, instruct him to keep his head up and look at second base as he runs toward it. If he spends too much time looking at the catcher, he'll slow himself down. When he reaches second base, watch to make sure that he doesn't go into his slide too early or too late — the former reduces his chances of success, and the latter increases the risk of injury.

After you go through a few repetitions of this drill, you can increase the difficulty level for the catcher. Have a player stand in the batter's box so your catcher can practice making throws while dealing with a player in his way. You also can add a first baseman to the mix so your pitcher can practice holding the runner.

From Dirt Stains to Grass Stains: Defensive Drills

A defensive unit that shows skill and knowledge in all areas of the game makes it challenging for an opposing team to get runners on base, move them along, and score runs. After many practices and a few games, your players will start to excel in the basics of the defensive side of the game. In this section, we present an array of drills to help your players upgrade their defensive skills at many positions. The more skills a player has in his arsenal, and the better prepared he is to handle different situations, the more enjoyment he'll experience when playing the game. (For specifics on the proper techniques required to play the defensive positions, check out Chapters 10 and 11.)

Closely monitor how often you incorporate throwing drills into your practices, and keep tabs on how many throws your youngsters are making. The muscles, tendons, and bones in kids' arms are growing and developing; you need to limit the stress you put on their arms so that you don't put them at unnecessary risk of injury.

This section starts off with standard infield/outfield practice, and it then introduces some specific drills for the battery, infielders, and outfielders.

Infield/outfield practice

This drill is a great warm-up for practices and games because it gives all your infielders quality practice fielding grounders and making throws, and all of your outfielders practice making catches and delivering throws — in a relatively short period of time.

What you need: One coach and eight players.

How it works: The kids take their positions in the infield and outfield (the pitcher isn't included in this drill). You begin by hitting a fly ball to the left fielder, who makes the grab and throws it in to the third baseman. He throws it to the shortstop and the ball continues around the horn until the catcher receives the ball from the first baseman. While the left fielder makes the throw you hit a ball to the center fielder. He makes the grab and fires it to the third baseman, who sends it around the horn. Repeat with the right fielder. Go through another rotation hitting balls to the outfielders, but this time they throw to the second baseman. He catches the ball and relays it to the catcher. The next rotation the outfielders catch the ball and throw home to the catcher.

You then move on to the infielders. (Your outfielders can stay put and practice backing up plays on the infield.) Hit a ground ball to the third baseman, who throws to first. The shortstop and second baseman also throw to first. The first baseman throws the ball home. On the next rotation, the third baseman, shortstop, and first baseman field grounders and throw to the second baseman, and he throws the ball home. On the next rotation, the third baseman fields the grounder and throws the ball home, while the shortstop and second baseman each flip the ball to the other to turn double plays. The first baseman throws to second.

And, finally, roll a ball out in front of the catcher, who fields it and throws to first. Give him two other balls to handle, which he delivers to the second and third basemen.

Coaching pointers: On balls hit to the outfield, make sure all your players are rotating correctly to back up the play and serve as cutoff men. (Refer to the diagrams in Chapter 15 to see the proper rotation.) On grounders to the infield, make sure each player is using proper form and making accurate throws. (See Chapter 10 for all the infield — and outfield — fielding fundamentals.) Feel free to tweak the number of balls each player gets and where they make the throws. For example, early in the season, you might want to give extra attention to outfield practice, with balls hit to all areas of the outfield, so that your team can get accustomed to rotating properly, covering the necessary bases, and making cutoff throws.

Pitchers and catchers

You can add the following drills to your practice plan to help your pitchers and catchers hone their throwing mechanics and reflexes. One of the drills, the bunt bonanza, gives the members of your battery all-important fielding practice, which many coaches tend to overlook at these positions.

Target throws

Having the proper mechanics is vital for delivering a pitch properly. One of the most important mechanics for accuracy is a youngster's ability to rotate his hips while throwing. The target throws drill helps young pitchers practice rotating their hips and executing a good follow-through.

What you need: One pitcher, one catcher, and five baseballs.

How it works: Have a pitcher set up about 30 feet away from home plate (facing the plate), kneeling down on his right knee with his left foot planted and pointing toward home plate (for a right-handed pitcher). Put a ball in his glove, and place another ball 6 inches in front of his left foot.

Ask the catcher to assume his normal position behind home plate. You put three baseballs in front of home plate: one ball in the center and the other two on the corners.

The setup is complete. Now the catcher points to the target (one of the three balls) in front of him that he wants the pitcher to deliver the ball over.

The pitcher, keeping his knee on the ground, rocks his body backward while rotating his body to the right and delivers the pitch. During his follow-through, he scoops the ball in front of his left foot.

Coaching pointers: You place the ball in front of a right-handed pitcher's left foot to encourage good extension on the follow-through. Make sure the pitcher keeps his eyes on the target during the drill. Ideally, his head should wind up in front of his left knee after the throw.

Bunt bonanza

A pitcher who can get off the mound quickly to field bunts and weakly hit ground balls is a major asset to a defense, as is a catcher who can pounce on balls around the home-plate area. The bunt bonanza drill is great for helping young pitchers and catchers get comfortable with the responsibilities of fielding balls and making throws to different bases.

What you need: A pitcher, a catcher, a first baseman, and a coach.

How it works: A youngster goes to the pitcher's mound, and the catcher and first baseman assume their normal positions. The coach should stand off to the side of the catcher. The pitcher delivers a pitch, and as soon as the ball hits the catcher's glove, the coach rolls a ball in front of the pitcher's mound. The pitcher and catcher move toward the ball, communicate with each other on who should handle it, and deliver a throw to first base.

Coaching pointers: You should mix up the location of the balls you roll toward the pitcher so he has to move to his left, to his right, and forward. To increase the difficulty of the drill, you can add a second baseman and third baseman to the mix. As soon as the pitcher starts to scoop up the bunt, you (or a catcher) yell out which base you want him to throw to. This wrinkle in the drill simulates game action, because the pitcher and catcher often have to make a split-second decision on which base to throw to when fielding bunts. For more details on each player's responsibilities covering bunts, check out Chapter 15.

Quick mystery throws

Quick hands and good reflexes are assets catchers really benefit from having. The following drill helps build up these assets so that your catchers can make the plays that make the catching position so much fun, such as tagging out runners at home plate and calling out assignments for other infielders.

What you need: One catcher, three helpers, and three buckets of baseballs.

How it works: The catcher, wearing his full gear, takes his normal position behind home plate. Your three helpers, who can be teammates, assistant coaches, or parents, stand in a horizontal line in front of the catcher about 25 feet away with the buckets in front of them. The first player in line throws a ball to the catcher, who catches it and quickly rolls it off to the side. As soon as the ball leaves his glove, the next helper throws a ball to the catcher. The drill continues in rapid succession.

Coaching pointers: The key to this drill is to keep it fast-paced. The quicker the balls fly to the catcher, the better his reflexes and hands become. Ask your helpers to throw the balls to the catcher's left and right so that he gets practice moving in both directions. You also can have them bounce balls in front of the plate, forcing your catcher to deal with game-like situations.

Infielders

Playing in the infield — and having lots of success there — requires assorted catching and throwing skills. The more comfortable kids are with these skills, the more difficulty opposing teams will have reaching that coveted destination known as home plate. The drills in this section zero in on skills all infielders need.

Hit the target

The two most common throws a first baseman has to make during a game are to home plate and second base. The following drill gives first basemen the opportunity to field grounders and make quick adjustments to deliver the ball to home plate and second base.

What you need: A first baseman, a second baseman, a catcher, and a coach.

How it works: Have your first and second basemen and catcher take their normal positions. The coach should take a position off to the left side of home plate. When everyone is set, the coach hits a grounder to the first baseman. As the ball nears the player, the coach yells out where he wants him to throw the ball. Much like during a game, the first baseman has to make split-second decisions and quick throws — two key abilities for handling the responsibilities of the position.

Coaching pointers: Make sure the youngster in the field watches the ground ball into his glove instead of lifting his head too early to peek at the base the coach has called out. You can turn the target drill into a competitive game for the kids by awarding points for cleanly fielded balls and on-target throws. You can also mix the drill up a bit by including a third baseman and having the first baseman field some bunts and deliver throws to third.

Speedy double plays

The bulk of the responsibilities for executing double plays fall in the young laps of the second baseman and shortstop. If you want to give them plenty of practice turning double plays to shore up your defense, you should make some room for the following drill in your practices.

What you need: A shortstop, a second baseman, a first baseman, a coach, and a bucket of baseballs.

How it works: The three players take their normal positions in the infield. The coach grabs the bucket of balls and takes a position between the pitcher's mound and second base. He begins the drill by throwing a ground ball to the shortstop. When the coach releases the ball toward the shortstop, the second baseman should run to cover second base. He receives a throw from the shortstop, forces out the runner at second, and relays the ball to the first baseman.

When the second baseman releases his throw, the coach throws a ground ball to the second baseman's vacant position, which forces him to run several steps to his left. When he fields the ball, he turns and throws to the shortstop who's covering second base; the shortstop forces out the runner and then relays the ball to first base. When the shortstop releases the ball, you throw another ground ball to his vacant position, and the cycle begins all over again.

Coaching pointers: Make sure the player covering second base has his glove up, providing a clear target for the fielder to throw to. You can challenge the infielders to see how many consecutive double plays they can turn cleanly to keep them focused during this fast-moving drill. Run through the drill about ten times and then give the kids a breather.

Find the fly

The more range your middle infielders have moving back on pop ups that barely leave the infield, and the more comfortable they are at doing so, the tougher it will be for opposing players to reach base on tricky little bloopers that your outfielders can't reach. The following drill helps your players become more comfortable making tough over-the-shoulder catches.

What you need: A shortstop, a second baseman, and a coach with a bucket of balls.

How it works: The shortstop and second baseman take their normal positions, but they stand facing the outfield. The coach stands just behind the pitcher's mound. The coach begins the drill by lobbing a ball high in the air over a player's head and into the shallow part of the outfield. When the coach releases the ball, he yells "ball," which signals the player to locate the direction of the pop up and move to make the catch.

Coaching pointers: When the coach first begins the drill, he should keep the balls directly over the players' heads so they gain some confidence making the catches. When the players start to get comfortable with those grabs, the coach can bump up the difficulty level by tossing balls over the players' left and right shoulders. The coach also can toss some balls toward center field, which forces the players to communicate about who should take the ball.

Kids love making those diving catches they see their favorite Major Leaguers make on television, but the less often they have to attempt those really tough grabs the better off the team will be. So, be sure to stress that they need to focus on locating the ball as quickly as possible and getting under it to make the grab, if possible. Remind them that a routine putout is just as valuable to the team as a flashy one.

Choose the base

With runners on base, a third baseman often has to make quick decisions on which base to throw to when ground balls come his way. The following drill helps a third basemen practice evaluating situations properly and choosing the right base as his target.

What you need: One third baseman, one first baseman, one catcher, two base runners, and one coach.

How it works: The third baseman, first baseman, and catcher assume their normal positions. One base runner takes third base, and the other begins in the batter's box. The coach stands near the batter's box; he begins the drill by throwing or hitting a ground ball to the third baseman. As soon as the ball leaves the coach's hand or bat, the runner on third should break for home, and the youngster in the batter's box should take off for first base. When the third baseman fields the ball, he must determine which runner he has the best chance of throwing out and make the play to that base. You can also set up base runners on first or second so the third baseman is challenged with more options.

Coaching pointers: Make sure the third baseman gets a variety of throws that force him to move to his left and right and to come forward. Youngsters often feel tempted to throw the ball home — even when they have zero chance of getting runners out — because a play at the plate is more exciting than throwing a runner out at first. The throw to home also is shorter and often easier. Go over the importance of recording an out at first base when your players don't have a realistic opportunity to throw out runners at other bases.

You can turn this drill into a fun competition by challenging your third baseman to see how many outs he can record when fielding 15 ground balls.

Outfielders

You can use the drills in this section to take your outfielders' skills to the next level (above simply catching balls). Specifically, your outfielders work to improve their throwing techniques and accuracy, and they master the art of catching fly balls hit in front of them.

Throw home

Nothing makes an outfielder feel better — or puts a bigger smile on his face — than throwing out a base runner when his teammates are counting on him, especially at home plate (well, except for a diving catch that draws an "ooh!" from the stands). It makes a coach pretty happy, too; throwing out a runner who's moving into scoring position can provide a real boost to the defense. The following drill helps outfielders gain the confidence, and hone the techniques, to execute throws to the infield. (See Chapter 15 for some situational info on balls hit to the outfield.)

What you need: A base runner, an outfielder, a catcher, and a coach.

How it works: Position the base runner on third base, and have your outfielder and catcher take their normal positions. The coach begins the drill by hitting a fly ball to the outfielder. The runner tags up on third base, and as soon as the outfielder makes the catch, the runner takes off for home plate. The outfielder throws the ball to the catcher to attempt to make the out. You can also add a second and third baseman, as well as other base runners, to give your outfielders practice making these throws under pressure.

Coaching pointers: Keep a close watch on the base runner to make sure he doesn't leave the base too early. Instruct your outfielder to stay a couple steps back from where he thinks the ball will land. When the time comes, he moves forward to catch the ball with his momentum going toward home plate. If he catches the ball while standing still, he'll waste precious seconds in an attempt to gain momentum, which reduces his chances of throwing out the runner.

Also, encourage the outfielder to catch the ball on the throwing side of his body, which makes for a quicker transition from glove to throwing hand. For example, a right-handed player should catch the ball with his glove in front of his right shoulder. If your outfielders don't have the arm strength to deliver throws to the cutoff man on the fly, work with them on getting throws there on one bounce. You can also have your infielders, if they've got strong arms, venture a few steps farther out to shorten the distance of the outfielder's throw (which, of course, makes your infielder's throw that much longer).

To keep this drill moving, you can have a couple base runners waiting their turn to sprint home.

Basket catch

Sometimes, to make a tough catch on a short fly ball, an outfielder has to charge in and flip his glove over so the open mitt points toward the sky. The following drill helps your outfielders become more comfortable with making this type of grab when situations force them to.

What you need: Three outfielders, a coach, and a bucket of balls.

How it works: The coach stands on the edge of the infield with a bucket of balls. He lobs a ball in the air in front of an outfielder, who runs forward and performs the basket catch.

Coaching pointers: Make sure you lob the balls short enough that the outfielders don't have to slow down just to warrant the basket catch. To help increase your kids' concentration, you can turn the basket catch drill into an elimination game, where a dropped ball knocks an outfielder out of the contest. Or, you can break the kids into groups to see which group can make the most basket catches in a row or overall. Stress to the kids that if they're able to make conventional catches, that's the preferred route because the ball is less likely to bounce out of their gloves.

Considering Sample Practice Plans

Incorporating a variety of fun drills that enable your kids to learn and develop their skills is only one step toward conducting productive practices. You also have to organize your practices in a logical order that utilizes the entire field. Ideally, the more assistants or parent helpers you have, the more drills you can run at the same time with their help, and the smoother your practices will go. If you don't have much help, adjust your sessions and reduce the number of drills you have going at once so you can closely monitor what's taking place.

Anytime you're designing drills or practice sessions do your best to keep the kids' waiting to a minimum. The less standing-around time the kids have to endure the more fun they'll have.

Outlining your practice plans well before you arrive at the field is crucial for maximizing your usage of time and the field and for giving your kids the best opportunities to learn. In the sections that follow, we present two sample practices — both of which last an hour — that you can run with your team by using the drills we cover in this chapter (as well as those in Chapter 12).

Sample practice #1

5 minutes: Take 5 minutes for your warm-up period (flip to Chapter 16 to get the rundown on all the different stretches your kids should perform). The older your kids, the more important it is that they properly stretch all their major muscles. They shouldn't suffer needless injuries because you skip the warm-up period.

15 minutes: You can run Infield/Outfield practice for your infielders and outfielders, which allows them to get plenty of work on their fielding and throwing skills in a short amount of time. Off to the side, have your pitchers and catchers throwing.

20 minutes: Separate your team into groups of four (or close to it) and scatter the groups around the field, where they can perform the Pepper drill. Make sure the groups are spread far enough apart that errant balls won't pose injury risks for other groups. Use a watch or a stopwatch to give each child five minutes in the batter's role.

15 minutes: A great drill you can use to follow the Pepper drill is the Progression Hitting batting tee exercise. Not only does it give the kids a chance to hone their swings, but also involves the rest of the team. Players can work on their defensive skills when a teammate is at bat.

5 minutes: Conclude the practice with a brief cool-down period that includes some light stretching. Thank the players for doing their best and for following instructions.

Sample practice #2

10 minutes: Conduct your warm-up period (check out Chapter 16 for all the warm-up details).

15 minutes: Start with some old drills that the kids enjoy and that have been paying dividends in their development. For example, you can conduct the Strike Challenge in outfield foul territory; this drill helps your young pitchers learn to find the strike zone with their pitches (see Chapter 12). At the home-plate area, you can conduct the Find the Foul Ball drill for your catchers (see Chapter 12); you can use the infield for a Base-Throw challenge for your first and second basemen and shortstops (see Chapter 12); your third basemen can work on the Find the Pop Up drill (see Chapter 12); and you can test the outfielders with the Fly-Ball Frenzy drill (see Chapter 12).

Avoid filling your entire practice with all new drills, unless you're coaching an older team that you know will adapt quickly to your instructions. Of course, even with younger kids, during the first practice of the season every drill you introduce will be new to them. Just be sure to keep in mind that most of your practice time should feature the kids playing rather than listening to you explaining different drills.

15 minutes: For your shortstop, first basemen, and second basemen, you can conduct the Speedy Double Plays drill. Call your third basemen and catchers to work on the Ground-Ball Mania drill (which we discuss in Chapter 12).

When we introduce the Ground-Ball Mania drill in Chapter 12, we explain that the third baseman fields the ball and makes the throw to first base. Because the first basemen are occupied with the Speedy Double Plays drill, you need to make a slight alteration to incorporate the drill in another way. Being an effective practice planner means being able to tweak drills in order to keep your practices running smoothly.

For your outfielders, you can stand in foul territory and hit fly balls for a few minutes, and then you can switch to the Throw Home drill. You should call your third basemen to assume the base-running responsibilities for this drill, and have the catchers assume their normal positions. In a corner of the outfield, your pitchers can practice the Bunt Bonanza drill. You don't need a pitcher's mound to teach them the basics of fielding bunts and making accurate throws.

15 minutes: The Extra Base challenge is a fun way to conclude your practice. Divide your team in half and see which group fares better in the drill.

5 minutes: Conclude with a quick cool-down and team chat. Thank the players for their hard work, and compliment them on the areas where the team is showing improvement. Take this time to let them know about any schedule changes, and remind them about the next practice or game. Conclude with a team cheer and send them on their way!

Part IV
Playing Sound Situational Baseball

"We covered the basics today —
hitting the ball, tying our shoelaces
and why I have hair growing out
of my nose."

In this part . . .

Seeing your players learning and improving as your season progresses will bring a smile to your face, no doubt. But you need to be prepared to adapt to their ever-changing abilities. In this part, we cover the different plays, situations, and strategies you'll need to know. We offer a chapter on offensive strategies that will take your run-producing abilities to the next level, and we offer a chapter on defensive strategies that will upgrade your run-stopping capabilities.

Chapter 14

Coaching Offense 101

- -

In This Chapter

▶ Coaching good situational hitters

▶ Teaching how to run the bases in all situations

▶ Becoming your players' eyes and ears from the coaching boxes

- -

Collecting hits and scoring runs are some of the most popular elements of baseball in your kids' eyes. Teaching them the fundamentals of offense is one of your core responsibilities as a coach. However, teaching them offensive strategy — at the plate and on the bases — helps them become more proficient players and allows them to enjoy the game more. Plus, sound fundamentals coupled with thoughtful strategy generate more run-scoring opportunities!

In this chapter, we look at the best ways to help your players get on base, and we show them how to be aggressive on the base paths after they get there. We also cover the basics of base coaching so you and your assistants can be part of the action. Being successful in these areas creates opportunities for your team to break down the opposition. (The information in this chapter builds on the offensive fundamentals to make your kids and your team better.)

Becoming a Tough Out at the Plate

Good hitters understand that being successful at the plate requires more than simply being able to hold a bat properly and produce a level swing. Yes, hitting fundamentals are crucial — without them, players have little chance of reaching base often. The key to consistent success, though, is combining hitting fundamentals (which we cover in Chapter 9) with situational hitting elements, such as working pitch counts and handling the bat while handcuffed with two strikes. Implementing the situational facets of the offensive game, which we cover in the following sections, allows your youngsters to reach base safely a little more often. And more time on base equals more fun!

Stalking the pitcher in the on-deck circle

The on-deck circle is much more than a place for hitters to await their turns at bat and to chat up parents and teammates. (Check out Chapter 3 for more on the layout of the field.) When used properly, the on-deck circle helps your youngsters prepare for their trips to the plate and increases their chances of getting on base. Here are some tips to share with your players to help them get the most out of their time in the on-deck circle:

✔ **Get loose.** Players should take time in the on-deck circle to loosen up the muscles that they'll use to swing the bat. This is especially important on cooler days when muscles have a tendency to stiffen up, and for players who enter the game off the bench. Players can get loose by swinging a couple of bats at once; or they can use *donuts*, which are disks shaped like that breakfast favorite that slip over the bat to give the player extra weight to swing.

✔ **Be safe.** Never allow a player to stand in the on-deck circle without a batting helmet on.

A good team rule to enforce is that no player is allowed out of the dugout without a batting helmet on when your team is up at the plate.

✔ **Recognize the game situation.** The on-deck circle is a great place for your players to compose themselves and analyze what's unfolding in the game so they'll be better prepared to deliver what your team needs. For example, if you have a runner on third base and no outs, the player should be thinking about getting the ball out of the infield to get the run in.

✔ **Watch the pitcher.** The on-deck circle provides a great vantage point for gauging the speed and location of the pitcher's throws. Encourage your players to pay close attention to the pitcher's release point, which will help them zero in on the ball quicker when they step to the plate. Also, have them take their normal stances and execute full swings as if they're hacking at pitches from the batter's box so they can adjust to the speed of the pitches.

Encourage your players to share what they learn during their at-bats with their teammates in the dugout. Even if a player fails to get on base, he can help his teammates fare better on their trips to the plate. For example, say a youngster grounds out on the first pitch of his second at-bat, and he notices that each time the pitcher threw him a changeup on the first pitch. He can alert his teammates to this tendency, which prepares them to be on the lookout for that pitch. With all your players paying attention to the pitcher, you have many resources for comparison.

Developing your hitters' attitudes

Teaching your kids to make good decisions in the batter's box not only pays off in the form of hits and walks, but also safety and confidence. One of the biggest challenges you face is molding your hitters' attitudes at the plate. They need to know that different situations call for different hitting styles, and that every at-bat won't produce a heroic hit or exciting play. Keep the following pointers in mind when you're teaching your kids how to be successful in the batter's box:

- **Taking strikes is okay.** Kids have a tendency to think that they screwed up by not swinging at pitches that the umpire calls strikes, which isn't the case at all. You should applaud your players' patience and good eyes for taking pitches they aren't comfortable swinging at. (See the following section for tips on when taking pitches is good practice.)

- **A walk can be as good as a hit.** A walk is good for your offense; it just isn't nearly as exciting for the kids. You should constantly remind your players that getting on base — regardless of how they do it — benefits the entire team. Your players can capitalize on a pitcher's control struggles if they can curb some of their enthusiasm for swinging the bat.

- **Never take one for the team.** Certain fearless players on your team may let pitches hit them without trying to get out of the way so they can advance to first base. This is a big no-no. Advise all your players to dodge wild pitches any way they can. You can't risk injury to your players just to produce runs.

- **Don't assume failure against tough pitchers.** Hitting a baseball is tough enough as it is, but if a pitcher is throwing flaming fastballs, your kids may have even more trouble making contact. You can help your players fare better by having them move several inches back in the batter's box. Making this slight adjustment gives your kids an extra split-second to locate and react to the pitches.

    Likewise, against pitchers who throw slower or throw many off-speed pitches, have them inch up in the box so there is less time for the ball to spin and dart in different directions.

Working pitch counts

Enlarging and shrinking the strike zone is a big part of being a successful hitter. And what your players consider balls and strikes should depend on the counts they have against them. Use the following guidelines to help your players gain a command of different pitch counts they'll face:

- **The first pitch:** Because the count is even at 0-0 when the hitter steps to the plate, neither the hitter nor the pitcher has an advantage. Some coaches advocate hitters taking the first pitch. The theory is that they want the pitcher to prove he can throw a strike before the hitter starts to swing the bat. However, other coaches believe that if the pitcher delivers a toss that the hitter likes and can put a good swing on, the hitter shouldn't take the pitch and put himself in an 0-1 hole. (See Chapter 2 for more information on developing a coaching philosophy that works for you and your team.) Many other factors go into the approach you teach your players for dealing with the first pitch. For example, some players are more aggressive and like swinging at the first pitch because they may not fare as well when the pressure is on with one or two strikes against them. How the opposing pitcher is throwing that day also dictates strategy. If you've noticed that the pitcher is struggling with his control in the later innings and may be tiring, encourage your players to take some pitches, even if they're good first-pitch hitters.

When your players step into the batter's box during practice, have them visualize and develop a strike zone in which they're comfortable swinging the bat. If the pitcher puts the ball in that zone on the first pitch during a game, the hitter can take a whack at it. If the pitch misses the hitter's comfort zone, he can lay off the pitch and gain an advantage if the umpire calls it a ball. If the umpire calls it a strike, the hitter still has plenty of time to deal with other pitches.

✔ **Behind in the count:** The general rule when the batter is behind in the count — such as 0-1, 0-2, or 1-2 — is that he should go on the defensive and widen his strike zone to protect the plate. In this situation, batters don't have the luxury of waiting for pitches in the specific locations that suit them best. Instead, they should swing at anything close to the strike zone. Most coaches prefer aggressive players who go down swinging over players who take pitches and hope the umpires don't call out strike three. (See the following section for tips on when players benefit from choking up and protecting the plate.)

✔ **Ahead in the count:** When the hitter is ahead in the count — such as 1-0, 2-0, 2-1, and 3-1 — he can go on the passive offensive. In other words, he can be much more selective about the type of pitch that he wants to swing at. When the count is in his favor, a hitter can afford to let a pitch go by for a strike if it isn't exactly what he wants. However, if the pitch gets his attention because of its great location, he can take an aggressive crack at it (see Chapter 9 for more on teaching the fundamentals of hitting).

✔ **3-0:** With this count, the hitter is completely in the driver's seat. Whenever the hitter has this advantage, he should look for a specific pitch in a specific spot. If he gets it, chances are pretty good that he'll put a good swing on it — and hopefully make solid contact. If he doesn't get the exact pitch he's looking for, he holds off and lets the ball go by. Even if it's a strike he's still got the advantage, because the pitcher is still behind in the count. Many coaches, however, advocate automatically taking a 3-0 pitch because the chances for a walk are so high (and to keep over-aggressive hitters from swinging at a potential ball four).

Have your upcoming hitters pay close attention to a pitcher's control. If the pitcher walks a batter — especially on four straight pitches — he may be struggling with his control. Your hitters can use this knowledge to their advantage. For instance, the next batter may want to take a pitch or two so he can gain the count advantage. (Check out the "Stalking the pitcher in the on-deck circle" sidebar in this chapter for more observation and preparation tips.)

Protecting the plate

In many game situations, such as when a hitter is down 0-2 or 1-2 in the count (see the previous section), your players need to swing at any pitch close (within a couple of inches) to the strike zone. By protecting the plate this way, they give themselves a chance to put the ball in play, and they avoid being called out on strikes.

A batter with two strikes should also choke up on the bat, or slide his hands up the handle a couple of inches (for more on the topic, see Chapter 9). Choking up takes away some of a player's power, but in exchange, he gains more control of the bat, which is a great trade-off when the hitter needs to focus on simply getting the bat on the ball and putting it into play.

 During your hitting time in practice sessions, make sure your youngsters implement a specific number of choked-up and shortened swings to simulate game situations. When your players become comfortable with these swings, they'll be able to transfer them over to game day.

Sacrificing to produce runs

When your team is involved in a close game, the littlest things often make the biggest difference. A team's ability to sacrifice outs in exchange for runs fits into the category of "littlest things." The two most common sacrifices are the sacrifice bunt and the sacrifice fly. (See Chapter 9 for techniques on bunting and for info on scoring on sacrifice flies, or tagging up.)

The sacrifice bunt

With the *sacrifice bunt,* your goal is to sacrifice an out at first base in order to move runners into scoring position. Sacrifices can be a good weapon when you have runners on first, first and second, or second. (Chapter 9 provides a how-to on the bunting basics.)

In beginning-level leagues, you won't need to use the sacrifice bunt — just let your players swing away and have fun. But with more-advanced players, or more-advanced leagues, you can use the sacrifice to your advantage in the following situations:

✔ **Against a great pitcher:** When you're facing a really talented pitcher, runs may be hard to come by. But when you do get some runners on base, you can use the sacrifice bunt to move up the runners and maximize your chances of scoring.

✔ **In the late innings of a close game:** In a tightly contested game, one run may be the difference between winning and losing. You can use the sacrifice bunt to scoot up the base runners and set up a potential game-winning hit.

✔ **When a struggling hitter is up with runners on base:** If one of your hitters is slumping at the plate, sometimes making a positive play such as putting down a good sacrifice bunt can do wonders for his confidence — not to mention help the team win the game.

✔ **When a good bunter is at the plate.** Your players don't have to sport .400 averages to be a threat at the plate. Encourage players to work on their bunting skills and continually stress this important aspect of the game. If all your players become proficient in this aspect of the game, even players with lower batting averages than their teammates can make big contributions in clutch situations by laying down a bunt.

The sacrifice fly

If you have a runner on third base with fewer than two outs — especially in a close game in the late innings — you may ask your hitter to do his best to hit a sacrifice fly. A *sacrifice fly* occurs when a fly ball is hit, the runner on base tags up (see Chapter 9), a defender catches the ball, and the runner dashes for home. The hitter's prime responsibility is getting the ball into the outfield so the runner has the best chance to reach home. In this situation, you'll gladly trade an out with a sacrifice fly for a run (although runners can move from first to second or second to third on a fly ball as well).

Executing a sacrifice fly requires a swing modification to make sure the ball gets airborne. To deliver a sacrifice fly, your hitter must use a slight uppercut to hit underneath the ball. Before asking youngsters to deliver fly balls in game situations, try working on this skill in practice, having each child take several swings where he tries to hit a fly ball to the outfield.

Wreaking Havoc on the Base Paths

When it comes to base running, many different components combine to impact how successful a team can be. A team that produces at the plate but is inefficient on the bases won't score nearly as many runs as a team that understands how to benefit from certain situations, uses steals to its advantage, and recognizes the best times be more aggressive by taking extra bases, among other areas. In this section, you can find the information and advice you need to turn your players into savvy runners on the base paths (for tips on teaching the base-running basics, head to Chapter 9).

Practicing situational base running

Base running seems like an easy skill to master on the surface — just run from base to base, right? — but it's actually a tricky skill that takes concentration and plenty of practice to master. Therefore, you need to spend plenty of practice time on the skills we cover in the following pages. To be good base runners, your kids need to understand the following general ideas that apply to running from any base:

- **Know the situation.** A base runner who doesn't know the situation — such as the number of outs and whether he can be forced out at a base, for example — will be as effective as a painter without a brush. Remind kids to keep their concentration on the game to avoid committing those costly base-running blunders that can wipe out an inning.

  Let runners know that they must run with two outs, whether the batter puts the ball in the air or on the ground.

- **Watch for line drives.** Instruct your base runners to freeze on line drives to assess the situation. If the balls go through the infield or hit the outfield grass, they should hustle on to the next bases. If defenders catch the line drives, they need to scramble back to their original bases.

- **Tracking pop flies.** Determining when to advance on a pop fly, and when to stay put and tag up, are some of the toughest decisions base runners have to make. Compounding the challenge is parents and spectators in the stands yelling at runners to "go" when they should be staying put, and vice versa. To counteract these conflicting messages, stress to players the importance of listening to their first and third base coaches and ignoring all the other voices in the stands.

- **Be on the alert for wild pitches.** Wild pitches, or those that escape the catcher's grasp, are as good as a base hit because they allow the runners to move up a base — as long as he's paying attention. However, you must make sure your league allows runners to advance in this situation. (See Chapter 2 for more on finding out about your league's rules.)

- **Watch (and listen to) your base coaches.** Remind your players to watch for, and listen to, the instructions provided by the first and third base coaches. They're out there for a reason, which is to help direct the kids and let them know when to advance another base, when to hold up, and when to slide to avoid being tagged out, among many other reasons. (See the section "Coaching Your Runners on the Bases" for more.)

- **Stay away from the ball.** One of the main ingredients of sound base running is knowing where the ball is at all times. This principle is especially important on ground balls and line drives, because players need to be aware that if the ball touches them they are out.

Remind your players to tag up on any pop up in foul territory because the only way they can advance is if a defender catches the ball.

Running from first base

Runners who reach first base need to be aware of several potential situations and their responsibilities in each situation, which the following list details:

- ✔ **Run on a ground ball.** The runner on first must always run on a ground ball.

- ✔ **Try to break up double plays.** A runner can make the execution of a double play much more challenging for the defense by hustling down the base line and sliding into second base. Even if he has little chance to reach it safely, he can force the infielder to avoid his slide, which makes the throw over to first base a little more difficult. That may be all it takes to help the batter reach first base safely. (See Chapter 9 for sliding tips.)

  Make sure your kids slide straight into second base. Even though Major Leaguers aim for the infielder, you don't want to risk injury to either of the young players involved.

- ✔ **Decide what to do on a fly ball (with fewer than two outs).** On nearly every fly ball that sails to the outfield, the runner should move about halfway toward second base — only about a third of the way on fly balls to right field — and position himself so that he can clearly see the player trying to make the catch. If the defender catches the ball, the runner should quickly scramble back to first. If the ball drops in, the runner should advance.

Running from second base

When a player reaches second base, he's in *scoring position,* or in a prime position to score a run. Here are some tips you should relay to your players for when they occupy second base:

- ✔ **Watch the ground balls.** When first base is empty, the runner on second can be selective on whether he wants to advance or not. A good rule of thumb goes as follows: If the ball is hit at the runner or to his left, he should try to take third base; if the ball is hit to his right, he should wait to make sure it gets through the infield before advancing. If first base is occupied, the runner should head straight for third base.

- ✔ **Decide what to do on a fly ball (with fewer than two outs).** On fly balls hit to left field or shallow center field, the runner on second should move about a third of the way to third base and position himself so that he can see the player trying to make the catch. If the defender catches the ball, the runner should quickly scramble back to second. If the ball drops in, the runner should advance to third while keeping his eye on his third base coach.

  On balls hit to right field and deep center field, the runner on second should tag up and watch his third base coach for instruction.

Running from third base

Runners who occupy third base are tantalizingly close to scoring, so smart base running here is critical to your team. Go over the following points with your runners during practice:

- **Decide what to do on a fly ball (with fewer than two outs).** On any fly ball hit to the outfield, the runner on third should immediately tag up. With the help of his trusty third base coach (see Chapter 9), he decides whether to try to score when the defender makes a play on the ball.

- **Heading home on ground balls.** Scoring on infield ground balls is dictated, to a large degree, by how aggressive you want your players to be on the bases. A general rule is that runners advance home on balls hit to the right side of second base, simply because by the time the ball reaches the first or second baseman, they usually can't throw home in time to nab the base runner. Or, with good base runners, you can instruct them to run on contact. Be aware that a hard-hit ball to the third baseman may produce a throw home, so your players must look to get a good jump and be ready to slide into home.

- **Watching for wild pitches.** Smart base runners take advantage of every opportunity to advance, and wild pitches present great chances to score easy runs — if the player pays attention to where the ball is at all times. When the ball gets by the catcher, the base runner should be on the move forward. You want your players to be aggressive on the base paths, but you want to avoid making an out at home plate trying to score on a wild pitch with fewer than two outs, because even a sacrifice fly or infield ground ball may get him home. (Make sure you first check out your league's rules on advancing on wild pitches.)

Stealing bases

Teams that can steal bases effectively pose all sorts of problems for the opposition. Even the threat of stealing a base — without even actually attempting it — can cause major disruptions for the other team.

Make sure you know your league's rules regarding stealing. Nearly all leagues for kids 12 years old and younger require base runners to wait until the ball crosses home plate before they can take off. (If you'd like more info on stealing bases with leadoffs, Joe Morgan, one of the great base stealers of all time, provides lots of sage advice in *Baseball For Dummies*.)

The following list presents some tips for coaches regarding base stealing; if your league allows it, make sure you cover the strategy thoroughly during your practice time:

- **Adjust for the hitter.** It usually isn't good baseball strategy to have a base runner attempt to steal with two outs with a good hitter up at the plate. You're often better off letting the hitter try to knock in the run with a base hit rather than risk the runner being thrown out to end the inning. When good hitters step into the batter's box, you don't want to take away their chances to drive in runs.

- **Be mindful of the scoreboard.** You shouldn't attempt to steal bases when your team is comfortably ahead. Doing so is a real sign of poor sportsmanship. Even if the strength of your team is running, you should ease off the accelerator when going against a weaker opponent.

  Of course, even if your team is trailing by a bunch of runs, attempting to steal usually isn't worth the risk. In this situation, you're looking to patch together several hits to get a rally going. Having a player move up one base usually won't make that much of a difference.

- **Know your players.** Don't expect your slower players to be able to steal bases, so refrain from sending them too often. But with your faster players, you can be more aggressive and have them steal more often.

Challenging outfielders' arms

Evaluate an opponent's outfielders in order to know which ones possess strong and accurate arms and which ones you may be able to take advantage of. Your base coaches can use this scouting information to make decisions on sending runners. During pre-game warm-ups, keep an eye on the other team to get a sense of how strong the players' arms are. (You can have an assistant or parent do the scouting if you're too busy.) You also can pay attention to their throws during the early innings of the game. Even a routine fly ball can provide you with valuable information.

Coaching Your Runners on the Bases

Most youth baseball programs allow teams to have first and third base coaches, which is a real benefit for the kids and coaches. A base coach can relay valuable feedback and instruction in all different areas of the game, from offense to defense. Be sure the coaches you choose to man the base paths understand the situational base-running basics we outline in the section "Practicing situational base running" earlier in this chapter. The following sections discuss the roles and responsibilities of these coaching positions.

Sending them around: First base coach

The first base coach's responsibilities aren't nearly as complex as those required of the third base coach. Although the head coach usually coaches third base, many teams employ one of the players as the first base coach. (This often is the player who was the last batter in the previous inning.) Despite the second-class base coach status, the first base coach's duties are quite varied. The following list gives you a rundown:

✔ **Cheerleader:** When a player hits a ground ball in the infield, the first base coach provides vocal encouragement for the youngster to hustle down the first-base line. A player who hears positive encouragement is likely to have a little extra spring in his step as he sprints toward the bag.

✔ **Informant:** He lets a runner on first know how many outs your team has. Most kids lose track of the number of outs amid all the excitement of game day. When you have two outs, the coach reminds the player to run hard as soon as the batter makes contact; with fewer than two outs, he reminds him to sprint on a ground ball, freeze on a line drive, and go a certain distance on a fly ball (halfway on a ball to the outfield, a few steps in the infield, for example).

✔ **Director:** The first base coach gives information to hitters based on the nature of the hits:

• **Base hit:** He points toward second base while giving instructions to round first base. He reminds the player to keep his eye on the ball so that he can advance to second if the outfielder mishandles it.

• **Extra-base hit:** If he thinks the ball is an extra-base hit, he continues pointing and tells the batter to go to second before he nears first base so he continues to sprint around the bag.

Asking an injured player to coach first base is a great way to keep him involved in the game and feeling like a contributing member of the team. Just make sure that he understands his responsibilities and is wearing a batting helmet to protect against foul balls.

Bringing 'em home: Third base coach

Third base is where all the action takes place from a coach's perspective. A third base coach must make all sorts of split-second decisions that often shape the game's outcome. At most levels, the head coach handles the third base coaching responsibilities, because it allows him to be close to the action and interact easily with all the players. The following list gives you a look at the third base coach's duties:

✔ **Serves as the runner's eyes.** Because base runners who are heading to second base or coming into third base don't know what's happening behind them, they rely heavily on the third base coach to make all the decisions for them.

✔ **Sends runners who are tagging up.** On fly balls, he alerts the runner to get in position to tag up and lets him know when to head for home. (Check out Chapter 9 for more details on tagging up.)

✔ **Gives signals to batters and runners.** At the advanced levels of play, he uses signals, or signs, to let batters and base runners know to use a specific play, such as a sacrifice bunt. (See Chapter 7 for more on signs.)

✔ **Informs players about game situations.** For example, if the team is trailing by a run in the last inning with no outs, he lets a runner on third know not to be too aggressive and risk being thrown out on a hard-hit infield grounder directly at a player.

✔ **Makes quick decisions.** When you're standing in the third base coaching box, you don't have the luxury of time. You have no room to hesitate on whether to send a runner home or hold him up at third base.

Because you must make decisions in the blink of an eye, you can help yourself — and your players — by anticipating the play before it unfolds. For example, if you have a runner on second base and one out, start thinking about what you'll have the runner do if the batter hits the ball to left field, center field, or right field, based on your evaluations of the other team (see the section "Challenging outfielders' arms") and your players (see Chapter 5). If you notice the right fielder playing deeper than usual, you may want to send the runner home on a base hit in the fielder's direction. If you know the left fielder has a strong throwing arm, you may not want to challenge him on a base hit in his direction. Other factors to take into account are the game situation and who's up next in your lineup.

Chapter 15

Coaching Defense 101

. . . .

In This Chapter

▶ Playing smart in the field when the ball is in play

▶ Taking advantage of defensive strategies before the pitch

. . . .

Because your players will spend roughly half of every game in the field, knowing the ins and outs of playing good defense carries special importance. At first, collecting base hits and scoring runs may seem like the only glamorous parts of the game to many kids. After all, isn't defense just standing around and waiting for a ball hit your way? But after they develop a good understanding of all the intricacies of playing defense — above and beyond the basics of fielding grounders and catching fly balls — they'll gain just as much satisfaction from sniffing out an opponent's bunt opportunity and shutting out an opposing offense.

In this chapter, we dig into some of the most common strategic elements of defensive baseball — executing responsibilities on all batted balls, utilizing the cutoff man, fielding bunts with set plays, and adjusting positions based on the situation — and we give you the scoop on teaching these elements to your players.

Getting Defensive After the Ball Is in Play

Some days, your team will run into pitchers who shut you down and make base hits as rare as winning lottery tickets. That's just the nature of the game, and you can't control it. However, what you do have control over is how your team handles *its* responsibilities in the field.

The kids who excel in the field don't always have the strongest arms or the quickest feet. Sure, those abilities help, but one of the most underrated and important elements of good defensive play is preparation. A player should know what he's going to do in every situation before it occurs, and then execute his responsibility after the ball is put in play. A fielder should ask himself questions about where he should be if the ball gets hit to left field, or what his role is if the ball gets knocked into right field, for example. Kids who know where they're supposed to be as soon as the ball hits the bat will make it much more difficult for the opposing team to generate runs.

The sections and diagrams that follow, which illustrate defensive movement and cutoff men, don't really apply to T-ballers. These five- and six-year-olds usually all make a mad dash for every ball hit in play and end up in a big scrum fighting for the ball. With these guys, try to stress the concept that they should stick near their positions and field only the balls hit close to them. The only cutoff man you may want to use is an assistant coach to "cut off" any youngster who's had too many post-game snacks!

For the plays involving cutoffs, you want the cutoff man situated where he can receive the outfielder's throw on the fly. Through lots of repetitions in practice, your infielders will get a good gauge of each outfielder's arm and where they need to be positioned to receive throws from them.

In the following sections, we outline the basic responsibilities of each player in the field on singles, doubles, triples, and dying pop ups to the shallow outfield. By reviewing these duties with your players, you'll prepare them to know exactly what to do in any situation.

A main theme you'll notice in these sections is backing up other players. Backing up throws is one of the cornerstones of good — make that great — defensive play. If you can get your players in the habit of backing up their teammates, you can keep the damage caused by wild throws to a minimum. On the other hand, if you don't emphasize this aspect of the game — and many coaches don't give it the attention it deserves — you open the door for the opposition to run wild on throws that miss their marks.

Here's a quickie guide to the symbols and arrows in the diagrams in this section:

1B	First baseman
2B	Second baseman
3B	Third baseman
SS	Shortstop

LF	Left fielder
CF	Center fielder
RF	Right fielder
P	Pitcher
C	Catcher
->	Path of batted ball
→	Path of player

Assigning responsibilities on singles

On singles hit to the outfield, cutoff throws are vital for clamping down on runners who may try to take extra bases given the opportunity. (See Chapter 10 for the proper fielding technique). The *cutoff man* is the player who intercepts an outfielder's throw and makes a relay throw to another base. Where the cutoff throw goes depends on the number of base runners and the number of outs in the inning. The following sections outline the many possible scenarios.

Good communication between your players is vital to successful cutoff throws and relays. Because the cutoff man has his back to the infield to receive a throw from the outfield, he needs to hear constant instruction from the intended target so he knows what to do with the ball when he receives it. The cutoff man has three options:

- Let the throw go through
- Cut off the throw and hold the ball
- Cut off the throw and relay it to a base

For example, on plays at the plate, the catcher should yell out where he wants the cutoff man positioned, and then he should make it clear whether he wants the ball cut off, let go, or relayed. If he thinks the throw is strong enough to nab the runner, he can remain silent so the cutoff man knows to let the ball go through. If the catcher yells out "cut home," he wants the cutoff man to intercept the ball, turn around, and throw it home. And if the catcher yells "cut two" or "cut three," he wants the player to cut off the throw from the outfield and relay it to another base. You should devote some time in practice when going over the topics in this section to run through different cutoff scenarios.

Single to left field with the bases empty

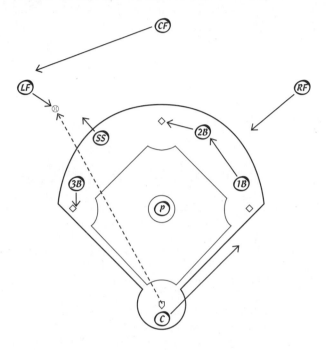

Catcher: Prepares to cover first base in case the runner strays too far from the bag.

Pitcher: Stays near the mound.

First baseman: Backs up a relay throw to second base.

Second baseman: Covers second base.

Shortstop: Handles the cutoff duties for the left fielder. He should set up in a direct line between the left fielder and second base.

Third baseman: Stays near third base in case an error is made and the runner advances.

Left fielder: On a routine base hit, scoops up the ball and throws it to the cutoff man (the shortstop). If he notices that the batter is trying to turn the hit into a double, he should throw the ball directly to the second baseman, if possible.

Center fielder: Backs up the left fielder by running behind him.

Right fielder: Moves to a position behind second base, in the line of the throw from left field, to back up the second baseman in case of a (really) poor throw.

Single to center field with the bases empty

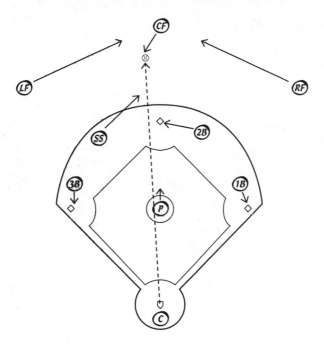

Catcher: Stays near home plate.

Pitcher: Stays near the mound and backs up any errant throws to second base.

First baseman: Covers first base in case the runner strays too far off the base.

Second baseman: Covers second base and takes the throw, either from the outfielder or cutoff man (shortstop)

Shortstop: Serves as cutoff man for the center fielder. He should set up in a direct line between the center fielder and second base.

Third baseman: Covers third base.

Left fielder: Backs up the center fielder.

Center fielder: Fields the ball and throws it to the cutoff man (the shortstop).

Right fielder: Backs up the center fielder.

Single to right field with the bases empty

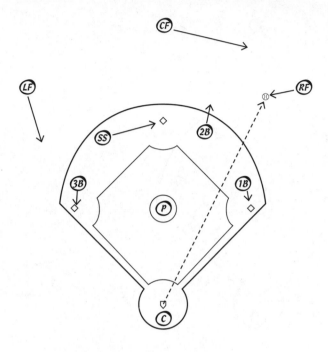

Catcher: Stays near home plate.

Pitcher: Stays near the mound.

First baseman: Covers first base.

Second baseman: Serves as the cutoff man, positioning himself in a direct line between the right fielder and second base.

Shortstop: Covers second base and awaits a throw from right field.

Third baseman: Covers third base.

Left fielder: Moves toward third base to back up the play in case of a (really) bad throw from the right fielder.

Center fielder: Backs up the right fielder.

Right fielder: Fields the ball and throws it to the cutoff man (the second baseman).

Single to left field with a runner on first or runners on first and third

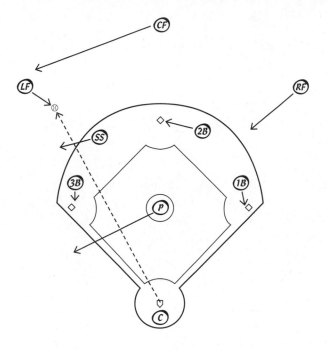

Catcher: Covers home plate.

Pitcher: Backs up third base.

First baseman: Covers first base.

Second baseman: Covers second base.

Shortstop: Positions himself between the left fielder and third base. If the left fielder has a chance to throw out the runner heading to third base and the throw is on line, the shortstop lets it go; if the throw is off target or too late, the shortstop cuts it off.

Third baseman: Covers third base and awaits a possible throw.

Left fielder: Fields the ball and throws it to the cutoff man (the shortstop).

Center fielder: Backs up the left fielder.

Right fielder: Moves in toward the infield to help back up any poor throws.

Single to center field with a runner on first or runners on first and third

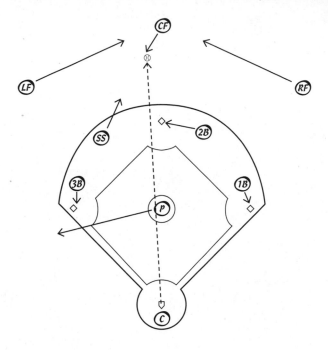

Catcher: Covers home plate.

Pitcher: Backs up third base.

First baseman: Covers first base.

Second baseman: Covers second base.

Shortstop: Lines up for the cutoff throw between the center fielder and third base.

Third baseman: Covers third base and awaits a throw.

Left fielder: Moves toward the infield to help back up the play.

Center fielder: Fields the ball and fires it to the cutoff man (the shortstop).

Right fielder: Backs up the center fielder.

Single to right field with a runner on first or runners on first and third

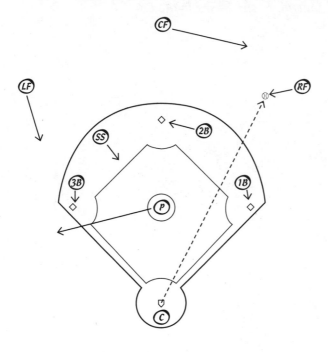

Catcher: Covers home plate.

Pitcher: Backs up third base.

First baseman: Covers first base.

Second baseman: Covers second base.

Shortstop: Lines up between the right fielder and third base to serve as the cutoff man.

Third baseman: Covers third base and awaits a throw.

Left fielder: Moves toward the infield to help back up the play.

Center fielder: Backs up the right fielder.

Right fielder: Fields the ball and throws it to the cutoff man (the shortstop).

Single to left field with a runner on second, runners on first and second, or the bases loaded

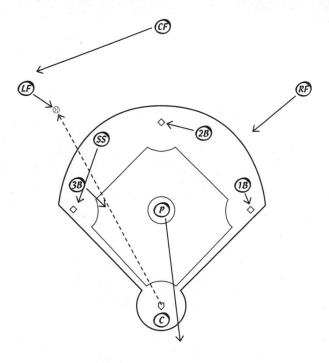

Catcher: Covers home plate and lets the third baseman know to let the ball go through, relay it home, or cut if off and throw to another base.

Pitcher: Backs up home plate.

First baseman: Covers first base.

Second baseman: Covers second base.

Shortstop: Covers third base.

Third baseman: Moves in toward home plate and lines up between the left fielder and the catcher to serve as the cutoff man. He lets the ball go through, relays it to the catcher, or cuts it off and checks to see if he can get a runner out at another base.

Left fielder: Fields the ball and throws it to the cutoff man (the third baseman).

Center fielder: Backs up the left fielder.

Right fielder: Moves toward the infield to back up any potential throws to second base.

Single to center field with a runner on second, runners on first and second, or the bases loaded

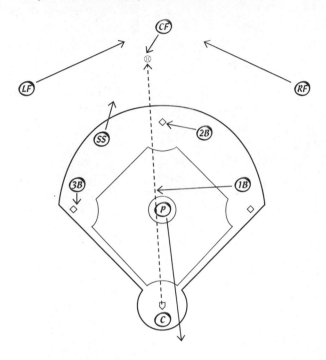

Catcher: Covers home plate and communicates with the first baseman (his respective cutoff man).

Pitcher: Backs up home plate.

First baseman: Moves across the infield and positions himself between the pitcher's mound and second base. You want him nearer to second base to eliminate the chance of the throw hitting the pitching mound and bouncing off target.

Second baseman: Covers second base.

Shortstop: Moves between the center fielder and third base to provide another cutoff option for the center fielder.

Third baseman: Covers third base and communicates with the shortstop (his respective cutoff man).

Left fielder: Moves to back up the center fielder. On his way, he watches what's happening on the bases and lets the center fielder know whether to throw to the first baseman or the shortstop.

Center fielder: Fields the ball and listens for instructions on where to throw the ball.

Right fielder: Backs up the center fielder.

Single to right field with a runner on second, runners on first and second, or the bases loaded

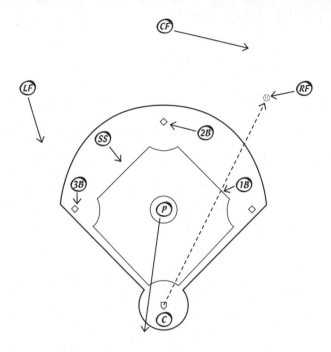

Catcher: Covers home plate and communicates with the first baseman (his respective cutoff man).

Pitcher: Backs up home plate.

First baseman: Lines up between the right fielder and home plate to serve as a cutoff man.

Second baseman: Covers second base.

Shortstop: Positions himself between the right fielder and third base to serve as a cutoff man.

Third baseman: Covers third base and communicates with the shortstop (his respective cutoff man).

Left fielder: Moves toward the infield to help back up the play.

Center fielder: Backs up the right fielder.

Right fielder: Fields the ball and listens for instructions on where to throw the ball.

Making adjustments on potential doubles and triples

Uncaught balls that are hit between — and past — your outfielders force your defense to react quickly. Getting the ball back to the infield swiftly helps keep opposing runners from advancing extra bases. Typically, these types of hits are doubles — and sometimes triples — for the batter. These sections outline the ballet of motion that your players go through on balls hit down the foul lines and into the *gaps*, the outfield areas between the left fielder and center fielder and between the right fielder and center fielder.

Ball hit to the left field corner with the bases empty or with runners on base

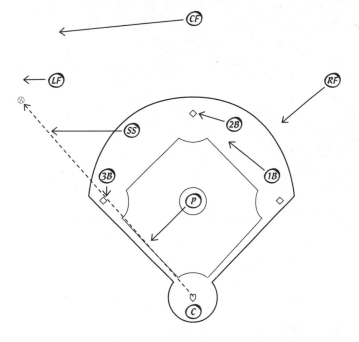

Catcher: Covers home plate.

Pitcher: Backs up third base.

First baseman: Backs up potential throws to second base.

Second baseman: Covers second base.

Shortstop: Goes out into shallow left field and positions himself along the foul line between the left fielder and third base to serve as the cutoff man.

Third baseman: Covers third base and communicates with the cutoff man (the shortstop).

Left fielder: Runs at an angle to track down the ball, then turns and throws to his cutoff man (the shortstop).

Center fielder: Backs up the left fielder.

Right fielder: Moves toward the infield to help back up the play.

Ball hit to the right field corner with the bases empty

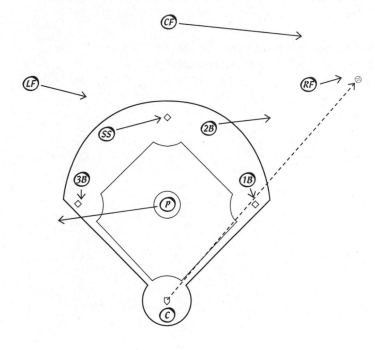

Catcher: Covers home plate.

Pitcher: Backs up third base.

First baseman: Stays near first base.

Second baseman: Moves out into shallow right field and positions himself between the right fielder and third base to serve as the cutoff man.

Shortstop: Covers second base.

Third baseman: Covers third base and communicates with the cutoff man (the shortstop).

Left fielder: Moves toward the infield to help back up a throw to second base.

Center fielder: Backs up the right fielder.

Right fielder: Runs at an angle to track down the ball, then turns and throws to his cutoff man (the second baseman).

Ball hit to the right field corner with runners on base

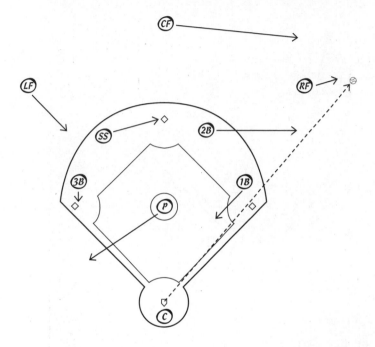

Catcher: Covers home plate.

Pitcher: Runs to the outside of the base path between third base and home. As the play evolves, he runs to back up the necessary base (either third base or home).

First baseman: Moves in toward home plate and positions himself between the right fielder and home plate as the second cutoff man.

Second baseman: Moves out into shallow right field and positions himself between the right fielder and home plate to serve as the first cutoff man. If he makes a throw home, he aims it toward the cutoff man in the infield (the first baseman).

Shortstop: Covers second base.

Third baseman: Covers third base.

Left fielder: Moves toward the infield to help back up the play.

Center fielder: Backs up the right fielder and lets him know which base to throw to.

Right fielder: Runs at an angle to field the ball and listens for instructions on where to throw the ball.

Ball hit to the left center field gap with the bases empty

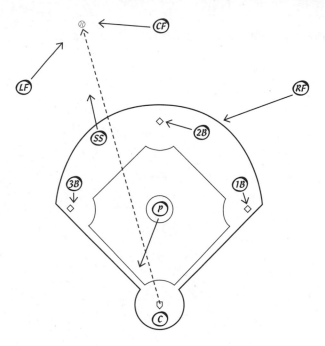

Catcher: Covers home plate.

Pitcher: Backs up third base.

First baseman: Stays near first base.

Second baseman: Covers second base.

Shortstop: Moves out to the outfield and positions himself between the outfielder making the throw — either the center fielder or left fielder — and second or third base to serve as the cutoff man.

Third baseman: Covers third base.

Left fielder: Runs at an angle to track down the ball and communicates with the center fielder to decide who should field the ball. Makes the throw to the cutoff man if he fields the ball.

Center fielder: Runs at an angle to track down the ball and communicates with the left fielder to decide who should field the ball. Makes the throw to the cutoff man if he fields the ball.

Right fielder: Moves toward the infield to back up any throw to second base.

Ball hit to the right center field gap with the bases empty

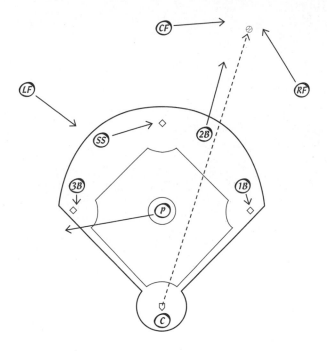

Catcher: Covers home plate.

Pitcher: Backs up third base.

First baseman: Stays near first base.

Second baseman: Moves out to the outfield and lines up between the outfielder making the throw — either the center fielder or right fielder — and second or third base to serve as the cutoff man.

Shortstop: Covers second base.

Third baseman: Covers third base.

Left fielder: Moves toward the infield to back up any throw to second base.

Center fielder: Runs at an angle to track down the ball and communicates with the right fielder to decide who should field the ball. Makes the throw to the cutoff man if he fields the ball.

Right fielder: Runs at an angle to track down the ball and communicates with the center fielder to decide who should field the ball. Makes the throw to the cutoff man if he fields the ball.

Ball hit to the left center field gap with runners on base

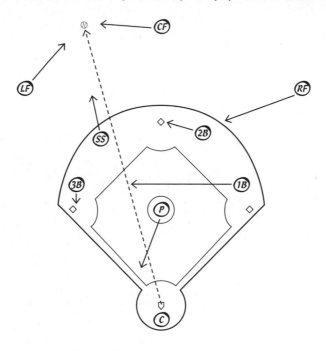

Catcher: Covers home plate.

Pitcher: Moves between third base and home. As the play evolves, he runs to back up the necessary base (either third base or home).

First baseman: Moves across the infield and positions himself between the shortstop and home plate to serve as a secondary cutoff man.

Second baseman: Covers second base.

Shortstop: Moves out into shallow left center field and positions himself between the outfielder making the throw — either the left fielder or center fielder — and home plate to serve as the cutoff man. He can go to second base, third base, or home with a throw.

Third baseman: Covers third base.

Left fielder: Runs at an angle to track down the ball and communicates with the center fielder to decide who should field the ball. Makes the throw to the cutoff man if he fields the ball.

Center fielder: Runs at an angle to track down the ball and communicates with the left fielder to decide who should field the ball. Makes the throw to the cutoff man if he fields the ball.

Right fielder: Moves toward the infield to back up any throw to second base.

Ball hit to the right center field gap with runners on base

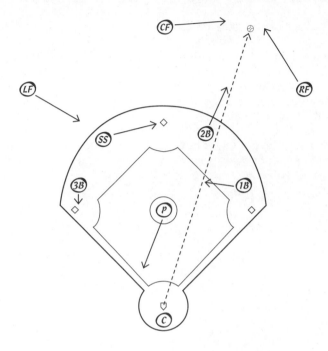

Catcher: Covers home plate.

Pitcher: Moves between third base and home. As the play evolves, he runs to back up the necessary base (either third base or home).

First baseman: Lines up between the second baseman and home plate to provide a cutoff option on a throw to home.

Second baseman: Moves out to shallow right center field and positions himself between the outfielder making the play — either the center or right fielder — and home plate to serve as the cutoff man.

Shortstop: Covers second base.

Third baseman: Covers third base.

Left fielder: Moves toward the infield to back up any throw to second base.

Center fielder: Runs at an angle to track down the ball and communicates with the right fielder to decide who should field the ball. Makes the throw to the cutoff man if he fields the ball.

Right fielder: Runs at an angle to track down the ball and communicates with the center fielder to decide who should field the ball. Makes the throw to the cutoff man if he fields the ball.

Ranging to cover the shallow outfield

Pop flies to the shallow outfield are tough plays because several players must communicate to decide who should try to make the play. Often, balls drop in for hits because of miscommunication among the infielders and outfielders.

If outfielders feel like they can make the catch, they must call for the ball ("I've got it! I've got it!") to tell the other fielders to back off. Likewise, if an infielder is calling for the ball, the outfielder can make the decision to back off, as well. If an infielder and an outfielder are *both* calling for the ball, which happens frequently, the outfielder must *call him off*, or continue calling for the ball until the infielder gives way. Work on this frequently in practice.

Pop fly to shallow left field

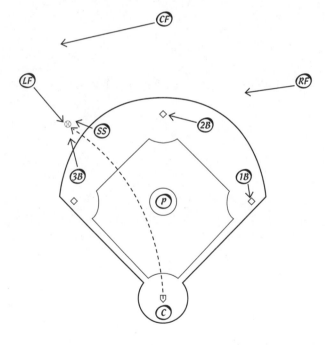

Catcher: Covers home plate.

Pitcher: Stays near the mound.

First baseman: Covers first base.

Second baseman: Covers second base.

Shortstop: Calls for the ball if he thinks he can make the play. Backs off if the left fielder calls for the ball.

Third baseman: Calls for the ball if he thinks he can make the play. Backs off if the shortstop or left fielder calls for the ball.

Left fielder: Calls for the ball if he thinks he can make the play. Infielders *must* yield to him.

Center fielder: Backs up the left fielder.

Right fielder: Moves toward the infield to back up any throw to second base.

Pop fly to shallow center field

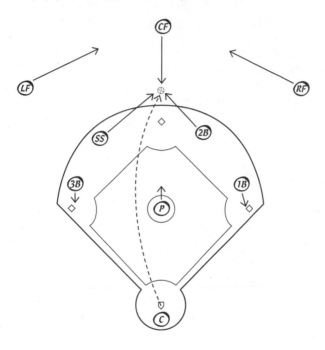

Catcher: Covers home plate.

Pitcher: Stays near the mound.

First baseman: Covers first base.

Second baseman: Calls for the ball if he thinks he can make the play. Backs off if the center fielder or shortstop calls for the ball, and retreats to cover second base.

Shortstop: Calls for the ball if he thinks he can make the play. Backs off if the center fielder or second baseman calls for the ball, and retreats to cover second base.

Third baseman: Covers third base.

Left fielder: Backs up the center fielder.

Center fielder: Calls for the ball if he thinks he can make the play. Infielders *must* yield to him.

Right fielder: Backs up the center fielder.

Pop fly to shallow right field

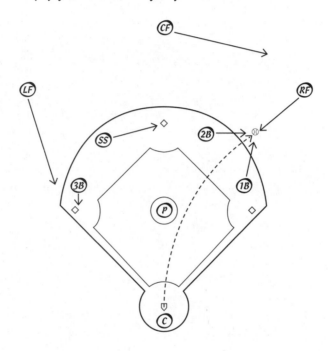

Catcher: Covers home plate.

Pitcher: Stays near the mound.

First baseman: Calls for the ball if he thinks he can make the play. Backs off if the second baseman or left fielder calls for the ball.

Second baseman: Calls for the ball if he thinks he can make the play. Backs off if the right fielder calls for the ball.

Shortstop: Covers second base.

Third baseman: Covers third base.

Left fielder: Moves toward the infield to back up any throw to second base.

Center fielder: Backs up the right fielder.

Right fielder: Calls for the ball if he thinks he can make the play. Infielders *must* yield to him.

Covering sacrifice bunts

An opposing coach may decide to utilize a sacrifice bunt in a close game when his team has a runner on base. With a *sacrifice bunt,* a team gives up an out to advance a runner into scoring position. The most common scenario is laying down a bunt with a runner at first base or with runners on first and second. How your defense handles the bunting situation makes the difference in whether the opposition can produce that valuable run or head to the dugout empty-handed.

Because the most effective bunts roll about halfway down the baselines — just far enough away that the pitcher, catcher, or infielders don't have easy plays on them — your best bet is to be aggressive by rotating your infielders. When you're involved in a tight game, and you expect the opposition to use a sacrifice bunt to move runners, you want your first and third basemen charging toward home plate as the pitch is thrown to field a ball hit in their direction. The following sections show you how, in the form of set sacrifice bunt plays.

On a sacrifice bunt, the defense's top priority is to make sure it gets one out. If a fielder can get the lead runner out, he'll make a big play for the team, but if the bunt is too well-placed, he shouldn't hesitate to settle for the out at first. You don't want your fielders trying to get the lead runner out when they have little chance to do so, because you'll set up the opposition with more runners on base. Be sure to work on your communication skills and decision making on sacrifice bunts during practice. (To find out how to teach *your* players to execute a sacrifice bunt, check out Chapter 9.)

As with all defensive plays, good communication is important for covering bunts. The pitcher, first baseman, and third baseman must coordinate who is going to field the ball by calling for it if they think they can make the play. The catcher plays the field general, yelling out to the fielders where to make the throw.

Sacrifice bunt with a runner on first

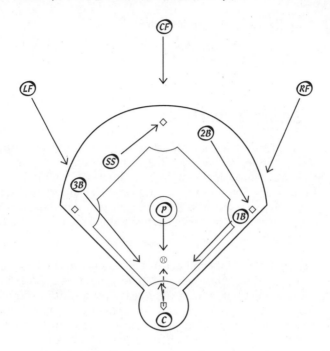

Catcher: Fields the ball if it's bunted close to home plate. If he doesn't field the ball, he tells the infielder or pitcher where to throw.

Pitcher: Charges in to cover the middle of the infield. If he fields the ball, listens to the catcher for instructions on where to throw the ball.

First baseman: Charges in to cover the right side of the infield. If he fields the ball, listens to the catcher for instructions on where to throw the ball.

Second baseman: Covers first base.

Shortstop: Covers second base.

Third baseman: Charges in to cover the left side of the infield. If he fields the ball, listens to the catcher for instructions on where to throw the ball. If he doesn't field the ball, he quickly retreats to cover third base.

Left fielder: Moves toward the infield to back up a throw to third base.

Center fielder: Moves toward the infield to back up a throw to second base.

Right fielder: Moves toward the infield to back up a throw to first base.

Sacrifice bunt with runners on first and second or runner on second

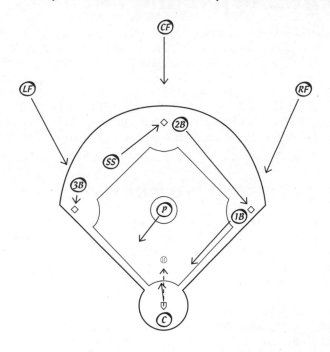

Catcher: Fields the ball if it's bunted close to home plate. If he doesn't field the ball, he tells the infielder or pitcher where to throw.

Pitcher: Charges in to cover the middle and left side of the infield. If he fields the ball, listens to the catcher for instructions on where to throw the ball.

First baseman: Charges in to cover the middle and right side of the infield. If he fields the ball, listens to the catcher for instructions on where to throw the ball.

Second baseman: Covers first base.

Shortstop: Covers second base.

Third baseman: Covers third base.

Left fielder: Moves toward the infield to back up a throw to third base.

Center fielder: Moves toward the infield to back up a throw to second base.

Right fielder: Moves toward the infield to back up a throw to first base.

Shifting Players before the Pitch

One of the fun things about coaching defense on a baseball team is that you can position your players in so many different ways before a pitch is even thrown. You can make minor adjustments, such as sliding players over a couple steps from where they normally play; or you can employ more radical changes, such as moving in players a substantial distance to prevent runs from scoring. These decisions — and when you want to make them — depend on your team's skill level and how the game is unfolding. We cover many of the adjustments you can make before the pitch in the sections that follow.

Moving in close to prevent runs

When your team is barely ahead in a close game or is trailing by a small margin, you simply can't afford to surrender any more runs. Therefore, you may have to resort to unique defensive measures to prevent runs from crossing home plate. One such measure is calling your entire infield closer to home plate when a runner is on third base with fewer than two outs.

To execute the strategy, you simply have every infielder take several steps forward, so that each player is approximately in the base path. In this position, if a ball is hit to an infielder, he'll have a better chance to stop the lead runner from scoring than he would in his normal position. On grounders hit directly at your infielders, they should be looking to throw the runner out at the plate; if they have to range several steps to their left or right to field the ball, their only option, in most cases, will be to throw the ball to first base. In certain situations, such as a tie game in the bottom of the last inning with a runner on third base and fewer than two outs, you'll also want your outfielders to scoot in several steps so they'll be able to make a throw to the plate on a short fly ball.

The biggest drawback of the in-close setup is that routine ground balls that your kids would field easily in their regular spots turn into hits. Your players have far less time to react to the ball when in close. Therefore, you should use this setup only when your team absolutely can't afford to give up a run.

Protecting a lead

The score and the inning dictate many of the decisions you make during games. This is especially true when it comes to protecting a lead late in the game. How you align your defense in the second inning of a two-run game may be drastically different than how you position your players with that same two-run advantage in the bottom of the last inning.

Consider employing the following strategies to ensure that an opposing team doesn't mount a comeback in the late innings of a close game:

- **Guard the lines.** Extra-base hits are rally-starters for the opposition. You can help your defense avoid getting stung by having your first and third basemen take a couple steps toward their respective foul lines next to their bases, so that they're each about a step off the line. Guarding the lines prevents hitters from collecting easy doubles and triples down the lines and getting into scoring position.

- **Retreat your outfielders.** Having your outfielders take a few steps backward prevents many balls from sailing over their heads, which reduces opportunities for extra-base hits. You want your defensive players to keep the ball in front of them at all costs in tight situations.

When you practice two-run (or more) game situations with your players, remind them to keep their attention on the batter rather than a base runner. The run the player on base represents can't hurt your team as long as your defense eliminates the hitters and kills rallies. For example, when the opposition has a runner on base, and a batter hits a ground ball on the infield, you want your players throwing to first base to get the sure out — unless they have an undeniably easy play available to get the lead runner. Big innings can materialize when teams get too greedy on defense.

Dealing with pull hitters

Many hitters, from T-ball to the big leagues, develop the reputation of being pull hitters. A *pull hitter* usually smacks the ball to the same side as his batter's box — a right-handed batter typically hits the ball to the left side, and a left-handed pull hitter goes to the right. After you play a team a few times during the season, you may begin to notice certain tendencies its hitters have that you can exploit on defense.

For instance, you can shift your players to deal with a pull hitter. The shift you use can be minor, such as moving all fielders a couple steps toward third base against a right-handed pull hitter. Or, you can call for a major shift against the same player, with the following moving parts:

- The second baseman moves all the way over to the shortstop side of second base.

- The third baseman hugs his foul line.

- The shortstop moves significantly to his right, in between the second and third basemen.

- All the outfielders move to their right, with the left fielder about five or six steps from the foul line, the center fielder shifted over into left center field, and the right fielder shifted over into right center field.

The only player who stays put in this major shift is the first baseman. Remember, he has to be close enough to cover first base on ground balls to the infield.

Even in the middle of a game against a team you're unfamiliar with, you can employ the shift. For example, if the opposing team's third hitter pulled the ball to left field his first three at-bats, you can give him a minor or major shift the next time he steps to the plate, depending on the game situation. (Check out Chapter 7 for tips on scouting the other team on game day.)

Part V
The Extra Innings

"Someone's got to break it to Mr. Swanzy that his son is just too young to play third base."

In this part . . .

*I*n this part, we offer plenty of information on keeping your players healthy and off the disabled list, and what to do if injury strikes. We also explain how you can effectively deal with some potential coaching headaches — the assorted problems that tend to pop up with players, coaches, parents, and umpires.

Chapter 16

Keeping Your Kids Healthy

• •

In This Chapter

▶ Preparing your team first-aid kit

▶ Helping your kids avoid injuries

▶ Coming to a player's aid in serious situations

▶ Keeping tabs on the weather conditions

▶ Consuming the right foods and liquids

• •

*T*he obvious coaching duties you perform, such as teaching technique, get all the attention from parents and players, but how you handle some of the less obvious aspects of the job often makes or breaks your players' season. Areas such as preventing, recognizing, and treating injuries; dealing with emergency situations; and stepping up to the plate — excuse the pun — to provide pre- and post-game eating tips all impact how much enjoyment the kids have during the season. After all, they can't enjoy baseball if they're hurt or sluggish due to a poor diet.

Don't worry, you don't need to be an expert in the fields of sports medicine or nutrition fields; you just need to have some general knowledge of these areas and how they influence kids' performances on the field. In this chapter, we give you the scoop on important but often overlooked areas of the game. We cover all the bases of keeping your players healthy, from doing what you can to prevent injuries to treating injuries when they occur. We give you some weather-watching basics so you can keep your kids out of harm's way. And we present some diet tips so you can make sure your kids are well-hydrated and energized for practices and games.

Packing Your Game and Practice First-Aid Kit

You probably cringe when you write a monthly check for your car insurance. You hope you'll never need it, but you feel safe knowing that you're covered if an accident happens. The same goes for preparing and toting a first-aid kit.

Sure, it may be a chore to put together, and you don't think you'll ever have to open it up. However, it's reassuring to know that you're prepared if something goes wrong on the field.

Your league may hand out basic first-aid kits to all its coaches, or it may leave the responsibility of first aid up to you. You need to find out about your league's policy before you ever take the field. No matter the policy, never conduct practices or coach games without having a stocked first-aid kit nearby.

What to pack

The following items are the basic materials that should be in every volunteer baseball coach's first-aid kit. You can use a toolbox or any other type of waterproof container to hold the supplies.

- **Antiseptic spray or wipes:** Use these to clean cuts and abrasions.

- **An assortment of bandages:** Use waterproof bandages to cover cuts or other wounds.

- **Athletic tape:** Use the tape to hold ice bags in place to reduce swelling around an injury.

- **Bee-sting kit:** You can pick up a bee-sting kit at your local pharmacy.

- **Cold spray:** Use to help reduce the pain of being hit by a pitch.

- **CPR mouth barrier:** For use in the event that a child needs mouth-to-mouth resuscitation.

- **Emergency tooth-preserving system:** Use when a players' tooth gets knocked out. You can look at a local pharmacy for this too, or you can check with your dentist for recommendations.

- **Freezer-type storage bags:** Plastic storage bags are great for holding ice packs.

- **Insect repellent:** To combat mosquitoes, which can be annoying during evening practices or games.

- **Latex gloves:** You need to wear gloves while dealing with bloody cuts.

- **Nail clippers:** These come in handy for addressing torn nails.

- **Prescriptions:** Make sure you have any prescription medicines that your players may need due to individual conditions. (As we cover in Chapter 4, you need to be aware of any medical conditions youngsters on your team may have. Before the season, find out if any of your players have any medical issues that you need to work with.)

- **Scissors:** You need scissors to cut bandages and athletic tape.

✔ **Sterile eyewash and prepackaged sterile eye pads:** You need these items to remove debris that becomes stuck in a child's eye.

✔ **Tweezers:** Use tweezers to remove any type of debris that becomes lodged in a child's skin.

In Chapter 4, we cover the importance of having parents fill out emergency-notification forms. With these forms, if something happens to a child and his parents aren't at the game or practice, you'll know how to reach them, another family member, or a friend. Keep these forms in a folder with your first-aid kit so you can easily access them in case of an emergency. Also, put any information about your players' personal medical needs in your kit, too, and consider the players' needs when stocking your kit.

How to pack it

Here are some other tips to keep in mind concerning your first-aid kit:

✔ **Stock reasonable amounts.** Be sure your kit contains a reasonable number of items so that you can treat a couple youngsters with the same ailment, if necessary.

✔ **Track your supplies.** You never want to be caught without the necessary supplies. When you must use an item in your kit to treat a youngster, restock the item before the next practice or game.

✔ **Be organized.** Clearly mark your supplies so you can easily identify what you need right away, and have some type of order so you don't have to dig around in your kit to find supplies. During an injury timeout, you may have to comfort an injured child, and an assistant may need to grab an item out of the kit. Being able to tell him the exact location of the item saves valuable time.

Plastic storage bags work great for keeping your supplies in order inside your first-aid kid, and you can write on them to help with easy identification.

Putting Prevention at Leadoff: Taking Steps to Avoid Injuries

All kids who step onto the field — from outstanding pitchers to role-playing infielders — are susceptible to injuries. Although eliminating the threat of injuries that may occur during practices and games is impossible, you can take steps to help reduce the chances of an injury disrupting a child's season.

A sound stretching and warm-up regimen — both before and after games and practices — goes a long way toward enhancing your kids' flexibility and providing added protection against unwanted aches and pains.

During your first few practices of the season, don't run your players ragged — regardless of what age level or ability you're coaching — until you can gauge what kind of condition they're in. Gradually work them up to more strenuous activity; by taking your time, you give their young bodies a chance to acclimate to the physical exertion. (See Chapters 6, 12, and 13 for more information about running a practice.)

Stretching before practices and games

Before every practice or game, your players need to be at the field early enough to stretch out. Enhancing a child's flexibility is essential not only for preventing injuries, but also for creating a solid foundation of strength, balance, and coordination — all important attributes for performing the basic skills of baseball. Having your youngsters go through a variety of stretches and exercises during your pre-practice and pre-game warm-ups prepares them for a successful and injury-free day on the field.

Giving players a chance to lead warm-ups is a great way to inject some fun into the activity, as well as help them gain valuable experience in leadership roles. Before each practice and game, designate a player or two to take positions in front of the team and guide the warm-ups. Don't be surprised to find that many of the kids will really look forward to assuming these roles. Just make sure that you plan these in advance so that every child gets an equal number of opportunities as the warm-up leader.

If you coach younger kids, your warm-ups don't need to be elaborate. You can simply have your players perform some jumping jacks and light running for no longer than five minutes before practices and games. If you're in charge of an advanced squad, however, your players need to do some light running and a wide range of stretches to properly loosen up all their muscles. You can run through a good warm-up in about ten minutes or less.

The warm-up exercises we present here concentrate on strengthening your players' cores. A player's abdominal, back, and shoulder muscles, along with his gluts, hip flexors, and chest muscles, comprise the core area of his body — the area that has the greatest impact on a player's performance. The muscles in the area contribute to the bulk of the force that the player generates while performing basic skills like throwing and hitting:

✔ **Butt kicks:** While running on the balls of his feet, the player exaggerates his leg kick and tries to touch his buttocks with his heels. At contact, the knees should be pointing down toward the ground. Have your players run down the first-base line for this drill, which warms up the hamstrings and gluts.

✔ **Forearm and wrist stretch:** The player stands with his feet shoulder-width apart. He extends his right arm straight out in front of him with his palm out and fingers up, just like he's motioning for someone to stop. Using his left hand, he grabs his right fingertips and gently pulls them back toward his body, holding for a five-second count. After the count, he rotates his right hand over so his fingers are pointing down and his palm is facing away from his body. He uses his left hand to gently pull the fingertips back toward him for a five-second count. The player does the same for the left arm.

✔ **Groin stretch:** In a sitting position on the ground, the child bends his knees and places the soles of his feet together, with his knees off to the sides. He slowly presses his torso and upper body forward with his forearms on his knees until he feels mild tension in his groin.

✔ **Hip-flexor stretch:** The child stands with his feet in a lunge position — imagine taking one really big stride, as though you're stepping over a big puddle of water to avoid getting wet — with his front knee slightly bent. He briefly pushes up onto the toes of his back foot, and then presses his hips forward while tightening his buttocks. At that point, he slowly lowers his body until he feels a stretch in the front of his hip. While he performs this stretch, the player's upper body should remain upright and centered directly over his hips. Alternate so each hip gets stretched out.

✔ **Neck stretch:** In a standing position, the child slowly turns his head all the way to the left and then all the way to the right. He then tucks his chin into his chest to stretch out the back of his neck.

✔ **Seated spinal stretch:** Sitting on the ground, the player extends his left leg straight out in front of him, with the heel of his foot touching the ground and his toes pointing straight up. He takes his right foot and crosses it over his left knee, while twisting his waist and lower back to the right. He moves his left arm across his body and places his left elbow on the outside of his right knee. He holds this position for a five-second count before repeating with his other side.

✔ **Side-hurdle stretch:** The player begins standing with his legs spread apart — well beyond shoulder-width. He bends his right knee and leans his body to the right, resting his right hand on his right knee. He keeps his left leg extended straight out, with his left hand resting lightly on the outside of his left knee. The player holds this position for a five-second count and then repeats with his other side.

✔ **Standing spine twist:** The player stands with his feet together, his legs straight, and his hands on his hips. Without moving his feet or legs, he twists his waist to his right and looks down toward his right heel. He holds this position for five seconds before repeating to the left.

✔ **Triceps shoulder stretch:** The youngster stands with his feet shoulder-width apart and his knees slightly bent. He moves his right hand behind his head, bending his elbow, and places the palm of his hand in the middle of his back. He then reaches across his head with his left hand and gently applies pressure to his right elbow, which stretches out his triceps and rear-deltoid area. Repeat with the other arm.

✔ **Upper-back stretch:** In a standing position, the child stretches both arms behind his back — interlocking his fingers and resting his hands against the middle of his back — while puffing out his chest. He holds this position for five seconds and then releases.

Breaking a sweat during warm-ups

Because baseball requires short running bursts, long sprints, long throws, quick throws, and many other exhilarating activities, the warm-up you create must get your kids' hearts pumping to prepare them for the exertion. If you incorporate some skills that your players will use during the practice or game, you maximize your time with the kids and beef up the learning that takes place. Here are some activities your players should complete during warm-ups:

✔ **Acclimating the arms.** Pair players up and have them lightly toss balls back and forth to their partner, throwing at about half speed to begin with, about 30 to 40 feet apart. As they get loosened up, gradually have them move farther away from each other and pick up the pace of their throws.

✔ **Loosening the legs.** After some light jogging to get their hearts pumping, have them run the bases a couple of times to loosen up their legs. Make sure they use good base-running technique, that is, taking the proper angles approaching each base and hitting the inside corner of each base. (See Chapter 9 for more base-running basics.)

When you're conducting warm-up drills, remind your players to refrain from fully exerting themselves. Players should work at about 50 percent of their normal speed during warm-ups so they'll have full tanks of energy to call on throughout the practice or game. Here's a couple other tips to keep in mind:

✔ **Minimize the standing-around time.** When your players are warmed up, you need to make sure their bodies don't cool down before they step onto the field. Your warm-up loses its effectiveness if the kids stand off to the side for several minutes, waiting to take the field, which often happens when a preceding game runs long. If you must wait for any reason, encourage your players to lightly toss balls back and forth, jog in place, or perform stretches on their own to stay loose.

✔ **Adjust for hot weather.** If the weather is extremely hot or humid, shorten the warm-up period to preserve your kids' energy. Also, make sure they consume plenty of water to stay hydrated (see the section "Staying hydrated" later in the chapter). Also, see the section "Considering the Weather Conditions" later in this chapter for more on this topic.

Cooling down after practices and games

The pre-practice and pre-game warm-ups get most of the attention because of their obvious importance in preventing injury and enhancing performance, but most people don't realize that the post-practice and post-game cool-downs are equally important. Cooling down your players maintains the long-term health of your team.

Have your kids perform some light stretches after practices and games; they can use the same stretches they performed before the practice or game. This cool-down does the following:

✔ Helps prevent your players' muscles from tightening

✔ Reduces soreness

✔ Aids circulation

Get your youngsters in a routine of going through a cool-down following every practice and game. The process doesn't have to be nearly as detailed as the warm-up session, because you want the kids to wind down from the activity rather than build up to another.

From Coach to Coach, MD: Recognizing and Treating Injuries

Eliminating injuries that take place during practices and games — or even just the threat of them occurring — is impossible, on every level of the game. So, as the coach, you need to be prepared to treat many types of injuries on the spot, and you need to know what to do when a player experiences a severe injury. How efficiently you handle injury situations impacts not only the kids' health, but also how they (and their parents) feel about continuing to play the sport.

You have two responsibilities whenever you provide treatment for any type of injury a player suffers:

✔ Tell his parents exactly how the injury occurred and what you did to treat it.

✔ Log (in a notebook or your practice planner) the nature of the injury, how it happened, and what treatment you provided.

Complete these tasks on the same day as the event occurs, while the situation is still fresh in your mind, and hang onto the documentation for several years. Unfortunately, we live in a lawsuit-happy society, so having an accurate account of what transpired helps protect you in a court of law. Having detailed practice plans, with dates, also helps to show that you safely and properly taught your players specific skills.

In the following sections, we show you how to treat common injuries that occur on the baseball field. We explain what you need to do during emergency situations. Finally, we let you know what to do with your players during injury situations. (First things first: Be sure you have a well-stocked first-aid kit with you at all practices and games, as we instruct in the "Packing Your Game and Practice First-Aid Kit" section earlier in this chapter.)

Treating common baseball injuries

Most injuries that occur on the baseball field consist of bumps and bruises or cuts and scrapes. Occasionally, a player will get a twisted ankle from sliding into a base. Most injuries may seem minor to you, but they can be quite traumatic to a youngster who suddenly sees blood trickling down his leg or a welt forming on his arm after getting hit by a pitch. Unfortunately, youngsters also face the risk of serious injury on the field — most notably facial injuries. As a coach, you're responsible for administering the proper treatment — and comforting the youngster — in most situations. In cases of serious injury, you need to do what you can at the scene and get your youngster to professionals as soon as possible. In the following sections, we present the information you need to know to treat common injuries that occur on the baseball field.

Although providing first aid for your team is your responsibility, you can assign an experienced parent to help out, if one is available. Having an assistant takes some of the pressure off you and reassures the other parents that you have control over anything that happens on the field. (See Chapter 4 for more info on recruiting parents to help out during the season.)

Cuts and scrapes

Little cuts and scrapes can lead to big tears with young players. If the wounds are minor, you can dig into your first-aid kit (see the section "Packing Your Game and Practice First-Aid Kit") to treat them quickly and effectively. As long as the player is mentally ready, he'll be back on the field in no time. Keep the following steps in mind when administering aid to a cut or scrape:

1. **Put on latex gloves.**

   Always use some type of blood barrier when you deal with a cut or open wound.

2. **Apply direct pressure to the wound with a clean dressing to stop the bleeding.**

   If you have trouble stopping the bleeding, elevate the child's injured area above his heart while maintaining the direct pressure.

3. **Clean the wound.**

   Pre-moistened towelettes work well for cleaning minor cuts and scrapes. You also can use over-the-counter alcohol swabs or antibiotic creams.

4. **Cover the cut with a bandage or piece of sterile gauze, and secure the covering in place with adhesive tape.**

   Securing the bandaging is particularly important if the child wants to continue playing.

5. **Put your gloves, and any other materials that came in contact with blood, in a sealed bag, and place the bag in the trash.**

   You don't want anyone else coming in contact with these potentially hazardous materials.

You need to be aware of the risks involved in treating an open wound, but the risks shouldn't prevent you from providing help to an injured player. If one of your players has AIDS, or is HIV-positive, his parents need to make you aware of his condition during your preseason parents meeting (which we discuss in Chapter 4). The knowledge of a disease, however, shouldn't affect the treatment a player receives; wearing latex gloves provides the protection you need to treat any injured child. You put yourself at risk only if you allow the blood of an HIV-positive person to come into contact with an open wound of your own.

A child who suffers a serious cut may require stitches. Wounds that span an inch or longer generally call for stitches, as do deep cuts where the edges of the skin fail to touch each other. If a player suffers a serious cut, get the child to a doctor right away for care.

Twists, sprains, and strains

Baseball requires many sudden stops and starts — on the base paths, in the batter's box, and in the field — and these movements can induce muscle strains and sprains. Many baseball injuries involve the foot, ankle, hands, or fingers. Common injuries include sprained or twisted ankles, sprained wrists, strained muscles (quadriceps, hamstrings), and pulled groins. With these types of injuries, the child will experience pain, discoloration around the area, and swelling.

When a player strains a muscle or twists an ankle or wrist, stick with the *RICE* (**R**est, **I**ce, **C**ompress, **E**levate) *method* for treatment:

- ✔ **Rest:** Take the child to the dugout to rest the injury. If he has twisted his ankle, for example, ask an assistant coach or a parent to help you carry him off the field so he doesn't put any additional pressure on the injured area, which may cause further damage.

- ✔ **Ice:** Apply ice to the injured area to reduce the swelling and pain. Wrap a bag of ice in a towel and then place the towel on the injured area for 20 minutes. Never apply the ice directly to the skin. Instruct the player to ice the area four to eight times a day in the coming days.

- ✔ **Compress:** Compress the injured area by using athletic tape or another type of adhesive to hold the ice bag and towel in place. You can rewrap the injured area with a bandage to help further reduce the swelling.

- ✔ **Elevate:** Have the child elevate the injured area to a position above his heart level to prevent blood from pooling in the area.

The player can return to action after the swelling, discoloration, and pain subside. If any of these symptoms are present for more than a couple days, the player should see a physician before you allow him back on the field. You can't let a child return with an injury that hasn't completely healed because he may re-injure the area and miss even more game action.

Other minor injuries

Your players may encounter some other common minor injuries; here are some tips for treating them:

- ✔ **Debris in the eye:** If a player has debris in an eye, you'll see tearing and redness, and the player will complain of pain. You usually can remove flecks of dirt, or any other foreign substance, with a cotton swab and saline wash. If the surface of his eye isn't seriously injured and his vision isn't impaired, the player can return to competition after you remove the object. If the irritation doesn't go away, the child will need to see an eye specialist for an evaluation.

✔ **A poke to the eye:** Examine the player's eye after the poke. If he isn't in significant pain and you see minimal redness and no discharge or bleeding, clean the area with cool water and have him rest for awhile before returning to play. If you see any type of discharge or blood coming from the eye, though, get the child to a doctor immediately.

✔ **Nosebleed:** Gently squeeze the player's nostrils together to stop the bleeding, and tilt his head slightly forward. If the bleeding doesn't stop after a couple minutes, get the child to a doctor, because he can have a serious injury, such as a nasal fracture.

✔ **Shin splints:** The general cause of shin splints is weight pounding down on the shins. Other factors that can contribute include muscle weakness, poor flexibility, improper warm-up and cool-down exercises, and improper footwear. You can easily identify the symptoms, because the athlete constantly complains about pain on his shins. If a player develops shin splints, apply an ice bag wrapped in a towel to reduce pain and swelling, and eliminate any weight-bearing activities to allow the affected area(s) time to heal. A week of rest usually is enough to cure a mild case of shin splints. *Note:* If you don't properly manage the injury, shin splints can result in a stress fracture.

✔ **Getting his wind knocked out:** A youngster who has the wind knocked out of him for the first time (and probably any other time) is likely to panic when he has trouble breathing. Comfort the youngster, and ask him to take short, quick breaths and pant like a dog until he can breathe normally again.

Serious injuries

At the more advanced levels of play — around age 13 or 14, when the kids start to gain strength and speed — the chances of serious injuries occurring rise. Here's a quick look at some injuries that require immediate medical attention:

✔ **Concussion:** A *concussion* is a jarring injury to the head that results in a disturbance of the brain. Concussions are classified as mild or severe, but both require that you get help for a player immediately. Possible symptoms include the following:

- A brief loss of consciousness
- Headache
- Grogginess
- Confusion
- Glassy-eyed look
- Memory loss
- Disturbed balance
- Slight dizziness

If you suspect that a child has suffered a mild injury, such as bumping heads while colliding with a player on the base paths, remove him from the game and make sure an adult is in attendance to provide careful observation. Parents should carefully monitor the child at home for several days; alert them to be on the lookout for persistent headaches, dizziness, irritability, and memory or vision changes — conditions that can suddenly appear following a head injury. If these symptoms appear, they should take their child to a doctor.

Mild concussions usually require a week for full recovery; a physician must make the decision about when the child can return to action. Severe concussions usually require at least four weeks of recovery; only a head specialist should give permission for the child to return.

If you or the child's parents see any evidence of more serious symptoms, such as unconsciousness, change in pupil size, or convulsions, call for immediate medical attention.

- **Injury to the eyeball:** A direct injury to an eyeball is an immediate medical emergency. Symptoms include extreme pain, loss of vision, hazy or double vision, trouble with colors, and obvious lacerations or abrasions. You should put a dry, sterile eye patch or a piece of gauze on the eye, along with a bag of soft, crushed ice. With these treatments in place, take the youngster to an emergency facility immediately.

- **Orbital fracture:** An *orbital fracture* is a break in the bony frame around the eye. All facial fractures are serious and require expert medical treatment. Symptoms of the fracture include severe pain and vision problems, such as double vision. The fracture may be accompanied by cuts, abrasions, bleeding, or black-and-blue marks. If you notice any of these symptoms, transport the youngster to an emergency facility for X-rays so doctors can determine whether a fracture has occurred.

- **Knocked-out tooth:** If a child has a tooth knocked out, try to retrieve it, and then utilize the tooth-preserving system in your first-aid kit (see the earlier section "Packing Your Game and Practice First-Aid Kit"). If you don't have the system, place the tooth in a sterile gauze pad, add some saline, and take the child to a dentist right away.

- **Broken or dislocated bones:** You may suspect that a child has suffered a broken or dislocated bone if he's in a lot of pain. You need to be careful and immobilize the area by using a splint. For example, if a child has a broken finger, put on a splint and wrap it with tape to hold it in place. When you have the area immobilized, take the child to a doctor. If the child has a broken or dislocated leg or arm, call for immediate medical attention.

If a broken bone is protruding from the child's skin, don't try to push it back in. Call for medical personnel and cover the area with a dry, sterile dressing until help arrives.

You need to proceed very cautiously when dealing with an injury that involves the head, neck, or spine. If you think a player may have an injured neck or spinal cord, never attempt to move him while he's lying on the ground, because doing so can cause further damage. Call for medical assistance immediately.

Acting fast in an emergency/ first-aid situation

You spend time practicing all types of baseball scenarios, so it makes sense to do the same with regard to handling emergency situations. Your kids' safety is just as important as them being able to execute a safety squeeze. How you respond to an emergency situation can make the difference in saving a youngster's life. Hopefully, you'll never have to deal with such a situation; if you do, however, you need to be able to assess the situation and then provide the proper treatment (or call people who can).

Assessing the situation

Being able to assess injuries isn't a fun or easy part of coaching baseball, but it is important. The acronym *COACH* gives you a handy reminder of how to respond when approaching an injured child during an emergency situation:

✔ **C:** Determine whether the child is *conscious*.

✔ **O:** Is the child breathing and getting *oxygen?*

    Look at his lip color, feel his chest, and put your cheek next to his nose. Feel for a pulse in his neck or wrist. If he has a pulse but isn't breathing, begin mouth-to-mouth resuscitation without chest compressions. If he isn't breathing and you can't find a palpable pulse, initiate CPR and ask an assistant to call for immediate medical assistance. Be especially careful not to press down on the lowest portion of the child's breastbone, which can injure his internal organs.

✔ **A:** If the youngster is conscious and breathing, *ask* him where he's hurt.

✔ **C:** *Control* the area that's painful.

✔ **H:** Ask yourself what type of *help* is required. Decide whether you need to call for immediate medical assistance and have the child taken to the hospital.

We strongly recommend that you and your assistant coaches become certified in CPR. You can receive CPR and first-aid training from the American Red Cross or another nationally recognized organization. At every practice and game, you're responsible for the safety and well-being of your players. You can do your team and yourself a huge favor by taking the time to go through the class.

Taking action

After you assess the situation, you need to act. Taking action can mean treating the child on your own, calling medical professionals, or both. It also comes with other responsibilities. Keep the following pointers in mind:

- **Know your location.** Make sure you know the name of your league facility and its address. When you call 911, you need to be able to provide as much information as possible so that emergency medical personnel will arrive at the location fast.

- **Have easy access to your team's emergency information.** The important medical forms we discuss in Chapter 4 are crucial in emergency events. Medical personnel will need to know whether the child is allergic to any type of medication. Always carry your players' medical forms in your first-aid kit and have them easily accessible.

- **Provide first aid.** While you await the arrival of medical personnel, provide the first-aid care that you're trained to perform.

- **Comfort the child.** If the child is conscious, comfort him by talking in a calm and relaxed voice. Let him know that he'll be okay and that medical help is on the way.

- **Call the parents.** If the child's parents aren't in attendance, appoint one of your assistant coaches to call them and let them know what's going on. Your first responsibility is to the child; if you designate someone you trust to make the call to the parents, you don't have to waste unnecessary time.

Accounting for your kids during an injury stoppage in play

When you see a car accident, you give in to curiosity and slow down to check it out. The same goes for young kids when an injury occurs on the field. Your players naturally want to take a look. Even though they may be showing genuine concern for their teammate, you need to keep them back away from the injured youngster. Having the entire team crowded around him and staring can make the child more panicked than he already is. Have your assistant coaches keep players back while you tend to the injured player.

If a player on an opposing team experiences a serious injury during a game, instruct your team return to its dugout area. You need to check on the injured child with the other coaches and provide any help you can. You don't want your players being a distraction or getting in the way of the player's treatment.

Considering the Weather Conditions

You should never take Mother Nature and the power she wields lightly, particularly when young children are involved — children who count on you for their safety and well-being. Different weather conditions — from humidity to approaching storms — present different types of risks to youngsters. You don't need to be a meteorologist to protect your players, but you do need to be aware of the weather. The following sections give you advice on what to look for.

Tracking storms

When storms are closing in during games, and lightning may be lurking in the area, don't wait for a league administrator or the umpire to stop the games. If you think the kids' safety is in jeopardy, get them off the field right away. Whether you're playing the first game of the season or the championship game, you shouldn't try to squeeze in one more inning simply to avoid the hassle of rescheduling (see Chapter 2 for more on rescheduling). During a practice, the responsibility of keeping your players safe is squarely on your shoulders. Even a light rain can pose injury risks to children, because they'll be more likely to lose their footing moving on wet grass or have a slippery bat fly out of their hands. Whenever Mother Nature disrupts your practices, you're always better off getting the kids off the field and trying again another day.

Lightning poses a big safety threat because it can show up so swiftly — and strike even more quickly. If lightning catches you by surprise, retreat to a safe place with the kids. Here are some go's and no go's for lightning safety:

- ✔ **Go's:** Enclosed buildings, fully enclosed vehicles with the windows up, and low ground
- ✔ **No go's:** Trees, water, wide-open areas, metal bleachers, light poles, fences, and any other metal objects

If a tornado approaches your area, immediately move your players inside a building, if one is available. Otherwise, have the kids lie down in a ditch or some other low-lying area. Instruct them to use their arms to protect their heads and necks.

Beating the heat

The bulk of the baseball season usually occurs during the dog days of summer. Because of this, you need to take precautions to protect your kids — and your coaching staff — from heat- and sun-related injuries.

Kids don't acclimate to heat as well as adults do; their sweat glands aren't as developed, and they don't have the tolerance. When the thermometer climbs or the humidity rises, the conditions put extra stress on players' bodies. As a general rule, when the humidity rises above 70 percent and the temperature is above 80 degrees, you need to take extreme caution with your team and make sure your players and coaches drink extra water (see the section "Staying hydrated" later in this chapter). When the temperature tops 90 degrees, combined with humidity hovering in the 70- to 80-percent range, the dangers of heat illness enter the picture. During these conditions, you should suspend practices or games, or at the very least significantly reduce the time spent on the field. If playing or practicing for a short time, the kids should wear only cool, porous clothing.

Be aware, though, that playing or practicing in hot and humid conditions can lead to several heat-related injuries:

✔ **Sun exposure/sunburn:** It's never too early to get kids in the habit of protecting their skin. Every moment spent in the sun adds up, and over-exposure to the sun can lead to skin damage and skin cancer. Encourage your players to use sunscreen with an SPF of at least 30. Ask the parents to lather up the kids with sunscreen before any game or practice that will take place in the midday sun.

✔ **Heat exhaustion:** *Heat exhaustion* is caused by dehydration; its symptoms include profuse sweating, nausea, headache, chills, dizziness, and extreme thirst. If you notice these symptoms in one of your players or coaches, seek medical attention. In the meantime, move the person to a cool, shaded area and provide cool fluids. You also should apply ice to the neck and back to help cool the body.

✔ **Heatstroke:** *Heatstroke* happens when the child stops sweating, which pushes his body temperature to dangerously high levels. Warning signs of heatstroke include red or flushed skin, rapid pulse, rapid breathing, vomiting, seizures, unconsciousness, and cardiac arrest.

You must call medical personnel immediately if you notice these symptoms. After calling for help, cool the player's body with wet towels, or pour cool water over him. Apply ice packs to the neck, back, abdomen, armpits, and in between the legs. If the player is conscious, provide cool fluids. If he's unconscious, roll him onto his side so that if he vomits, the matter won't block the passageway in his throat.

Hammering Home the Importance of a Healthy Diet

When you begin to teach your players how to hit for power and make backhanded plays on grounders, you shouldn't neglect talking to them about nutrition and hydration and how they impact their performance. After all, you can't muster any power or concentrate at the plate or in the field if you're sluggish or dehydrated. Although you can't control what your players eat before practices and games, you can do your best to influence their decisions on whether to reach for potato chips and soda or fruits and water. These types of discussions are more applicable for the older kids, many of whom will constantly be searching for ways to improve their performances and can utilize the information to their advantage.

Children get their information from many self-serving sources — including television commercials that push candy bars and other sugar-laden snacks — so you need to keep diet and hydration information in perspective for them. The more time you spend talking about eating healthy, the more likely it is that your players will put the right foods and drinks in their bellies before and after they hit the field.

Your best chance of getting your kids' attention, and keeping it, when it comes to chats about nutrition is to put your discussion in simple terms and keep it in the present. Let them know that what they put in their stomachs this morning will affect what they can do in the field and at the plate this afternoon. Also, inform them that their diets affect how quickly their bodies recover before the next practice or game.

The following sections cover what your players should be putting in their mouths during, before, and after practices and games. We also give hydration its own section because of its great importance.

How to maintain energy during games and practices

One nutrition factor you can control is what your players ingest during practices and games. The two primary ingredients you can use to fuel a child's muscles during practices and games — both of which the body uses up the longer an activity goes on — are the following:

- ✔ **Fluids:** Kids lose fluids through perspiration, so water is a key ingredient for keeping their body temperatures from rising during an activity. The longer your players exercise without replacing their lost fluids, and the hotter the conditions become, the more likely heat-related illnesses become, and the less effective their performances will be. Sports drinks are also ideal for keeping kids hydrated. If players prefer the taste of those over water, have mom or dad fill their bottles with those types of drinks. (See the upcoming section "Staying hydrated" for more on the topic.)

- ✔ **Glucose:** This sugar, derived from carbohydrates, is important for fueling muscles. The more carbohydrate fuel children lose during competition, the less energy they have to perform at their peak.

Good snacks for the kids to munch on to keep their bodies fueled while they're sitting in the dugout include dried and fresh fruit and energy bars. The key with mid-game snacks is you want them to be easy for the kids to grab and take a few quick bites.

What to eat before games and practices

Players who show up for practices and games without the proper nutrition are setting themselves up for failure. Not only will their energy levels be down, but also their ability to perform and their concentration. Consuming nutritious pre-game meals or snacks — packed with plenty of carbohydrates — opens the door for them to play at their best.

Carbohydrates convert into energy more quickly and efficiently than other nutrients. For the most nutritional punch, youngsters should opt for the following foods before a practice or game:

Meals: Pastas, breads, cereals, whole grains, fruits, and vegetables

Snacks: Bagels, yogurt, dried fruit, fresh fruit, energy bars, fruit granola bars, and whole-grain crackers with peanut butter or cheese

Usually, when players tire easily or appear sluggish in the later innings of games or practices, you can trace the problems back to their diets. Tell your players (and their parents) to stay away from the following pre-game foods:

Candy, cookies, donuts, burgers, fries, and other greasy foods

Let your kids and their parents know that they should eat their pre-game or practice meals a couple of hours before the opening pitch or the start of practice. If they eat too close to the action, their bodies will digest the food during the first few innings or practice drills, which will negatively impact their performance.

What to eat after games and practices

What you say to your kids following games and practices — and how you say it — impacts their confidence and self-esteem. Similarly, what your players chow on after games and practices affects their bodies and how they feel. Rewarding kids with tasty snacks for doing their best is fun, but giving them junk food sends the wrong message about the importance of a healthy diet. Having the occasional pizza party or taking a trip to the ice-cream shop is fine, of course, but steering your players toward sound nutritional habits can lead to a lifetime of healthy eating. Here are some post-game tips that you, your players, and their parents can chew on:

✔ **Concentrate on carbs.** Youngsters benefit the most from foods rich in carbohydrates that also have some protein value. The post-game meal or snack should resemble the pre-game meal (see the previous section), only in smaller portions. Turkey sandwiches, fresh fruit, and crackers with cheese are great options for replenishing worn-out bodies.

✔ **The sooner the better.** Carbohydrate-rich foods provide the most benefits for youngsters when they consume them within about an hour of the most recent activity. At this point, their metabolism is at its highest performance level, and their muscles absorb the most nutrients from the food.

✔ **Recruit parents.** During your preseason parents meeting (see Chapter 4), try to recruit parents to be in charge of organizing post-game snacks for your players. Offer some suggestions from this list to guide the parents so they don't show up with bags of candy bars every game.

✔ **Set out snacks for all.** Treating your players to a snack after a big game or a hard practice is a nice way to conclude a fun day of baseball — but only if every player can have the snacks you provide. One of the keys to being a good coach is ensuring that you meet the needs of every player on your team, whether you're doling out praise or food. A child who's lactose intolerant, for example, won't have any fun watching his team-mates devour ice cream on a hot day. During your preseason parents meeting (which we cover in Chapter 4), find out if any of your players have food allergies that you should be aware of. Having this information allows you and the other parents to hand out treats without leaving any youngster out of the fun.

Staying hydrated

Making sure your players consume plenty of fluids during a game or practice — and consume the right kinds — is very important for their health and perform-ance. Kids exert a ton of energy during games and tough practices, which increases their body temperature. The younger your players are, the less they'll sweat, because a young person's sweat glands aren't fully developed. Because of this, their bodies soak up more heat during games or practices that take place in high temperatures. Children who don't consume adequate amounts of water or sports drinks during games or practices — especially those contested in hot and humid conditions — are at risk of bodily harm due to dehydration, muscle cramps, heat exhaustion, or, even worse, heat stroke.

Gloves, bats, and mouthpieces are important pieces of equipment that kids need to bring to your practices and games — and the same goes for water bot-tles, too. Remind your players of the importance of bringing those bottles — filled with water or their favorite sports drink — to the field. A good rule of thumb is to encourage your kids to drink water or a sports drink whenever possible. A player can down a glass of water with his pre-game or practice meal, take sips out of his water bottle during warm-ups, and replenish while he sits in the dugout during the game.

You can quench your knowledge regarding fluid intake by reviewing the following additional tips:

- ✔ **Go with specifics.** Even if you constantly remind your players to drink water, chances are they won't consume enough. Try to get more specific with your instruction. For example, when you switch to a new drill in practice, or when the kids are in your dugout during your team's at-bats, tell them to take five sips of water. Giving specific instructions ensures that they get the proper amount of fluids into their bodies.

- ✔ **Encourage steady drinking.** Encourage your kids to drink throughout a practice or game, whenever opportunities for grabbing water bottles present themselves — such as when you're delivering a pre-game speech, announcing the batting lineup for a game, or praising the kids' efforts after the game.

- ✔ **Bring extra water.** Always have extra water on hand so your kids can refill their water bottles when needed. You can go so far as to designate different parents each week to bring extra water to practices and games. You never want to have a shortage of water.

- ✔ **Say no to caffeine and carbonation.** Beverages with caffeine act as a diuretic, which is exactly the opposite of what you're trying to accomplish in keeping the kids hydrated. Also, keep kids away from carbonated drinks, because carbonation discourages drinking.

Never withhold water as a form of discipline — no matter how serious the infraction or how upset you may be. Water is too important for your kids' health. Choose another form of discipline that gets your point across, such as taking away playing time (see Chapter 17 for more on discipline).

Chapter 17

Overcoming Challenges That Every Coach Faces

- -

In This Chapter

▶ Addressing problems posed by parents

▶ Combating difficult coaches

▶ Solving disciplinary problems on your team

▶ Helping players struggling with skills

- -

Some of the obvious responsibilities of being a youth baseball coach are teaching — the basics of hitting, throwing, fielding, and base running — motivating, and making things fun for the kids. A not-so-visible aspect of the job is having to handle the different types of problems you encounter with parents, opposing coaches, your assistant coaches, and your players. You're in charge of a wide range of kids (who come with an equally diverse group of parents), so chances are good that problems will flare up occasionally.

This chapter digs into the common challenges that youth baseball coaches face. Among other issues, we give you tips on handling discipline problems with your players; solving disagreements you have with assistants; toning down overly involved parents; and dealing with opposing coaches who will do anything to win. Hopefully, few of these unpleasant situations will arise, but if they do, the information in this chapter will prepare you to remedy the situations quickly and smoothly.

Dealing with Problematic Parents

We've all seen comedic displays of angry parents who disrupt youth sporting events on television or in the movies. However, we can assure you that having a parent disrupt a youth baseball game is no laughing matter in real life. It embarrasses the child, your team, and you. You can do your part to ensure that parents behave appropriately — before their children ever step into the batter's box — by explaining to them at a preseason meeting what type of behavior you expect. (We cover how you can pull off one of these preseason parent meetings in Chapter 4.)

Often, the simplest solution for nipping problem behavior in the bud is to offer a friendly reminder to the parent(s) in question. Simply voice your concern with them after the game (or practice), and often you'll resolve the issue without any further trouble.

Many baseball leagues have implemented parent sportsmanship programs — some voluntary, some mandatory — to inform parents of their roles and responsibilities and to help ensure that the kids have positive and rewarding experiences. Knowing your league's rules, which we cover in Chapter 2, is extremely important. If your league doesn't have a parent program in place, you may want to recommend to your league director that it considers adopting one.

However, despite all your efforts to ensure model parental behavior, some adults simply can't control their emotions after the opening pitch is delivered; therefore, you need to be prepared to step forward at the first sign of trouble. The following sections examine some common parental behaviors you may come across. Along the way, we explain which approaches work best for ensuring that the kids' experiences are memorable for all the right reasons, and we let you know which tactics to avoid at all costs.

Win-at-all-cost parents

Some parents pile unrealistic expectations on their children — and even on you and your other players — to perform at ridiculously high levels and win an unreasonable number of games. Being pressured to be the star and win the championship is one of the fastest routes to baseball-induced misery for a young player.

These "win-at-all-cost parents," blinded by thoughts of their children hoisting a first-place trophy, focus on making sure the wins come and on their youngsters being a big reason for the success. How do you recognize such a parent? A parent in this mold will shout remarks at umpires when calls don't go your team's way, and he or she will criticize everything from your batting order to your game strategy when the wins don't come. With this behavior, these parents bury the fun and unearth frustration.

How do you deal with folks who are a wee bit too competitive? Here's how:

✔ **Be aware that you're a target.** A win-at-all-costs parent will critique your coaching style when the team loses, question your strategies, and dissect your lineups. Regardless of the age or experience of the youngsters, the parent will confront you about the importance of playing the more athletic kids (of which the parent's child is one) and benching the lesser-skilled players. The parent will even provide unwanted input on everything from base running to pitching changes.

If a parent begins to infringe on your coaching duties, have a friendly — but firm — chat in private, clearly stating that at this level your responsibilities are to give all the kids equal playing time. Also, inform them that the team's won-loss record isn't nearly as important as making sure everyone learns and develops skills — and has lots of fun doing so. Encourage them to coach next season if they're interested; or to sign their child up for a more advanced or competitive league if that is what they think is most appropriate for their child.

✔ **Keep your players focused on what's most important.** Make sure that you always stress having fun, learning skills, and being good sports. In order for these lessons to take hold, you can't allow overly competitive parents to infringe on the season and trample what you want to teach.

If a child lets you know that what his parents are saying is different from what you're teaching, or if a child tunes you out because of his parents, pull the parents aside before a practice (or arrange to speak with them in private away from the field) and reinforce that winning is not the main focus of the season. Remind them that you outlined your coaching philosophy at your preseason parents meeting (covered in Chapter 4) and that you won't stray from fun and skill development as your focal points. Let them know that going against your teachings confuses the youngster, curbs their learning, and slows down their development.

✔ **Don't allow parents to interfere on your time.** Although you can't control what parents say to their children at home, you can control what's said while you're coaching a game or a practice. Picture the baseball field like a classroom and yourself as the teacher. In an English class, the teacher wouldn't allow parents to disrupt what she wants to teach the kids, and neither should you as you teach the kids important aspects of baseball.

During practices or games, you can calm the storm of a meddling parent without causing a scene (on your end, anyway) by reminding them that your job is to coach — and their job is to provide nonstop support and encouragement. If they can't control their emotions, you'll have them removed from games or barred from practices. Let them know that you are committed to ensuring that their behavior doesn't disrupt any child's experience playing.

Closing down your baseball baby-sitting service

Many parents lead hectic lives, so they cram their evenings and weekends with the duty of chauffeuring their kids to a variety of activities. Some parents may view your practices and games as a baby-sitting service, where they can drop off their children with you and use the off time to catch up on other areas of their lives. Invite parents to be an active part of the team, if at all possible.

Parents who attend practices regularly get a good sense of which areas of the game come pretty easily for their children, and they find out which areas they may need to work on a little more at home. They also see firsthand how their youngsters interact with other kids and if they listen and follow directions.

One of the best ways to get parents to hang around for practice is to invite them to be a part of your drills (we give you some great tips, if we do say so ourselves, in Chapter 6). Parents who aren't in the habit of staying for practices are likely to stick around when they see other parents actively involved and having fun with all the kids on the field.

As kids get older, however, parental involvement at practice becomes far less important. At this point, you can use parental involvement from time to time to shake up your practices. At the more advanced levels of baseball, kids become more competitive, so finding unique ways to quench their competitive desires — with the occasional help of parents at practice — is great for spicing up the season. Give mom a bat and see how she fares at the plate, or put some dads in the infield for a ground-ball drill. Your kids will have fun trying to outperform their parents, and they'll gain the added benefit of working on their skills.

Of course, some parents can't be on hand for your practices most of the time. If a parent lets you know that this is the case, inform the parent that his or her presence is very important on game day, so they shouldn't skip that part of the experience, too.

Parents who complain about playing time

Parents who are disappointed over the amount of playing time their kids receive can give youth coaches big headaches. Complaints about playing time are some of the most common complaints you'll hear. You need to understand that parents get as much enjoyment out of seeing their children sitting on the bench as they get from having a root canal. Every parent wants to see his or her kid on the field and involved in the action.

Some parents view their child's status on the team as a reflection of their parenting skills — as crazy as that may sound. In their eyes, their child's playing time is a status symbol that they can show off to other parents in the stands.

Other parents have an unrealistic view of their child's baseball skills. The minute they see him sitting on the bench, the parents get swept up in fears that you're compromising their son's athletic future and that his baseball scholarship is slipping away.

The parents of your players need to understand the league you're in and the team concept of the game. Here are some tips to keep in mind when dealing with the sensitive topic of playing time:

- ✔ **Follow the rules.** Let your parents know that although you'd love to be able to give their children more playing time, the league's rules dictate that all players receive an equal amount of time (or at least a certain amount of time). Let the parents know during your preseason meeting that you're going to follow the rules and allow everyone equal playing time (see Chapter 4 to find out about this meeting).

- ✔ **Document playing time.** Keep careful track of how you distribute playing time each game so that when a parent questions you about his or her child not getting a fair share, or about another player getting too much time, you can show the parent your balance chart.

- ✔ In advanced leagues, stress to parents that playing ability equals playing time. At the more competitive levels of baseball, the kids with more talent receive the bulk of the playing time. This presents new challenges for you as a coach, because sometimes you may have to explain to some upset parents why their child isn't in the lineup. Delivering that message to parents is tough, and the message is even tougher for parents to hear. You can soothe some of the parents' hurt and disappointment by stressing their child's positive aspects, how he is improving in specific areas of the game, and what an asset he is to the team in different areas.

Sometimes, a player may be reluctant to go into a game or to participate in practice, and you and his parents may not be aware of the situation. Maybe he injured his leg sliding into a base but is afraid to admit that he's hurt. Or maybe he got hit by a pitch earlier in the game/practice and is fearful that it can happen again. If you discover that a child is hesitant to step onto the field, don't force him, threaten him, or embarrass him. Speak with the child privately after the game to find out what happened and what you can do to ease his fears before the next practice or game. Be sure to alert his parents of the situation so they know why their child didn't play the number of innings he usually does.

Disruptive parents

The vast majority of parents who show up at baseball complexes to watch their kids participate do a wonderful job of keeping the situation in perspective and providing positive support and encouragement. Yet, it takes only one parent shouting, cursing, or criticizing to ruin the experience for all the kids, umpires, and coaches. Why some parents choose to behave in an inappropriate way is out of your control. But what you do have control over is making sure that the parent never disrupts another game or practice.

What do you do when a parent starts yelling at the home-plate umpire? What are your options when tensions are running high among a group of parents in the stands? In the following sections, we provide you with some strategies to deal with these situations and more. And, because you're only human, we give you advice on what not to do as well.

Here are some tips for negating inappropriate behaviors and keeping your games and practices distraction-free for the kids:

- **Address the inappropriate behavior as soon as possible.** Never turn your back on a disruptive situation. You don't want to send the message that you condone this type of behavior and that everything you talked about during your preseason parents meeting about setting a good example (see Chapter 4) was meaningless. Being swift in your response lets the parents know that if they cross the line, they'll hear from you. During games, you have a responsibility to the kids on the field, but between innings you can pull the parent aside to give them a friendly reminder to keep his emotions in check.

- **Diffuse tension.** When addressing an upset or overzealous parent, maintain a calm and friendly demeanor at all times. You want to avoid the chance that the situation will unravel into bickering and verbal sparring. If the parent is being unreasonable and saying inappropriate things, you'll find it challenging to refrain from saying what you're really thinking. But you have to control yourself for the sake of the kids. Never surrender to your frustration and lose control of your emotions.

- **Choose the right tone.** When coaching up your kids, your body language and the tone of your voice pack a pretty powerful punch. These factors have a pretty big impact when dealing with parents, too. When dealing with an upset parent, always pay close attention to your body movements and how you deliver your words.

  For example, if a parent asks you why her child played in only half the game, don't put your hands on your hips before responding; if you do, the parent will think you're upset before you even respond to the question. Collect yourself before you answer, and pay attention to how you're standing and the sound of your voice when you give your reasons. Mixed body-language signals and a negative tone are quick routes to unproductive and unhealthy conversations.

- **Keep your ears open.** If you're not willing to listen to what an upset parent has to say, you can't expect the parents to listen to you and your guidelines. If you give parents opportunities to express their feelings — and you listen intently to what they have to say — you'll find that the parents will be much more likely to hear what you have to say, and they'll be much less likely to lash out during games and practices to express themselves. To keep the communication lines open with the parents consider setting aside time after your practices for them to bring up any issues, concerns, or questions they may have. Your willingness to keep them informed — and tackle all the tough questions — greatly reduces the chances of problems materializing and disrupting the season.

✔ **Banish problem parents.** No coaches want to have parents removed from the stands, but if you face a time when removal is the only option left that will protect the interests of the youngsters and ensure their safety, you shouldn't hesitate. Just realize that having a mom or dad escorted away from the field is embarrassing for the whole family, so this action should be a last resort. In most cases, take this type of measure only with parents who have been problematic in the past and have done nothing to tone down their behavior.

On the other hand, when a problem with a parent begins to spin out of control and becomes a major headache, you may be tempted, out of sheer frustration, to try any tactic to solve the problem. We suggest that you steer clear of the following tactics, which may only worsen the issue:

✔ **Don't embarrass the parent.** Whenever you hear a seemingly random and inappropriate comment shouted from the stands, it may take only a quick glimpse over your shoulder at the offending parent to imply that he or she needs to tone it down.

Don't trot out to the on-deck circle and lecture the parent in front of everyone. Meet privately with the parent after the game and remind him or her that negative comments detract from everyone's enjoyment of the game. Try something along the following lines: "I know the umpire shouldn't have called your son out at third base, but not all calls are going to go our way this season. Please remember that I need you and the other parents to set an example of good sportsmanship."

✔ **Don't take out your frustrations on the player.** A child can't control his mom or dad's behavior, so you need to refrain from taking out your frustration with the parent on him. For example, you shouldn't chop his playing time in half in hopes that this punishment will translate into the improved behavior of his mom or dad.

✔ **Avoid parking-lot confrontations.** When a parent is visibly upset, the chances of you having a calm and productive conversation are greatly reduced. When a hot parent confronts you in the parking lot immediately after a game or practice, tell him or her that you'll be happy to speak in private the following day. Explain that a heated discussion won't do anyone much good — especially in front of his or her child and the other players and parents.

✔ **Never resort to violence.** *Never* allow any situation to escalate into violence. When tempers begin flaring and violent behavior appears to be a possibility, evaluate your options. Some leagues require that you call the league director when problems arise; other programs have police officers patrolling the fields in case physical altercations or threats occur. Of course, in any emergency situation, you shouldn't hesitate to call the police or 911.

Pitting Yourself against Problematic Coaches

Because all different types of adults volunteer to coach youth baseball teams — from the guy whose son's team desperately needs a coach, to the overprotective mother who wants to keep an eye on her son, to the overbearing father who wants another championship trophy — chances are pretty good that you'll encounter a coach who just doesn't get it when it comes to kids and baseball. Typically, bad situations arise with an opposing team, but you should also be aware that an assistant coach whom you thought was reliable and had an even-keel temperament may disrupt your dugout. Regardless of the age or experience level of the players you coach, problematic coaches can appear anywhere — and at any time.

Your job is to handle all situations maturely and with good sportsmanship. Your players will take their cues from you, so how you act when tension rises and blood pressures climb is important. In the following sections, we present the different types of inappropriate behaviors you may come across this season, both from opposing coaches and from your assistants, and how you should handle them.

Opposing coaches

Most of the coaches of the teams you'll be squaring off against this season will (hopefully) share many of your qualities, including encouraging the kids to play hard but fairly and displaying good sportsmanship at all times, among others. Chances are, regardless of the age or ability level of the league you're involved in, you'll encounter coaches who will spend more time yelling rather than encouraging; who will glare at umpires and question many of their calls; and who will treat every outing like it's the seventh game of the World Series. This section takes a look at some of the problems that can appear from the opposing dugout.

The behaviors in this section may also apply to your assistants (see the upcoming section "Dissenting assistants"). If you notice your assistants exhibiting problematic behaviors with your players, act immediately.

Encouraging unsafe play during the game

One of your top priorities is doing everything you can to ensure the safety of your players. If you discover that an opponent is employing unsafe tactics that are jeopardizing your players' well-being — such as players sliding into bases with one foot raised with their cleats directed at your infielders — you need to act swiftly. Keep in mind, if only one player demonstrates poor behavior, he may just not have a good handle on the fundamentals of this particular aspect of the game. Never hesitate to act when you notice a safety concern; try taking these steps:

✔ **Speak with the umpire.** In a respectful manner, approach the umpire and share your concerns that the other team is putting your players at unnecessary risk. Be clear that you're voicing your concern for the safety of all the kids on both teams. One of the umpire's most important responsibilities is ensuring the safety of all the players, so work with him to correct the problem.

Don't approach the opposing coach during a game because emotions are often more difficult for many coaches to keep in check after scoreboards are turned on and play is underway. Instead, rely on the umpire to solve any problems you see. Confronting the opposing coach creates the potential for more conflict to develop. He may misinterpret your intentions — viewing your concerns as a ploy to affect his team's play, particularly if his team is winning — or he may feel threatened or embarrassed that you're questioning his coaching techniques in front of everyone. If you're friends with him, you have more room to maneuver and a between-innings chat may be all that is needed to iron out your differences.

✔ **Contact a league official.** If a league director monitors games at the facility, speak with him about your concerns. Because several games are usually going on at once, chances are if a league official is on-site to watch over games he may not be at your field when an incident occurs. Alert the umpire that the director's presence is needed at the field. If the situation warrants, dispense one of your assistants, or even a parent, to locate the official and get him over to your field right away.

✔ **Stop the game.** Stopping a game should be the last resort. If your discussions with the umpire and league officials haven't cleared up the problem, and the other coach continues to allow his team to play dirty, your only option is removing your team from the field. If a league official isn't available before you take this measure, meet with him as soon as possible to explain your concerns and why you felt stopping the game was in the best interest of your kids. Don't base this decision on the score of the game or where your team is in the league standings. The safety and well-being of your players always takes precedence over winning games.

Modeling poor sportsmanship

You need to be prepared for opposing coaches who treat every game like it's the seventh game of the World Series. These coaches are pretty easy to spot: They conduct their pre-game warm-ups like a drill sergeant, continually question every ball and strike call, and go into convulsions when one of their players misplays a ball or strikes out.

Poor sportsmanship by coaches (or anyone, really) makes a baseball game a pretty miserable experience for all involved. Here are some pointers on how to keep your cool when the other coach is heating up:

- **Maintain your composure.** An opposing coach's unsportsmanlike behavior will challenge your patience and test your poise. Take a deep breath, count to ten, or use any other tricks at your disposal to keep your emotions under wraps. If you react negatively to what's taking place, you've allowed the other coach to lure you into behaving in a distasteful manner, too. Approach the umpire between innings and share your concerns with him so that you make sure he's aware of what is unfolding on the field.

- **Turn the fury into a teachable moment.** Your players hear and see the antics going on in the opposing dugout, so instead of acting like everything is okay, you can use the situation to reinforce the importance of good behavior. Point out to your team that by rising above the poor behavior and continuing to be good sports — regardless of what the opposing coach and players are saying — they come out looking classy and mature.

- **Maintain your team's focus.** Keep your players focused on their responsibilities within the game, and keep the positive comments flowing — just like you would during any other game. Don't allow the opposing coach's loud-mouthed behavior to distract your players from achieving your team's goals (see Chapter 8 for more on setting goals).

- **Meet with the league director.** Anytime you observe inappropriate behavior by an opposing coach that impacts your youngsters' experiences, be sure to let your league director know about it right away. If you don't say anything, you allow that coach to behave exactly the same way during the next game. Explain to the director that the offending coach is setting a poor example for the kids on his team and that without a change in demeanor, he shouldn't be coaching in a youth baseball league.

Dissenting assistants

You must think of your assistant coaches as extensions of you. They must teach what you want your kids to learn, and they must provide what you want your kids to take away from their experiences this season. Assistants whom you can trust to follow your lead are extremely valuable. However, recruiting outside help can open the door to problems. When you bring in other adults with other viewpoints and personalities into the coaching picture, you take the chance that they may stray from what's best for the players. (Chapter 4 offers pointers on how to choose assistants wisely so you can try to avoid any problems.)

Many problems can surface as a result of your assistants' agendas:

✔ **He eyes more playing time for his kid.** A parent may step forward to coach so he can try to secure more playing time or a desired position for his child.

✔ **He criticizes you behind your back.** This is common at the more competitive levels of play — particularly if your team isn't winning. Whenever this back-stabber gets the chance, he'll trash your techniques and criticize your strategies in front of the other parents to pile the blame on you for the team's won-loss record.

✔ **He causes unnecessary commotion.** Some parents — even the most laid-back ones — display crazy personalities when the scoreboard lights up. An assistant you choose can turn into a screamer and become a real disruptive influence to your coaching and your team's play.

✔ **His philosophy clashes with yours.** Hopefully, your assistants will agree that although your team will strive to do its best and win games, winning must take a back seat to skill development and having fun. When you mentioned this philosophy during the preseason meeting (see Chapter 4), a parent may have nodded his head enthusiastically in agreement; yet, as soon as the scoreboard is switched on and the kids take the field, you may discover that your new assistant doesn't share those views anymore.

During your first couple practices and games, keep a close watch on how your assistants interact with the kids, and observe how the youngsters respond to them, as well. If an assistant doesn't stick to your plan and follow your philosophies, have a private talk with him right away to reinforce your goals for the season. Usually, this chat is enough to get the assistant back on the right track. If the problems continue, however, thank him for his efforts, and let him know that it's in the team's best interest for him to step aside and become a supportive parent in the stands. The well-being of your players is too important to let problems with an assistant linger.

Disciplining Your Players

Working with kids, teaching them skills, and seeing them develop in all different areas of the game are some of the many aspects that make coaching baseball so much fun. Disciplining misbehaving players falls at the opposite end of the spectrum, but it's a part of the job, too. This section explores ways to keep your kids in line and your season running smoothly. (See Chapter 5 for more on understanding the different personality types — including some of the disruptive ones — on your team.)

The perpetually late child

Dealing with kids who show up late for practices and in the third inning of games can be very aggravating. Late players present all sorts of problems, ranging from missing warm-ups and your pre-practice instructions — which can put the child in danger of injury, especially at the more advanced levels — to throwing your lineup into disarray.

Pull the child aside to discuss his tardiness and the reasons behind it. Anytime you talk to a child regarding this issue, be sure to include the parents. The tardiness may be out of the child's control. Perhaps the parents' schedule prevents the child from being on time. Sometimes, it may be a simple case of negligence: The parents don't realize how disruptive their child's late arrival is for the rest of the team. Among other things, let the parents know that the tardiness

✔ Negatively affects the teams' schedule

✔ Hinders their child's development because of the need to build on skills

✔ Takes away from the child's playing time (which often is based on practice time)

Some parents may be in a real scheduling bind, and they can use a helping hand. Get the lowdown on their situation, and see what options you can come up with for the benefit of their child. Maybe they live nearby, so another parent can pick up the child on the way to practice or games. Facilitate the meeting between the parents and provide the avenue for this solution. You can also do your part to motivate the kids to be on time; kids can be quite persuasive if they really don't want to miss out.

Anytime you have to deal with player problems, you have the final and most important say, because you control playing time. You'll be amazed at what the threat of being benched can do to turn around a child's attitude. Use the playing-time factor to your advantage to try to get the behavior you want, regardless of the level you're coaching. Even at the beginning levels of play you can use playing time to your advantage, because most kids won't enjoy sitting on the bench for an extended period of time while watching their friends and teammates having fun. This tactic is no different than disciplining a child on the playground and forcing him to sit and watch while others climb monkey bars and go down slides. Missing out on all the action — and fun — for an inning or two usually does wonders for changing a child's behavior.

General advice

Dealing with behavior problems presented by your players can pose real headaches for you and cause major disruptions for the team, if you're not prepared to handle them. Keep the following pieces of advice in mind when addressing these issues:

✔ **Don't use running as a punishment.** When kids misbehave, you may be tempted to punish them with conditioning drills, sprints, or laps around the field. Do your best to avoid taking this route; you don't want your kids to associate conditioning and running with punishment and develop a negative outlook on the activities.

✔ **Don't waver on your rules.** Disciplining kids isn't fun, so you may be tempted to not go through with it. No matter how much you hate dealing out the discipline, though, you must follow through on your rules to maintain your authority and respect among your players.

✔ **Never play favorites.** A coach can kill team chemistry by playing favorites — in other words, allowing some youngsters to get away with bad behaviors and punishing their teammates for the same infractions. If you give special treatment to certain players — usually to kids who hit better, throw more accurately, or run the bases faster — you send the message that some kids are more valuable and important to you than others. Always apply your team rules evenly so you don't alienate any of your players.

✔ **Be reasonable.** Make sure that any punishment you hand out fits the crime. You shouldn't give a child who's five minutes late to practice the same punishment as a player who uses foul language after striking out during a game.

✔ **Leave some wiggle room.** Allow yourself some room to maneuver when special circumstances complicate matters. For example, taking away playing time is a common punishment for misbehavior, and you can vary the amount of time you take away to adjust to the severity of the infraction.

✔ **Inform the team about your decisions.** When you discipline a child, let the rest of your team know that a teammate won't be joining the game until the fifth inning, for example. Inform them about the punishment to reinforce that you won't tolerate bad behavior, which will reduce the chances of others behaving unacceptably. You also want to prepare the other kids for the game, because some of them will have to shuffle to different positions and places in the batting order.

✔ **Move forward.** When the disciplinary period ends with the child, sweep the incident to the side and move on so your relationship won't sour. It isn't fair to the child to hold a grudge for the rest of the season or to treat him differently than you did prior to the misbehavior. You can start by praising him right away for something he does well so he'll know that the past problems have been forgiven.

✔ **Don't discipline kids for playing miscues.** Never discipline a kid who commits a throwing error or makes a base-running mistake during a game — even if the miscue contributes to your team losing the game. Making mistakes, and learning from them, is a part of playing baseball.

If a player intentionally tries to hurt an opposing player or teammate — by sliding into him maliciously or trying to hit him with a pitch, for example — immediately remove him from the game or practice. This type of behavior has no place in youth baseball and sets a dangerous precedent if you don't deal with it the moment it occurs. If the event warrants further disciplinary action, deal with that after the game or the practice with the child's parents.

Employing the three-strike technique

You need to address all discipline problems at the first sign of trouble and do your best to resolve them right away if you want to maintain team order — and your sanity. The *three-strike technique* often works well for disciplining players. This approach gives your youngsters a little disciplinary wiggle room; in other words, they won't ruin their seasons the first time they cross the line. They'll have ample room to adjust to your expectations and adhere to your rules.

Always inform your kids' parents about the procedures you plan to follow throughout the season. Do this before any problems materialize so that everyone fully understands how you'll hand out punishment (the preseason parents meeting is a great place for this conversation; see Chapter 4).

The following sections give you the rundown of how the three-strike technique works.

Strike one! Issue a verbal warning

Give the player a verbal warning the first time he crosses the line to let him know that you're unhappy with what he said or did. Make sure he knows that if it happens again, you'll punish him for his behavior. Some examples of behavior that merit strike-one consideration include

- Throwing a batting helmet in the dugout after striking out
- Cursing after an error
- Making fun of a teammate's shortcomings

After seeing how serious you are, most kids won't repeat the problem behavior again. Of course, some youngsters may want to test your authority by venturing into an entirely different area of misbehavior. For example, say you issue a verbal warning to a child who swears during a game, and then he follows that up by refusing to shake hands with the opponent after the game. This child has stepped squarely into strike-two territory.

Strike two! Discipline the player

If a kid chooses the path of disobedience over following your instructions, you have to bump up the severity of the punishment to derail the problem behavior before it becomes a distraction for the team. The most effective punishment in many cases is to take away a portion of the child's playing time in the next game. This sends a strong message that if the player doesn't stop his bad behavior immediately, he won't get back on the field. Let the player know that if he continues to misbehave, he'll jeopardize his future with the team.

If a problem arises again in a short span of time, do a little digging. Find a time to talk to the culprit away from his teammates. Ask direct questions about what's bothering him, and see if you can trace the reasons for his behavior to problems at home, school, or with his teammates. Then find out what you can do to help him.

When you hand out a strike-two warning, you need to meet with the player's parents to let them know what's happened. Explain why you're taking away some of their child's playing time, and outline how much time the child will miss. Share with them exactly what you told their child so that they can follow up with some discipline at home. At the younger levels, where the league policy often dictates equal playing time for each child, check with the league director to find out if you can take playing time away from youngsters or if you'll need to come up with other types of punishment. If needed, you can designate those kids to pick up all the equipment at the end of practice or get all the bats and balls out of the equipment bags at the start of your practice sessions.

Strike three! Remove the player from the team (at least for now)

In rare instances where a youngster, for whatever reasons, continues to behave unacceptably, you may have to remove him from the team. This should be a last-resort punishment, and you never want to reach this point, but you have a responsibility to all the kids on your team. You can't allow the behavior of one child to disrupt the experiences of everyone else.

Before you excuse the child, meet with his parents again to explain the situation. Let them know that their child's options are running out. You also should meet with your league director to detail what's taken place. The director may be able to explore other options for getting the child back in line.

If you remove a youngster from your team, you can leave the door cracked open slightly for his return if you want. After he has some time away from the team and the game to think about his behavior, he may be willing to turn his act around. If he comes to you and the team with a sincere apology for his disruptive behavior, and if he promises to obey your instructions and team rules, you may decide to welcome him back. Kids can learn many valuable life lessons on a baseball team, including humility, obedience, and forgiveness.

Assisting Your Befuddled Players

As your season moves along, most of your players will learn new skills, make improvements, and have a lot of fun. However, some of your kids may not develop a comfort level with certain basics of the game, such as swinging the bat or sliding into a base. One of the real challenges of coaching a youth baseball team is not only recognizing that your players develop at vastly different rates, but also being prepared to help them overcome their difficulties so they don't feel disappointed and inadequate.

How you handle struggling kids, and the progress you make with them, is a true indicator of your coaching ability. In the sections that follow, we assist you in analyzing problems you may face and provide possible ways to deal with certain issues.

Analyzing problems

If you notice that certain players are having trouble picking up a skill, your job is to figure out a way to help them improve. Begin by taking a closer look at how you interact with the kids. Maybe you spend too much time talking and don't giving them enough time to practice the skill. Perhaps you fill their heads with too many thoughts about what to do instead of keeping your instructions really simple. If you're getting maximum effort out of the kids, and you know that they genuinely want to learn and improve, chances are good that you can trace the central problem to how you're teaching them.

Try out these tips to help your youngsters get back on the right track:

✔ **Move kids around.** Perhaps a child who's struggling really wants to play in the outfield, for example, but you have him playing third base instead. Try mixing things up. Sometimes, all it takes is a new position to spark a youngster's enthusiasm. As an added benefit, teaching your kids many different positions, and the skills that go with them, ensures that they'll be well-rounded players (see Chapter 10 for more on working with defensive positions).

✔ **Never make a child feel bad.** If a youngster is struggling with some aspect of the game, don't add to his misery by embarrassing him or making him feel inferior to his teammates. Most children know exactly where they stand in comparison to the other kids on the team, so they don't need you to highlight their deficiencies (by calling them out for extra work on the sidelines, for example).

Instead, find creative ways to help them without shining the spotlight on their difficulties. If a child is having problems catching fly balls high in the air, you can make adjustments during a drill that will go unnoticed by other players while helping this child in the process. For example, every time you hit a ball to this outfielder, don't put it up in the air quite as high as you do for the other players. After the youngster gets comfortable making these catches on shorter fly balls, he'll have a little more confidence to tackle those balls hit higher in the sky.

✔ **Maintain an even tone.** Don't allow the tone of your voice to divulge any frustration or disappointment you may be feeling. Keep that in mind with your body language, too. Patience and composure are invaluable when helping a child work through any difficulties he may have.

✔ **Stick by them.** Never turn your back on a youngster or give up hope just because he isn't picking up the game as fast as others. You have to stick by your kids, encouraging and applauding their efforts every step of the way. Struggling kids need you now more than ever. Who knows, years from now you may see a child who's still involved with the sport because of the efforts you made to help him out. What a good feeling!

You never want your focus to stray from making sure that every child is learning and developing. Losing track of some kids and overlooking their problems can happen easily if your season is going great and the team is playing well together. Don't let wins blind you to the problems of certain players.

Recognizing physical issues

How much progress a child makes in a sport may be dictated, to a certain degree, by a pre-existing condition he has. All sorts of ailments or disorders can affect children involved in sports.

One of the more common disorders is Attention Deficit Hyperactivity Disorder (AD/HD). A child's lack of focus may be the result of AD/HD. Some of the most common characteristics of AD/HD are

✔ Distractibility and poorly sustained attention to tasks

✔ Impaired impulse control

✔ Excessive activity and physical restlessness

If you think a player on your team may be displaying signs of AD/HD, talk to his parents about your observations. Or, if you know that a child has AD/HD, work with the parents and child to find ways to ensure that he has a rewarding experience on your team.

As we mention in Chapter 4, one of the most important reasons to hold a pre-season parents meeting is so you can find out if any of the children on your team have special needs. For example, if you don't discover a child's hearing problem, you won't like the obstacles lying ahead for you and the youngster. By making yourself aware of the situation, you can respond accordingly; for instance, you can always make sure the child can clearly see your lips when you're giving instruction.

Past injuries also can affect a child's development. For example, a youngster who suffered a broken leg a year or two ago may be limited in how he can perform a bent-leg slide (see Chapter 9). Again, finding out this information before the season is imperative. With knowledge of his condition, you can teach the child to perform a head-first slide instead.

Part VI
The Part of Tens

The 5th Wave   By Rich Tennant

"Can I use it coach? My dad made it for me
from an old telephone pole."

In this part . . .

If you're looking for some innovative ways to make the season fun and memorable for your players or child, you've come to the right place. In this part, we offer ten tips for relaxing your players before games. We present ten ways you can make your players remember this season forever. And we list ten suggestions for ending the season on a high note so your players want to continue playing this great game.

Chapter 18

Ten Pre-Game Tips to Relax Your Players and Keep Them Focused

. . . .

In This Chapter

▶ Recognizing that nerves and mistakes are part of the game

▶ Focusing on having fun

▶ Reminding the player that sportsmanship counts

▶ Offering words of encouragement

. . . .

*W*hat you say to your team before games, and how you choose to say it, can make a big difference in your players' attitude before stepping on the field and how the season unfolds for all of you. You want your players to experience a fun day of baseball, no matter what else is going on off the field, and you don't want them handcuffed by pre-game nerves, tension, or worries about their performance. In this section, we give you the scoop on what you can say to your players, and what topics to avoid, to help them relax and perform to the best of their abilities.

You Want to Be a Little Nervous

Adults get nervous before making big presentations to clients, trying to close business deals, or asking the boss for a raise. Why? Because we genuinely care about what happens (especially when it comes to getting a boost in the paycheck!). Kids experience those same jitters before baseball games because they want to do well. Let your kids know that having sweaty palms or butterflies in their stomachs before the opening pitch is okay and normal. Nervousness is a good sign that indicates that they care about the game. Even pros get nervous before games!

To combat pre-game edginess, tell your players to take a few deep breaths, which helps calm the body and relax the muscles.

Remember the Tasty Post-Game Treats

Whether the team plays one of its best games of the season and wins by several runs, or turns in its worst performance of the year and gets clobbered by a dozen runs, all of your players should always receive the same treatment, support, and positive reinforcement. You don't want to fall into the dreaded performance trap of only rewarding kids when they play well. Doing so sends an awful message; a child will think that doing his best and having fun really aren't what's most important to you.

You can give all the players support right off the bat by reminding them that the team will enjoy a tasty post-game snack together afterward. This reminder makes clear that win or lose, good performance or bad, your support will never waver.

Don't Worry about Making Mistakes

The Major Leagues' best players drop routine fly balls, bobble easy grounders, and make base-running blunders all the time. Make sure your players recognize that making mistakes is part of the game. Let them know that failing three out of ten times at the plate in the pros makes you an All-Star.

If you're coaching a team that has your own child on the roster, watch some televised major league games with him. When a player makes an error, use the situation to your advantage by not only pointing out to the child that mistakes happen all the time at all levels of play, but also by showing him how the player responds to the mistake. Kids become better equipped to handle their own miscues when they see that professionals don't hang their heads or pout (at least not that often).

Be a Good Teammate

Kids who have the support of their coaches and teammates will perform better and be more motivated to do so. You can talk to the kids about the roles they can play in setting a positive tone for the team. When other players hear their teammates offering encouraging words to them and applauding and giving high-fives, they'll be much more likely to adopt positive behaviors as well. Discussing this topic is particularly beneficial if the team you're coaching is older and more advanced. Also, if you have players on your team who are clearly the most popular, and the other kids look up to them, consider talking to them and encouraging them to be more vocal and supportive. Some kids respond better to motivation supplied by a teammate who is well-liked rather than a coach.

You also can confide in certain players to help boost a struggling teammate who can use some encouraging words during pre-game warm-ups. A talk from a teammate can have a bigger impact than a speech from you.

Remember to Be a Good Sport

If a child has one of those days where nothing goes his way on the field, he may feel like venting his frustration in negative ways. You don't want to see him throwing his batting helmet, pouting, or hanging his head in disappointment. Give your players gentle reminders about the importance of being good sports — whether the team wins or loses or whether he has a great day or a sub-par day. (For more details on the importance of being a good sport, check out Chapter 7.) Also, let your youngsters know that you want them to show respect toward opponents and umpires; ask them to treat others exactly as they want to be treated. You can really drive this point home by handing out post-game sportsmanship awards to your most deserving players. Also, keep in mind that your actions speak much louder than any words. Back up everything you say by being a good sport — win or lose — yourself.

In One of My Little League Games, 1 . . .

By laughing, having fun, and sharing some of your stories from your childhood sports experiences, you help your kids to remain calm, relaxed, and in the right frame of mind before the opening pitch. You can help players see that they're just playing a game that they should enjoy. If the coach can laugh at himself, a child can laugh along with him and will be less likely to take himself so seriously.

Visualize Success

Encourage players to visualize success in order to increase their chances of achieving it. For example, when players are in the on-deck circle awaiting their turn at bat, remind them to take a moment to visualize producing a good swing and making solid contact. Seeing it first is believing it can be done.

I Can't Wait to See You in Action Today

Kids want to play well to make their parents and coaches proud, so when you let them see that you have confidence in them and are eager to watch them perform, you give a big boost to their self-esteem. Try talking to the players about a particular skill they worked on in practice the past week and improved upon, or discuss some area of their game that you've noticed improvement in over the past few practices. Tell them that you're excited to see their work pay off in the game and that you're proud of their effort.

What Are You Looking Forward to Most?

A player, for whatever reason, may not be in a talkative mood before a game. A great conversation igniter is asking him what he's looking forward to most about the game. Be prepared, because you may be surprised by what tumbles out of his mouth! Maybe he has a bunch of friends on the opposing team who he can't wait to play against, or perhaps he's just excited to try out his new bat or pair of cleats!

You also should prepare yourself for the chance that he may say something that sends a warning signal to you that something is wrong. For example, say he mentions how good your opponent is. This belief may provide you with some insight about how the entire team is feeling. If you get the sense that your kids are too preoccupied with winning and losing, you can make it a priority to defuse the tension and refocus your players on just doing their best and having fun.

Have a Lot of Fun Today

Telling a child to have fun during the game is simple, straightforward, and to the point, but the advice is one of the most important points you can make to a child. You simply can't say it enough. Participating in organized baseball — at any age or ability level — must be fun. Make fun one of your top coaching priorities, and stress it every chance you get; doing so clears the way for a great day (and season) of baseball.

Chapter 19

Ten Ways to Make the Season Memorable (In a Good Way)

*Y*ears from now, your players won't be able to recall your team's won-loss record or how many hits they notched, but they'll clearly remember the time they spent with you and whether it was enjoyable, so-so, or downright miserable. One of your goals at the beginning of a season is to do your best to make sure that when your players look back on the season, they smile. This chapter shares ten interesting ways you can inject fun into your season. Hopefully, these tactics will have your players — and even some kids on opposing teams — begging to play for you next season.

Bring in New Faces to Practice

One of the best ways to liven up a practice is to bring in different baseball people to work with your kids. If you take a look around your community, you'll probably discover all sorts of resources. Check the following resources, depending on where you live:

✔ A local high school baseball coach

✔ A well-known high school baseball player

✔ Coaches or players from a nearby college team

✔ Coaches or players from a minor league team in your town or in a nearby city (contact the team's public-relations office about having someone come out to one of your practices)

Providing new voices for your kids to listen to and learn from can refresh and reenergize your team. Encourage the guests to participate in your practice and to be actively involved in the drills. (See Chapter 6 for tips on how to run a good practice.)

Try a Crazy Uniform Day

Young kids will get a real kick out of getting the chance to wear their shirt backward or inside out during a practice. You and your assistant coaches can also join in and do the same to demonstrate team camaraderie. For older kids, have them wear the cap or shirt of their favorite major league team.

Invite Guest Speakers

As a coach, you have the opportunity to make a big difference in a child's life — beyond helping him learn to catch pop flies and hit fastballs. One way you can make a difference is to bring in guest speakers to talk to your kids about other topics that relate to their performances on the field. For example, you can have a sports nutritionist give your kids the rundown on proper diet. Other guest-speaker options include a personal trainer, who can discuss topics from proper stretches to effective off-season workout plans, or a sports psychologist, who can share insights on how to concentrate more intensely or conquer pre-game nerves. Before making any arrangements clear it with your parents to make sure they're all on board.

Try soliciting feedback from your team to see if your players would like to hear a particular expert speak. If they're excited about a speaker, you can proceed with confidence.

Make sure you know exactly what the guest speaker's message is before he stands up in front of your team. You don't want to be surprised and have someone preach the opposite of what you've stressed to your players all season.

Change the Practice Scenery

Try taking a trip to the local batting cage to mix up your team's practice routine and to give the kids a change of scenery. If you coach younger kids, make sure you keep a close eye on them and provide positive feedback and instruction, just like you would at the field. With older kids, you can turn the batting cage into a fun competition. Break your team up into mini-groups of three or four players and keep track to see which group can produce the most solid hits out of a set number of swings.

Because changing scenery requires extra expense, be sure to check with the parents well in advance to make sure they're okay with the excursion.

Pit the Kids versus the Coaches

Kids will welcome the chance to put their skills to the test against you and your coaching staff if given the chance. The prospects of playing and beating you will energize even the most mundane practice. (See Chapters 12 and 13 for more fun fundamental drills.) The following list presents some of the many challenges in which players and coaches can compete:

- ✔ **Base-running sprint:** Begin in the batter's box and run a timed sprint around the bases. See if the kids can beat your time.

- ✔ **Base-path chase:** Have a youngster stand in the batter's box while you line up halfway between home plate and first base. On your signal, you should both beginning running around the bases. The youngster should try to catch up and tag you before you get all the way to home plate. If you like, you can reverse the starting position so you get to chase the player.

- ✔ **Long throw:** Give your kids five chances to throw, and take their longest throws. After they finish, you get one throw to try to beat them.

- ✔ **Target throw:** Place a target on the field, such as a trash can, at a reasonable distance. See who can hit the target first or who can come the closest out of a set number of throws.

Give Your Players a Voice

Giving your players the chance to voice their opinions, and be heard, is an ideal way to make them feel like they're integral parts of the team. You show that you respect them as baseball players *and* young people, and you prove that you value their thoughts and feedback. You also can use feedback as a great reward for when your players have been working hard in practice recently. Here are a few options for giving your players a voice:

- ✔ Let the team vote on all the drills that you'll run during an upcoming practice.

- ✔ Let the team create the team cheer they'll yell out before they take the field.

- ✔ Prior to the season starting, if your league allows it, let your kids vote on your team nickname or the color of your uniforms.

Hold Contests

Holding contests at practice that target different aspects of the game of baseball is a great way to hone your players' skills and provide fun at the same time. Older and more advanced kids will enjoy the competition and the thought of putting their skills to the test against their teammates'.

Although you *can* run the contests as individual competitions among all your players, a better approach is to pair your players into two-person teams. Make sure that the teams are balanced so that you create an even competition. Use a variety of competitions that challenge the kids to perform various skills. You want to give your players an appreciation for how difficult other positions on the field are; being able to value the skills of teammates is a great attribute for a ballplayer to have.

You can use some of the activities outlined in the "Pit the Kids versus the Coaches" section earlier in this chapter, or try some of these:

- **Toss and catch:** Line the kids up in two parallel lines, facing their partners, with each partnership about 10 yards apart. Have them make a set number of throws back and forth. Anytime a ball hits the ground, due to a bad throw or a missed catch, the twosome it belongs to is eliminated from the game. You can increase the difficulty of the throws by gradually moving the players farther from each other.

- **Target bunts:** Set up a couple of targets in front of home plate — towels work well — for hitters to attempt to get their bunts to land on. In this contest, each pair gets a total of ten bunts (five per player). A partner should pitch the ball to a partner to avoid any grievances over bad pitches! Award three points for any bunt that comes to rest on a towel and one point for any bunt that touches a target at all.

- **Base-running bonanza:** Have one partner start in the batter's box with a bat, and have the other partner stand on second base. You deliver a batting-practice pitch to the batter, and as he makes contact, he takes off on a sprint to first base and keeps going until he slides into second base. The base runner on second takes off on contact and rounds third base and slides into home. An assistant coach starts the timer as soon as the batter makes contact with the ball and stops the clock when the players reach home plate and second base, respectively. Make it into a fun competition to see which twosome turns in the fastest time.

Solicit Reviews of Your Work

The best way to gauge what type of impact you're having on your kids is to come right out and ask them. Around the season's halfway point, you should get the lowdown on what your players think of you, your practices, your drills, and so on. Do this by putting together a list of questions that you distribute to the kids; they'll take the lists home, answer the questions, and bring them back to your team's next practice. Be sure to stress that you don't want them to put their names on the forms so you can get the most honest feedback possible. Encourage parents to let their child answer the questions so you get honest feedback from them on how their season is going. Here are some basic questions you can include on your form:

✔ What have you liked best about the season so far?

✔ What have you liked least about the season so far?

✔ What's your favorite part of practice?

✔ What's your least favorite part of practice?

✔ What can I do to make practices more fun for you?

✔ What can I do to make game day more fun for you?

If you want, you can even include a spot on the form to get parental feedback by asking questions such as what you can do to help make the season more fun or which areas of the game they would like to see you devote more attention to, among others. Keeping these lines of communication open with parents, which we discuss in Chapter 4, is key for keeping the season headed in the right direction.

Use the responses you get to become a more effective coach. Don't take anything personally!

Encourage Nickname Mania

After you get to know your players, you can give them cool nicknames, or you can let them come up with nicknames for themselves. Younger kids, especially, love the attention that nicknames generate. You'll be happy to see that calling out their nicknames as you praise them for hustling on the base paths splashes big smiles across their faces. Nicknames also give older kids a chance to build team camaraderie and have fun with each other. You'd be surprised at how long a nickname can stick with a player, so don't take this option lightly!

Don't leave yourself, or any of your assistant coaches, out of the mix. Let your players come up with nicknames for you and your assistants.

Hand Out Progress Reports

Issuing progress reports to your players at the midpoint of your season is a great way to let them know that you notice and appreciate their efforts. Kids love being recognized for any improvements they make. A simple, handwritten note can really lift a youngster's spirits and give him the confidence to continuing working hard.

A progress report can be equally effective for an older player. You can take the process a step further by addressing a specific area of the player's game. You can challenge him to get better in a certain area, which will serve as great motivation, and you can point to an area where he excels.

Chapter 20

Ten Fun Ways to End the Season on a High Note

In This Chapter

▶ Wrapping up the season with fun activities and honors

▶ Recognizing all the kids for their efforts and achievements

*P*izza parties, trips to the ice-cream parlor, and team gatherings at the local arcade are some traditional ways that youth baseball coaches end their seasons. With a little effort, though, you can make yourself stand out and be known as one of the coolest coaches in the league by doing something a little less ordinary. In this chapter, we present ten clever activities you can organize to put big smiles on your kids' faces and wow the parents.

Staging a Carnival Day

Kids love going to carnivals, playing games, and winning prizes. With minimal effort, you can create a carnival day at the field during one of your last practices of the season that will have your kids raving about you for months. Ask the parents to chip in a little money for candy or other small prizes to give to the kids as they rotate through the different games. You can design all sorts of fun games on your own or with the help of your assistants and parents, such as the following:

✔ Set up an older table, place empty plastic bottles on it, and let the kids throw baseballs at the bottles to try to knock them off the table.

✔ Lie a large trash can on its side at home plate, facing the outfield, and station the kids at a spot in the outfield. Tell the kids to try to hit the can on one bounce.

✔ Set up a hitting station where the kids take swings at a set number of pitches, trying to hit targets that you've placed around the infield and outfield.

  ✔ Set up a pitching station where the kids have to throw a ball through a large piece of cardboard with different-sized holes.

Presenting Individual Awards

Handing out individual awards to your players is a great way to spotlight their season-long contributions. Coming up with the honors just takes a little imagination on your part. You can create all sorts of awards to recognize your kids' skills, attributes, and positive attitudes. For example, you can hand out an award for Most Likely to Dive and Stop a Ground Ball, or Most Likely to Beat Out an Infield Grounder. Awards that go beyond Most Valuable or Most Improved are great ways to recognize kids whose efforts otherwise may have been overlooked.

Be sure that if you choose to hand out individual awards, you recognize each of the kids in some way. Don't just hand out a Most Valuable Player and then leave out most of the kids.

Try recruiting a parent who has time to print certificates on a home computer. Or, if all the parents agree, collect money and order miniature trophies or plaques engraved with the players' names and the names of the awards.

Creating Team Trading Cards

Kids enjoy collecting and trading baseball cards with their friends, so you know they'll really get a kick out of trading their own cards. If you can raise the resources with the parents, contact a local photographer who can take the shots. Try to include some information on the back of the cards. You can stick to the basics — age, height, and position — or you can include more clever info, like what nicknames you call them. Give each youngster a dozen or so cards so all the kids can swap with their teammates, send some to grandparents, and show their neighborhood or school friends.

Recording Team DVDs

Thanks to today's technology, you can create amazing keepsakes that will hold a child's attention. One such gift is a team DVD. Your kids — as well as their parents and grandparents — will enjoy this special piece of memorabilia for years to come (or until DVDs become obsolete!). Recruit a parent to shoot video of your games and practices to collect all the necessary footage. Or, if all the parents are willing to chip in to cover the cost, you can hire a professional to do the job. Just make sure that the finished product has ample coverage of every child on your team. Bring up this idea at your preseason parents meeting (see Chapter 4) to gauge the interest level.

Showing Highlights with Player DVDs

Individual DVDs you give to each child, featuring action footage of great hits and sound plays in the field, make for neat season-ending gifts — as long as all the parents agree that the cost is reasonable. You can make a big deal of handing out the DVDs by holding a special team get-together after the season. Play each DVD for all in attendance before you present it to the child. The gathering will make for a memorable evening for everyone involved.

Organizing a Team Photo Album

A team photo album is a great keepsake that will stand the test of time, no matter what advances in technology take place — and an album really isn't that difficult or expensive to put together. At the start of the season, designate a parent — or several if many show interest — to take shots of all the kids in action and in play. Pick out the best shots — making sure you have the same number of photos for each child — and arrange them in photo albums.

If the parents of your players are really creative and have plenty of time to devote to the project, you can create individual albums for the players. These albums can feature a team photo along with a variety of action shots.

Handing Out a Baseball Memento

Any type of baseball memento usually goes over big with young kids. You don't have to come up with anything extravagant, either. You can give each player a baseball medal that they can display in their bedrooms. Other options include miniature bats with their names, the team name, and the year carved on them, or baseballs emblazoned with the kids' photos, which will look great on their bedroom shelves.

Forming a Team Newsletter

Kids of all ages love seeing their name in print. Putting together a team newsletter is a great way to help your kids remember the season and their accomplishments. The newsletter can recap the season, highlight all the positives that took place, and recognize the players and parents.

How detailed you make the newsletter is up to you. You can go the simple route and include the name of each player and a brief quote about how you enjoyed coaching him, what he meant to the team, and where he made the biggest improvements. However, if you or a volunteer parent has ample time, you can make an in-depth newsletter. You can include photos of each player, with brief bios that list their favorite Major Leaguers, favorite teams, and the names of their parents. You can even write a column that talks about what a joy it was to coach the kids and thanks the parents for helping to make the season a success.

Conducting Personal Meetings

Most kids look up to their coaches, and they devour their praise quicker than Halloween candy. You should take full advantage of your position as a key role model in your players' lives all season long, through your teachings and the example you set. After the season, spend a few minutes with each player to chat with them in private. Use the chats to pat your players on the back for their hard work, motivate them to stick with the game, and gently encourage them to work on certain areas of their games that may need more attention.

Taking Trips to Cool Places

A lot of kids love watching baseball games almost as much as playing in them, so chances are taking a trip to a ballgame together will go over big with them. Going to a major league game is a great experience for the kids, especially those who have never seen a professional game in person. If a major league team isn't in your area, attending a minor league or collegiate game can be just as much fun.

Make sure all the parents sign off on a trip first. And don't forget to arrange for plenty of chaperones to monitor the kids (shoot for about a four-to-one kid-to-parent ratio.

Index

• E •

rules, league *(continued)*
  knowing before you start, 12, 25
  for makeup games, 26
  for older kids, 41–42
  in personal packets, 64–65
  for playing time, 40, 41, 43, 313
  for recreational leagues, 27–28
  for removal of parents, 62–63
  for rescheduling practices, 26–27
  for substitutions, 115
  for youngest kids, 39–41
rules of baseball
  for base-running, 46–48
  for batting, 44
  batting order, 43
  changing for scrimmages, 92
  communicating to parents, 11, 64–65
  for getting on base, 44–45
  innings, 43
  knowing before you start, 12
  for making outs, 45–46
  in personal packets, 64–65
  softball versus baseball, 42
run batted in, 52
rundowns, 52, 169–170
runners on base, coaching, 256–258
runners on base, fielding with
  bases loaded, 268–270
  doubles or triples, 271–272, 273, 276–277
  first and second, sacrifice bunts, 283
  first and second, single hits, 268–270
  first and third, single hits, 265–267
  first, double plays, 174, 175–176
  first, sacrifice bunts, 282
  first, single hits, 265–267
  sacrifice bunts, 281–283
  second, sacrifice bunts, 283
  second, single hits, 268–270
  third, double plays, 174
running
  basic form for, 148
  for pre-game warm-up, 108
  as punishment, avoiding, 321
running bases. *See also* sliding; stealing
      bases
  avoiding double plays, 154
  base coaches, 256–258
  basic running form, 148

breaking up double plays, 158, 254
drills for, 213–215, 232–234
evaluating outfielder's arms, 256
to first base, 148–149, 154
from first base, 254
on fly balls, 254, 255
going outside base lines, 46, 149
on ground balls, 254, 255
hand signals for, 114
importance of, 148
leading off, 151
leaving the batter's box, 148–149, 154
legging out a ground ball, 149
rounding the bases, 150–151
sacrifice bunt for, 140–143, 251–252
sacrifice fly for, 252
scoring on wild pitches, 255
from second base, 254
situational tactics for, 253–255
strategies, 252–255, 256–258
tagging up, 48, 53, 151–154, 254
from third base, 255
troubleshooting, 153

NESS, CAREERS & PERSONAL FINANCE

0-7645-9847-3

0-7645-2431-3

Also available:
- Business Plans Kit For Dummies
  0-7645-9794-9
- Economics For Dummies
  0-7645-5726-2
- Grant Writing For Dummies
  0-7645-8416-2
- Home Buying For Dummies
  0-7645-5331-3
- Managing For Dummies
  0-7645-1771-6
- Marketing For Dummies
  0-7645-5600-2

- Personal Finance For Dummies
  0-7645-2590-5*
- Resumes For Dummies
  0-7645-5471-9
- Selling For Dummies
  0-7645-5363-1
- Six Sigma For Dummies
  0-7645-6798-5
- Small Business Kit For Dummies
  0-7645-5984-2
- Starting an eBay Business For Dummies
  0-7645-6924-4
- Your Dream Career For Dummies
  0-7645-9795-7

ME & BUSINESS COMPUTER BASICS

0-470-05432-8

0-471-75421-8

Also available:
- Cleaning Windows Vista For Dummies
  0-471-78293-9
- Excel 2007 For Dummies
  0-470-03737-7
- Mac OS X Tiger For Dummies
  0-7645-7675-5
- MacBook For Dummies
  0-470-04859-X
- Macs For Dummies
  0-470-04849-2
- Office 2007 For Dummies
  0-470-00923-3

- Outlook 2007 For Dummies
  0-470-03830-6
- PCs For Dummies
  0-7645-8958-X
- Salesforce.com For Dummies
  0-470-04893-X
- Upgrading & Fixing Laptops For Dummies
  0-7645-8959-8
- Word 2007 For Dummies
  0-470-03658-3
- Quicken 2007 For Dummies
  0-470-04600-7

D, HOME, GARDEN, HOBBIES, MUSIC & PETS

0-7645-8404-9

0-7645-9904-6

Also available:
- Candy Making For Dummies
  0-7645-9734-5
- Card Games For Dummies
  0-7645-9910-0
- Crocheting For Dummies
  0-7645-4151-X
- Dog Training For Dummies
  0-7645-8418-9
- Healthy Carb Cookbook For Dummies
  0-7645-8476-6
- Home Maintenance For Dummies
  0-7645-5215-5

- Horses For Dummies
  0-7645-9797-3
- Jewelry Making & Beading For Dummies
  0-7645-2571-9
- Orchids For Dummies
  0-7645-6759-4
- Puppies For Dummies
  0-7645-5255-4
- Rock Guitar For Dummies
  0-7645-5356-9
- Sewing For Dummies
  0-7645-6847-7
- Singing For Dummies
  0-7645-2475-5

ERNET & DIGITAL MEDIA

0-470-04529-9

0-470-04894-8

Also available:
- Blogging For Dummies
  0-471-77084-1
- Digital Photography For Dummies
  0-7645-9802-3
- Digital Photography All-in-One Desk Reference For Dummies
  0-470-03743-1
- Digital SLR Cameras and Photography For Dummies
  0-7645-9803-1
- eBay Business All-in-One Desk Reference For Dummies
  0-7645-8438-3
- HDTV For Dummies
  0-470-09673-X

- Home Entertainment PCs For Dummies
  0-470-05523-5
- MySpace For Dummies
  0-470-09529-6
- Search Engine Optimization For Dummies
  0-471-97998-8
- Skype For Dummies
  0-470-04891-3
- The Internet For Dummies
  0-7645-8996-2
- Wiring Your Digital Home For Dummies
  0-471-91830-X

rate Canadian edition also available
rate U.K. edition also available

le wherever books are sold. For more information or to order direct: U.S. customers visit www.dummies.com or call 1-877-762-2974.
tomers visit www.wileyeurope.com or call 0800 243407. Canadian customers visit www.wiley.ca or call 1-800-567-4797.

 WILEY

SPORTS, FITNESS, PARENTING, RELIGION & SPIRITUALITY

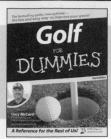

0-471-76871-5

0-7645-7841-3

Also available:
- Catholicism For Dummies
  0-7645-5391-7
- Exercise Balls For Dummies
  0-7645-5623-1
- Fitness For Dummies
  0-7645-7851-0
- Football For Dummies
  0-7645-3936-1
- Judaism For Dummies
  0-7645-5299-6
- Potty Training For Dummies
  0-7645-5417-4
- Buddhism For Dummies
  0-7645-5359-3

- Pregnancy For Dummies
  0-7645-4483-7 †
- Ten Minute Tone-Ups For Dummi
  0-7645-7207-5
- NASCAR For Dummies
  0-7645-7681-X
- Religion For Dummies
  0-7645-5264-3
- Soccer For Dummies
  0-7645-5229-5
- Women in the Bible For Dummie
  0-7645-8475-8

TRAVEL

0-7645-7749-2

0-7645-6945-7

Also available:
- Alaska For Dummies
  0-7645-7746-8
- Cruise Vacations For Dummies
  0-7645-6941-4
- England For Dummies
  0-7645-4276-1
- Europe For Dummies
  0-7645-7529-5
- Germany For Dummies
  0-7645-7823-5
- Hawaii For Dummies
  0-7645-7402-7

- Italy For Dummies
  0-7645-7386-1
- Las Vegas For Dummies
  0-7645-7382-9
- London For Dummies
  0-7645-4277-X
- Paris For Dummies
  0-7645-7630-5
- RV Vacations For Dummies
  0-7645-4442-X
- Walt Disney World & Orlando
  For Dummies
  0-7645-9660-8

GRAPHICS, DESIGN & WEB DEVELOPMENT

0-7645-8815-X

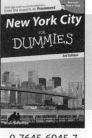

0-7645-9571-7

Also available:
- 3D Game Animation For Dummies
  0-7645-8789-7
- AutoCAD 2006 For Dummies
  0-7645-8925-3
- Building a Web Site For Dummies
  0-7645-7144-3
- Creating Web Pages For Dummies
  0-470-08030-2
- Creating Web Pages All-in-One Desk
  Reference For Dummies
  0-7645-4345-8
- Dreamweaver 8 For Dummies
  0-7645-9649-7

- InDesign CS2 For Dummies
  0-7645-9572-5
- Macromedia Flash 8 For Dummie
  0-7645-9691-8
- Photoshop CS2 and Digital
  Photography For Dummies
  0-7645-9580-6
- Photoshop Elements 4 For Dumn
  0-471-77483-9
- Syndicating Web Sites with RSS F
  For Dummies
  0-7645-8848-6
- Yahoo! SiteBuilder For Dummies
  0-7645-9800-7

NETWORKING, SECURITY, PROGRAMMING & DATABASES

0-7645-7728-X

0-471-74940-0

Also available:
- Access 2007 For Dummies
  0-470-04612-0
- ASP.NET 2 For Dummies
  0-7645-7907-X
- C# 2005 For Dummies
  0-7645-9704-3
- Hacking For Dummies
  0-470-05235-X
- Hacking Wireless Networks
  For Dummies
  0-7645-9730-2
- Java For Dummies
  0-470-08716-1

- Microsoft SQL Server 2005 For Dur
  0-7645-7755-7
- Networking All-in-One Desk Refe
  For Dummies
  0-7645-9939-9
- Preventing Identity Theft For Dum
  0-7645-7336-5
- Telecom For Dummies
  0-471-77085-X
- Visual Studio 2005 All-in-One De
  Reference For Dummies
  0-7645-9775-2
- XML For Dummies
  0-7645-8845-1

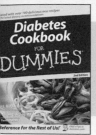
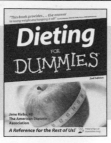
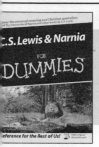